RESEARCHING RACISM IN EDUCATION

RESEARCHING RACISM IN EDUCATION
POLITICS, THEORY AND PRACTICE

Edited by
Paul Connolly and **Barry Troyna**

Open University Press
Buckingham · Philadelphia

Open University Press
Celtic Court
22 Ballmoor
Buckingham
MK18 1XW

and
1900 Frost Road, Suite 101
Bristol, PA 19007, USA

First Published 1998

A catalogue record of this book is available from the British Library

ISBN   0 335 19662 4 (pb)   0 335 19663 2 (hb)

Library of Congress Cataloging-in-Publication Data
Researching racism in education: politics, theory, and practice / edited by Paul
   Connolly and Barry Troyna.
        p.   cm.
      Includes bibliographical references and index.
      ISBN 0-335-19663-2 (hardcover). — ISBN 0-335-19662-4 (pbk.)
      1. Discrimination in education—Research—Great Britain—Methodology.
   2. Politics and education—Great Britain.   I. Connolly, Paul, 1966–   .
   II. Troyna, Barry.
   LC212.3.G7R47   1998
   306.43′2—dc21   97-23199
                                                                            CIP

Typeset by Type Study, Scarborough
Printed in Great Britain by St Edmundsbury Press Ltd, Bury St Edmunds, Suffolk

Contents

The editors and contributors

Maud Blair is Lecturer in Education at the Open University. She is Chair of the Open University course ED356 *'Race', Education and Society*, and of the MA course E826 *Gender Issues in Education: Equality and Difference*. Her publications include: *Racism and Education: Structures and Strategies* (Sage 1992, with Dawn Gill and Barbara Mayor); *Identity and Diversity: Gender and the Experience of Education* (Multilingual Matters 1995, with Janet Holland) and *Debates and Issues in Feminist Research and Pedagogy* (Multilingual Matters 1995, with Janet Holland).

Paul Connolly is Lecturer in Sociology at the University of Ulster. He has published a number of articles on racism and education and is author of *Racism, Gender Identities and Young Children* (Routledge 1998). He is currently researching sectarianism among children in Northern Ireland and is working on a book (with Brendon Murtagh) entitled *Researching Racism and Ethnic Relations: Methodology after Postmodernism* (Sage).

Sean Demack is a statistician and trained secondary mathematics teacher. He has just begun a PhD at Sheffield Hallam University entitled 'Race, gender and social class differences in education and the youth labour market'. The research will involve the analysis of data drawn from The Youth Cohort Study of England and Wales and focus on the 16–19 age range. His interests include cooking, writing and listening to loud techno music.

David Drew is Head of the Survey and Statistical Research Centre at Sheffield Hallam University. His experience of social survey research includes work on crime, demography, education, employment, and housing. His particular interest is in the study of 'race' and ethnic differences in education and the youth labour market. His most recent book, based on a longitudinal study for the Department for Education and Employment of 28,000 black and white young people, is entitled *Race, Education and Work: The Statistics of Inequality*

(Avebury 1995). This work is being continued with Sean Demack. Other new work includes a study of racism in football at Sheffield United Football Club and a study of ethnic differences in the links between education, unemployment and deprivation.

David Gillborn is Reader in the Sociology of Education at the Institute of Education, University of London, where he is Associate Director of the Health and Education Research Unit (HERU). David has researched extensively in the field of race and racism in schools. His most recent publications include *Racism and Antiracism in Real Schools* (Open University Press 1995) and *Recent Research on the Achievements of Ethnic Minority Pupils* (HMSO 1996, with Caroline Gipps). He is editor of a new international journal *Race, Ethnicity and Education*.

Martyn Hammersley is Professor of Educational and Social Research in the School of Education at the Open University. His main substantive area of research has been classroom interaction, and teachers' and pupils' perspectives in secondary schools. However, in recent years most of his work has been concerned with the methodological issues surrounding social research. He has written several books: *Ethnography: Principles in Practice* (Tavistock 1983, with Paul Atkinson, second edition 1995); *The Dilemma of Qualitative Method* (Routledge 1989); *Classroom Ethnography* (Open University Press 1990); *Reading Ethnographic Research* (Longman 1990); *What's Wrong with Ethnography?* (Routledge 1992); *The Politics of Social Research* (Sage 1995); and *Constructing Educational Inequality* (Falmer Press 1996, with Peter Foster and Roger Gomm).

Mehreen Mirza works in the Department of Education Studies at the University of Central Lancashire. She is currently completing some research in the area of 'race', gender and educational decision-making in the North West of England.

Sarah Neal is lecturer in the School of Sociology and Social Policy at Middlesex University. Her publications and research interests are in the areas of equal opportunities discourses and policies in organizations, race and higher education, concepts of whiteness and the interface between gender, race and sexuality. She is currently completing her book on equality policies in higher education.

Anuradha Rakhit is Indian by origin and migrated to Britain in 1966. She has been teaching mathematics in secondary schools since 1973. Throughout her career as a teacher, she has been concerned with the limitations imposed on black and women teachers in teaching. She is committed to raising awareness and challenging racial and gender inequality within education.

Barry Troyna was, until his death, Professor of Education and Director of Research Development in the Institute of Education at the University of Warwick. He was editor of the *British Educational Research Journal* and a member of the editorial boards of the *Cambridge Journal of Education*, *Discourse* and the *Journal of Education Policy*. He had written extensively in the area of 'race' and education. His most recent books included: *Antiracism, Culture and Social Justice in Education* (Trentham 1995, with Morwenna Griffiths), *Researching Education Policy* (Falmer Press 1994, with David Halpin), *Racism and Education:*

Research Perspectives (Open University Press 1993) and *Racism in Children's Lives* (Routledge 1992, with Richard Hatcher).

Cecile Wright is Reader in Sociology at Nottingham Trent University. She has written and researched extensively in the field of 'race' and schooling. Her current research includes black school exclusions. Her forthcoming book *'Race', Gender and Social Class in School Exclusion* (Falmer Press) is based on her research findings.

Preface and dedication

The idea for this book was conceived during several conversations that Barry Troyna and I had during the summer of 1994. They were conversations provoked by a number of heated exchanges that were at that time taking place through a variety of academic journals concerning the current state of educational research on 'race' and racism. They were debates that ranged from how 'racism' could be defined and studied, to what constituted 'evidence' of the existence and influence of racism in minority ethnic students' lives, and included more fundamental questions concerning the political nature of the research process itself, the role of 'antiracism' within it, and challenges to the orthodox view that academic research can and should be 'neutral'. Both Barry and I had, to varying degrees, contributed to these debates and felt a strong, personal investment in them (see, for example, Connolly 1992; Troyna 1993, 1995). In many ways, these contributions reflected a longer-standing concern that we both had with the politics and ethics of research on racism and education. This was particularly true for Barry who had by this time written quite extensively on the subject (see Troyna 1984, 1991a, 1993, 1994c; Troyna and Carrington 1989). His commitment to, and defence of, antiracism in education and research provided a significant influence in relation to my own developing work (see Connolly 1993, 1996a, 1996b).

It was during these conversations that we realized that these debates were taking place through a number of academic journals and were, consequently, relatively hidden and only being read by a small number of educational researchers and practitioners. Because of the fundamental importance of the issues that were being raised we agreed that we should try and bring together the main contributors to these debates, along with some of the newer voices in the field of 'race' and education, into one volume. We felt that this would help to bring the wide range of controversies and critiques to the attention of a much wider audience while also providing a platform for those authors to make an important contribution to these ongoing debates. It was from this basis that Barry and I put together an outline for the present book and approached those that have since contributed to this volume.

Tragically, Barry died in February 1996 after a year-long fight with cancer, long before the manuscript for this book was completed. However, his commitment to these debates generally and to this book more specifically is witnessed in the fact that he endeavoured to complete his own contribution to the collection while seriously ill and within months of his death. The decision to include Barry's name as joint editor of this volume reflects the central role that he played in conceiving the project and in organizing the contributors into a coherent collection. This book would simply not have materialized without his involvement. However, Barry's premature death meant that he was unable to see and offer guidance and comments on the drafts of the chapters that eventually materialized and which are included here. The responsibility for any editorial mistakes or omissions must therefore rest with me.

On hearing of Barry's death, it was unanimously agreed by all of those contributing to this present collection that the book be dedicated to his memory. Barry has not only made a fundamental and sustained contribution to our understanding of racism and education but he has also, importantly, come to influence and shape the work of a significant number of researchers, academics and educational practitioners. His commitment to social justice issues within education was not just an academic one but also informed his relationships with the many people that he came into contact with. Barry was unfailing in the emotional and academic support that he gave. He played the role of critical friend for many, and for some, including myself, that of mentor. The legacy of Barry's work and of the important role he has played in many people's lives will remain with us for a very long time.

Paul Connolly

Acknowledgements

I would like to thank a number of people for their help, support and encouragement in the production of this book. First, I would like to thank the contributors to the book and Shona Mullen and all at Open University Press. Second, I would like to place on record my thanks and gratitude to Barry Troyna. He was my mentor as well as my friend. He believed in me. This book would just not have materialized without his encouragement and support. Finally, I am particularly indebted to Karen Winter for her continuing love and emotional and practical support. She makes it all worthwhile.

Introduction

Paul Connolly

There are not many areas within the social sciences that can equal research on 'race' and ethnicity in terms of the heated methodological debates and controversies that have been generated. The debates have not been restricted to those concerning the strengths and weaknesses of particular methods but have opened up much wider controversies and raised more fundamental questions about the very research process itself. Some of the more central points of conflict within these debates include: arguments surrounding the need for a more politicized research agenda and, in particular, the development of an antiracist methodology; questions over racial identity and experience and who is best placed to do meaningful research on 'race' and ethnicity; and, finally, the issue of which methods are most appropriate in the study of racism and racialized relations. As these three particular themes provide the central points of engagement for the contributors to this book, the nature and development of the arguments and controversies in each area are worth briefly outlining in turn.

Anti-racism and the politicization of social research

In the early 1980s a number of writers came to question the politics of existing research on 'race' relations (see, for example, Bourne 1980; Gilroy 1980). Rather than seeing research as objective and neutral, such writers drew attention to the value-laden nature of the work that had been done on 'race' relations and argued that those carrying out research needed seriously to consider the nature, purpose and implications of their work. Up to that point, it was argued, mainstream research had largely produced very stereotypical accounts of minority ethnic communities which tended simply to reflect and reinforce the racist assumptions of the wider population. As Parmar (1981) argued in relation to young South Asians, for instance, they were invariably portrayed as being 'caught between two cultures' – the strict and traditional one of their parents' and the more liberal and open one of the 'West' – a position that was seen as inevitably leading to a crisis of identity and a rebelliousness among the younger generations (see also Brah and Minhas 1985). Much of the research on black youth was also criticized for its tendency to reinforce popular racial stereotypes. A number of commentators drew attention to the way that such research often portrayed black youth as aggressive and confrontational, and attempted to explain this in terms of pathological accounts of the lack of strong family ties within the black communities and, in particular, the high incidence of single parent families (see, for instance, Lawrence 1982; Phoenix 1994b). This culturalist approach, as Lawrence (1982) argued, tended therefore to shift attention away from the racist and discriminating processes of society and, instead, sought explanations for the disadvantaged position of minority ethnic communities among their own cultural traditions and ways of life. For Lawrence, the political implications of such work were quite clear: 'in a situation where *state racism* has intensified, it is disingenuous for policy-oriented researchers to expect that their racist and patriarchal conceptualizations of black people will not be of interest to the state institutions which oppress black people' (Lawrence 1982: 134, original emphasis).

It was in this recognition of the implications of such work that Bourne (1980), among others, called for an explicitly antiracist research agenda where studies of 'race' and ethnicity should be overtly political and where the focus should be decisively shifted away from dubious studies of the 'black community' and onto 'white racism'. This shift of focus would, it was argued, help to prevent studies which only seemed to reinforce the 'otherness' of the black community and would, instead, problematize and attempt to challenge racism.

More recently, however, the growing influence of post-structuralism within the social sciences and on theories of 'race' and ethnicity more specifically (see, for instance, Hall 1992a; Cohen 1992; Rattansi 1994; Connolly 1997), have led to an important reassessment of the nature and form of antiracism generally. It has been argued that this central focus on 'race', to the exclusion of other social factors, has encouraged a number of crude and essentialist beliefs including, most prominently, that all white people are racist and all minority ethnic people share a common experience of racism. A number of writers have argued that such an antiracist politics fails to realize the complex nature of racism, its diverse and context-specific forms and the way that it is crucially intersected and transformed by the cross-cutting influences of gender, class, ethnicity and sexuality (Gilroy 1990; Modood 1990; Rattansi 1992; Gillborn 1995). As the Macdonald Inquiry into the murder of a South Asian boy in a Manchester school quite vividly illustrates, there are clear limitations to constructing a unified white, racist population and thus ignoring the ways in which white people's identities and experiences are equally influenced by factors such as class and gender as well as 'race' (Macdonald *et al.* 1989; see also Connolly 1994; Gillborn 1996).

This reassessment of the nature and form of antiracism at a more general level has, as yet, to influence more specific debates about research – and particularly educational research – in any systematic way. One of the key themes running through a number of chapters in this book, however, is the need to develop an antiracist research perspective that can also accommodate the complexities, contingencies and contradictions of racism.

The place of racial identity and experience

Alongside, and related to, these debates generated in the early 1980s concerning the need for a more explicit antiracist agenda in social research, there emerged other fundamental questions concerning, in particular, who was best placed to conduct research on 'race' and racism. For many of the writers referred to above, the culturalist focus on minority ethnic communities and the inability to problematize the institutionalized nature of racism were seen partly as being the result of the value base of those conducting the research. It was felt that because the majority of researchers were white and middle-class, this meant that they had very little experience or understanding of racism. It was therefore not surprising, it was argued, that these researchers would tend to overlook the importance of racism in minority people's lives and simply reproduce the assumptions and values that were taken for granted because they underpinned their own privileged social position. Rather than critiquing the white, middle-class 'norm' and the exclusionary processes and practices that formed its foundation, it was argued that many researchers simply used this 'norm' unquestioningly as the yardstick to examine and assess the lives and experiences of the minority ethnic population. It was of little surprise to find, therefore, that the research focus failed to problematize racism. As Bikhu Parekh argued: 'Most researchers in the field are white. They have no experience of what it means to be black, and lack an intuitive understanding of the complex mental processes and social structures of the black communities' (cited in Troyna and Carrington 1989: 209). Moreover, it was argued that the focus that did exist, with its concern with documenting and analysing the 'different' traditions and ways of life of minority communities, encouraged the production of pathological and stereotypical portrayals.

While such debates rarely went so far as to call for the exclusion of white people from researching 'race' and ethnicity, they often tended to privilege the 'black experience' and led writers such as Brar (1992) to argue that there should be a division of labour where white people, because of their 'insider' status, should focus on white institutions, and black researchers should focus on the black community as they are much more acutely aware of the nature and effects of racism in their lives.

However, the growing influence of post-structuralism has also come to demand a reassessment of these debates concerning racial identities and experience. There has emerged, for instance, a growing critique of the use of the term 'black' as a political identity to refer to all minority ethnic groups in a bid to signify their shared experiences of racism. For writers such as Modood (1988, 1992), the term 'black' is largely the product of the African Caribbean experience and does not adequately address the very real differences that exist between that and the diverse experiences of South Asian people. In relation to education, a number of important studies have also highlighted the very differing experiences of schooling that African Caribbean and South Asian students face and how these experiences are further delineated in terms of gender (Mac an Ghaill 1988; Gillborn 1990; Mizra 1992; Connolly 1998).

This growing acknowledgement of the complexities of racial identities and experience is now feeding through into debates concerning 'race'-related research (see Connolly 1996b). As Rhodes has argued, for instance:

> arguments for the exclusion of white researchers from research with black people as subjects assume a congruence of interests between black researchers and subjects which disguises internal conflicts and suggests an artificial harmony. The only significant dimension of exploitation is assumed to be that between white investigator and black subject. Other dimensions of social inequality may often be more significant to participants.
>
> (Rhodes 1994: 556)

The implications of this ongoing reassessment of the nature of antiracism and identity are only now reaching through into the sphere of educational research and provide a second, important thread to the contributions in this collection.

Methods in the study of racism in education

Finally, this growing awareness within the research community of the complex and contradictory nature of racism has led the debates on methodology full circle, back onto a reassessment of the uses of differing research methods and their appropriateness in the study of 'race' and racism. The early statistical analyses of racial inequalities in educational performance, found for instance in the Swann Report *Education for All* (DES 1985), were criticized for failing to identify and help understand the complex social processes and practices that led to these inequalities. As Troyna (1984) pointed out, the production of crude statistics comparing the average examination performances of African Caribbean students with their white and South Asian peers only helped to reproduce the notion of black 'underachievement' which, in the absence of an understanding of the complex racialized processes that tend adversely to effect African Caribbean students, can easily act to reinforce popular racist stereotypes about their academic commitment and abilities. Similarly, the statistical analysis of racist incidents and their presentation in tabular form as found in the work of Kelly and Cohn (1988) for instance, have also been criticized for failing to shed light on the social contexts within which these incidents occur. As Troyna and Hatcher (1992: 35) argue: 'like any other pattern of behaviour of children and young people these incidents can only really be understood in the contexts of their lives in home, school and community. The orientation of current research, with its obsession for statistical profiles, has led to a dislocation of racist incidents from these settings'.

It was within this context that a distinctive shift towards ethnographic methods was witnessed in research on racism and schooling from the mid-1980s onwards (see, for instance, Wright 1986; Mac an Ghaill 1988; Gillborn 1990; Mirza 1992). It was believed that such an approach with its use of a variety of methods including observation, semi-structured interviews and documentary sources was best placed to uncover and analyse the subtle range of processes, nuances and meaning that underpin minority students' experiences of schooling (see Mac an Ghaill 1989 and also Connolly 1996a).

This shift towards qualitative methods has brought with it more controversy however. The in-depth study of particular schools and groups of students and teachers within these schools has led some critics to question whether these studies offer sufficient 'convincing evidence' to support their claim that teacher racism plays a significant part in the schooling of minority students (see Hurrell 1995; Foster *et al.* 1996). This, in turn, has opened up a fierce debate concerning the notions of validity, how 'racism' is to be defined and what types of data are required to constitute 'proof' of its manifestation (for an overview of these arguments see Gillborn 1995).

Moreover, these debates have created the space where researchers are now reconsidering the role and purpose of particular methods in the study of racism and schooling. In relation to ethnography, for instance: What is its function? What sort of claims should it be making? How should it be assessed and judged? Of equal importance, especially with the increasingly sophisticated statistical techniques that have been developed over the last decade, what should the role of quantitative methods be? How can they be used in such a way as to avoid the crude stereotypes offered and criticized in the past? In what ways can they contribute to our understanding of the contemporary significance of 'race' and racism in schooling?

Structure of the book

These ongoing debates in relation to the nature and form of antiracist research, the place of racial identity and experience in 'race'-related research, and the appropriate use of particular methods in the study of 'race' and racism, provide central themes that run throughout the chapters that follow. The first three chapters offer a reassessment of the broader politics of educational research and critique. Chapter 1 presents a critique of what Maud Blair terms the 'myth of neutrality in educational research'. In building upon the earlier work of Bourne (1980) and Lawrence (1982) among others, Blair argues that all research analyses are inevitably a reflection of the researchers' own particular value bases and social positions. It is disingenuous, she contends, to assume that research can be objective and value-free as this relies upon a bogus notion of a hegemonic research community where its members all subscribe to and share a common (and neutral) set of values and beliefs about the nature and purpose of research. Rather, Blair argues that the dominant research community reflects the particular values of the established white, middle-class and male elite. For Blair, what counts as 'neutral' and 'objective' and what is therefore used as a yardstick to judge and assess research, is actually itself simply a reflection of the dominant values of the powerful elites within society. There exists a certain irony, she contends, in partisan researchers being criticized for being open and truthful about their own value base and the political intentions of their work, by commentators who proceed to hide behind the mask of neutrality and therefore consistently fail to accept their own value base. Blair argues that all researchers need to be reflective and not only assess the ways in which their own social position and identification with particular social groups affects their work, but also to bear in mind the political implications of their research. Being 'partisan' in this way does not mean that research has to be biased or unsystematic in its analysis, but rather that it represents no more than the researcher being truthful about their social position and its impact upon their work.

By contrast, in Chapter 2, Martyn Hammersley, in Chapter 2, rejects the whole notion of partisan research and argues that it is a contradiction in terms. Hammersley contends that once a researcher attempts to use their research in the pursuit of particular political goals, the quality and objective nature of that research will be inevitably compromised. He uses Mac an Ghaill's (1988) ethnographic study of the schooling experiences of black and South Asian students as an example of this. Hammersley argues that Mac an Ghaill's overt antiracist stance and his political identification with the minority ethnic students meant that his collection and analysis of the data was biased. In essence, Hammersley contends that Mac an Ghaill drew disproportionately upon the students' perspectives and reported them largely as 'fact', while at the same time tended critically to interpret and deconstruct the teachers' perspectives. For Hammersley, Mac an Ghaill has done no more than reverse the dominant hierarchy of credibility that Becker (1967) claimed existed, where the viewpoint of the subordinate groups (in this case the black and South Asian students) was now regarded as a more credible source of information than that of the dominant group (i.e. the teachers). Hammersley concludes by arguing that just because the viewpoints of dominant groups have been regarded as more credible than those of subordinate groups in the past, this is no excuse simply to turn the hierarchy of credibility on its head. Rather, researchers should be concerned with discovering what is *justifiably* credible, and this involves the use of basic methodological procedures that are objective and neutral and whose employment should form the basis of agreement among the academic community.

In Chapter 3, David Gillborn addresses the broader methodological critique of existing qualitative research on racism and schooling that has been undertaken by Peter Foster, Roger Gomm and Martyn Hammersley, and which has culminated in the recent publication of their book *Constructing Educational Inequality* (Foster *et al.* 1996). As Gillborn explains, their work has involved a sustained critique of all of the main qualitative studies of racism and schooling and has, in every case, concluded that the data used in such work has not proven the existence of racism 'beyond reasonable doubt'. In developing some of the arguments offered by Blair in Chapter 1, Gillborn argues that Foster and his colleagues' professed support of objective research actually betrays their failure to recognize the value base of their own position. Gillborn contends that it is a position that privileges the status quo and acts to protect current educational processes and practices. Moreover, it is a position that places the onus of proof for the existence of racism on those seeking to challenge the current distribution of opportunities and awards. It is a value position that is further reinforced, Gillborn argues, by the restriction of the definition of what counts as racism to overtly identifiable and intentional acts, and thus the effective denial of the existence of institutional racism and its more subtle, indirect and unintentional forms. Gillborn argues that such a restrictive definition and the emphasis on proving the existence of racism 'beyond reasonable doubt' denies the inherently uncertain nature of social research coupled with the complex nature of racism.

One of the main consequences of this approach, Gillborn argues, is that the work of Foster, Gomm and Hammersley not only tends to inadvertently defend and sustain racial inequalities but also, in offering alternative explanations to racism for educational inequalities, tends to pathologize minority ethnic students and perpetuate a number of popular racist stereotypes. In echoing the arguments of Blair's earlier chapter, Gillborn argues that all social research and critique must bear in mind the political implications of its work and the values upon which it is based. In attempting to make a distinction between science and politics, Gillborn concludes that Foster and his colleagues' methodological project represents a subtle but pernicious sleight of hand where their support of value-free and objective scientific procedures and its use to critique the work of others helps to mask the political nature (whether intentional or otherwise) of their own work.

The following five chapters shift their focus, to varying degrees, to the practice of doing antiracist research. What can be seen quite clearly in these contributions is the very different perspectives held on the importance of identity and the difficulties in engaging with and developing an antiracist research paradigm. To begin with, in Chapter 4, Anuradha Rakhit explains how her own identity as a South Asian woman and her experience of racism as a teacher in England has played a pivotal role in helping her to formulate her research design and develop a good relationship with the South Asian women teachers she studied. In offering a powerful account of the effects of racism in her own life, Rakhit goes on to demonstrate how it had important resonances in the lives of her respondents. She argues that the use of the life history approach, and the space this gave for the sharing of experiences between herself and her respondents, was a central element in developing a mutual trust and encouraging the South Asian women to speak openly and personally about their own experiences of racism. For Rakhit, therefore, her identity as a South Asian woman and her personal experience of racism in the teaching profession provided important aides in sensitizing her to the issue of racism in her research design, and gaining access to and consequently understanding and analysing the nature and effects of racism in the lives of her respondents.

In Chapter 5, Cecile Wright draws upon her own experiences as a black woman doing ethnographic research to highlight some of the problems and tensions that can emerge when researching a social setting which includes respondents from different social backgrounds and representing very different interests. While she found that she was able to relate quite closely to the black students in her research because of the shared understandings and culture they had in common, this created tensions with the predominantly white teachers in her study. The complexities and multi-layered nature of social identities are highlighted in Wright's chapter in the sense that the teachers not only saw her as black but also as an adult and therefore someone who should be 'on their side'. As a result, Wright describes how she was 'caught in the crossfire' in relation to the conflicts that ensued between some of the black students and their white teachers. In this, both the students and the teachers appealed to different parts of her identity and expected her to support them. This, Wright goes on to outline, presented a number of difficult problems including, in particular, a tension in her relationships with some of the white teachers, which she struggled to manage.

The complex nature of identity does not only create situations such as those described by Wright, but can also create important divisions between the researcher and the researched even where they are 'racially matched'. This is the focus of Chapter 6 where Mehreen Mirza draws upon her own experience of attempts as a South Asian woman to research South Asian girls and women. She highlights some of the problems of assuming the importance of racial symmetry and ignoring the many other competing factors that come to shape and influence people's identities. She recounts the difficulties encountered in attempting to implement a black feminist approach with its stress on 'black' women researching 'black' women. Mirza's research focuses on South Asian girls' and women's experiences of education in 'non-traditional' subject areas. She found, however, that her own identity as a South Asian woman was not enough to develop a rapport and reciprocal relationship with her respondents to the degree that Rakhit found. For a number of reasons, Mirza found that the South Asian girls and women she studied actually viewed her, in many respects, as an 'outsider'. As Mirza explains, her dress, the make-up she wore, the style of her hair, the fact that she lived on her own and that she came from a different geographical area within England all acted to encourage the construction of her as the 'other' in the eyes of many of her respondents. In contrast to Rakhit's experience, therefore, the more that Mirza attempted to develop a reciprocal relationship by sharing experiences and aspects of her own life with her respondents, the more it tended to exacerbate their perception of her 'strangeness'. It was a process that not only encouraged the South Asian girls and women to question Mirza's identity but also had the effect of forcing her to do so as well.

In Chapter 7, Barry Troyna develops these themes through a critical reflection of the influence of his 'whiteness' on two particular research projects he was involved in. In reviewing the critique levelled at white researchers by writers such as Gilroy (1980) and Lawrence (1982) outlined earlier in this introduction (some of which Troyna points out was actually directed at his own work of the late 1970s and early 1980s), he develops some of the arguments by Mirza in relation to the crude and essentialist nature of debates concerning racial symmetry. In particular Troyna draws attention to the complex and multi-dimensional nature of social identities and how, as a white researcher, he was still able to draw upon a number of aspects of his identity in relation to place, class, gender and culture that he shared with the black young men and which enabled him to develop a rapport with them. Troyna uses this to reject the arguments that he was unable, as a *white* researcher, to interpret accurately and with empathy the experiences and perspectives of the black respondents. However, he does go on to accept another aspect of the critique relating to his focus on the black community rather than white racism. In retrospect, Troyna argues that this was misconceived and, as he terms it, an 'anathema to antiracist goals'. He adds that this type of exclusive focus on minority communities runs the risk of reinforcing their 'otherness'. Troyna goes on to outline how his growing commitment to an antiracist agenda, with the attendant need to problematize racism and avoid voyeuristic accounts of minority ethnic groups, led him to re-evaluate his involvement in a different research project that he was involved in some years later.

Both Troyna and Mirza, in their respective contributions, highlight the problems of adopting a simplistic approach to antiracist research. For both of them, the problems appeared to arise when attempting to follow an antiracist strategy that did not fully take into account the complexities of social identities and the way in which 'race' is cut across with other social factors including ethnicity, gender, class and place. This reassessment of antiracist strategies and the need to open them up to the influence of other critical research approaches is developed further by Sarah Neal in Chapter 8. In particular Neal explores the contradictions and problems that emerge when attempting to move beyond the singular focus of 'race' to incorporate a gender dimension. She begins by outlining the commonalities and differences between the development of the antiracist and feminist traditions in research. She draws attention to how antiracism developed, in large part, as a challenge to the stereotypical portrayal of minority ethnic communities in social research, while feminist research emerged in response to the omission of women from social science inquiry. As such, Neal argues that while feminist research has essentially developed a reciprocal, subjective focus by encouraging research by women on women to allow them to redress their absence from social research, antiracist research developed a more confrontational style with the aim of shifting the existing focus away from the 'black community' and on to 'white racism'. It is from this basis that Neal goes on to explore some of the contradictions that were opened up and the problems faced in trying to reconcile what she describes as the essential 'femininity' of the feminist stance with the 'masculinity' of the antiracist approach. Such a reconciliation was made that much more difficult, Neal explains, by the fact that her own research involved an 'upward gaze' to the powerful, and overwhelmingly male, professionals within higher education. Neal argues that the difficulties that a number of researchers have identified in terms of attempting to challenge the racism expressed by their respondents, were made that much more difficult for her as this also involved her having to challenge the feminine role expected of her. That is, as one who would listen to, passively encourage, and facilitate male speech.

The final two chapters consider the appropriate use and the strengths and weaknesses of particular methods in the study of 'race' and education in the light of the increasing stress on the complex, contingent and contradictory nature of racism. In focusing, respectively, on qualitative and quantitative methods, both chapters set out the possible role and functions of these methods and enable the reader to see how they can be used in a complimentary fashion. In Chapter 9, Paul Connolly offers a reassessment of the role and purpose of qualitative methods, and ethnographic research in particular, in contributing to our understanding of racism in schools. Connolly begins by drawing attention to the way that ethnography has often been criticized for being unscientific and subjective and, because of its small-scale focus on particular schools or students within schools, how its findings have been criticized for having little relevance beyond that particular study. He argues that such critiques betray a fundamental misunderstanding of the nature and role of ethnographic research and how, in trying to demonstrate a wider relevance, ethnographers have either been drawn into trying to generalize from their results and/or have been criticized when they do not. Connolly argues that there is a need to reconsider the role of ethnographic research and how its relevance can be more fruitfully assessed. In this he contends that ethnographers should resist the temptation to generalize once and for all. In arguing that ethnography is incapable of offering any form of generalization, either from the sample school to other schools, or within the school in relation to generalizations about particular groups of students or teachers, Connolly argues that ethnography should, instead, be primarily concerned with identifying and understanding causal social processes – in other words, developing our understanding of what *caused* a particular person or group of people to behave in a certain way. In arguing this, Connolly offers an alternative way in which the role of ethnography can be understood and its relevance assessed.

In Chapter 10, David Drew and Sean Demack offer a comprehensive overview of the recent developments within statistical analyses and the opportunities these have now opened up for developing our understanding of the influence of 'race' and racism in education. They outline a number of statistical methods and models that have been developed and refined over the last decade and explain how these have been utilized in three particular areas: analysis of educational attainment; the educational and labour market transitions for those aged between 16 and 19; and studies of what has come to be termed 'school effectiveness'. While they are careful to offer a number of caveats and to highlight the limitations of a number of studies conducted in these areas, they develop a strong case for the future role of statistical analyses and quantitative methods more generally in research on racism and schooling. As they conclude, with the many advances in statistical techniques and computer technology, the problems that Troyna (1984) identified over a decade ago in relation to the crude analyses of educational attainment and the tendency that such analyses had for painting a simplistic and caricatured picture of South Asian success and African Caribbean underachievement have now long passed.

It will become clear, on reading this book, that there are no easy answers or resolutions to these debates. Rather it will be seen that, in the place of agreement and consensus, there is only continuing debate and controversy. In the last analysis, the contentious nature of these debates reflects the complexity of the subject matter, their inherently political nature and the central role that racism continues to play in the distribution of educational rewards and life chances. While there are no easy solutions it is clear that it is incumbent upon us all, as researchers and practitioners, to make it our task to continue to prioritize and work through these issues in relation to our own work.

1 | The myth of neutrality in educational research

Maud Blair

> Privilege keeps the terms of your privilege invisible.
> Michael Kimmel

Introduction

During a symposium on gender held at a conference of the American Educational Research Association in New York in April 1996, the participants (predominantly women), were asked to go into groups to talk about how they might become more supportive of each other in the academy. The group I attended went into a long discussion about how women from minority ethnic groups felt let down in different ways and sometimes betrayed by their white women colleagues. Examples were given of racist assumptions held by white colleagues, of white women colluding either actively or passively with racially discriminatory decisions, not registering their objections to racial slurs, and so on. The 'scribe' (a white woman) took notes and also wrote up, for a report back to the plenary, 'ways forward' for all women. These 'ways forward' included the need to question assumptions about 'others', for white women to recognize that they had more power than minority women in predominantly white institutions, and the need to use such (albeit limited) power to advance the interests of women generally.

After the discussion had gone on in this vein for some time, the question was posed as to why after all these years of feminism and of debates about racism within feminism, the same assumptions about 'others' still existed, the same practices were prevalent and the same discussions were still taking place. It was suggested that perhaps it was time we stopped looking only at *what* happened and *how* these negative relations happened, and began to examine *why* they were continuously being reproduced. The speaker continued with the suggestion that perhaps a focus on how social identities, and in particular how white identities were produced and reproduced, might help to shed light on some of the factors which created boundaries between women and mitigated against an inclusive sense of sisterhood. Examples were given of studies which had begun to look beyond merely how men behaved, to studies of masculinity which sought to understand the discourses which produced 'men' and 'women' and helped to sustain gender inequalities. It was suggested that in addition to the recommendations already agreed, a further recommendation that we examine the notion of white identity be put forward. At this point the conversation ground to a halt, the 'scribe' handed her notes to the Chair of the group declaring that she did not know what to write and did not therefore know what to report back to the plenary. The other groups reported back their discussions and resolutions, which were all couched within the same somewhat soporific 'good intentions' framework, and our group did not report.

What does this story have to do with research theories? To begin with, it is important to make the distinction between *striving* for neutrality and *guaranteeing* neutrality. What the above story seems to me to illustrate is that no matter what our good intentions, we cannot guarantee neutrality in our interpretations and analyses. This is because our histories and memories are shot through with gendered, classed, racialized and other 'excluding' understandings which give us our particular perspectives on the world. Most of the participants at the conference, and certainly all those in the group described above, were academics or students and either had been or were currently engaged in research. There is no reason to suppose that they conducted their research with anything other than integrity, honesty and rigour. It is necessary, nevertheless, to ask to what extent researchers' definitions and interpretations can be neutral given the 'blindspots' that seem to arise when the 'gaze' is transferred from the 'other' to one's subjective self and the group with which one identifies? How easy is it for members of powerful groups to 'decentre' and make, not only the powerful group, but one's own personal investment in belonging to that group the object of inquiry in order to assess the extent to which this influences and affects the knowledge one produces? Laura E. Perez (1993: 270) states that constructions of identity are not only different but 'heavily invested in a *difference of interests* [her emphasis]'.

It is of course not only in relation to 'race' and ethnicity that blindspots of this kind can occur. According to hooks: 'Often brilliant political thinkers have had such blindspots. Men like Fanon, Albert Mennin, Paulo Freire and Aimé Césaire whose works teach us much about the nature of colonization, racism, classism, and revolutionary struggle often ignore issues of sexist oppression in their own writing' (hooks 1984: 39). Such blindspots occur when researchers conduct their research without also acquainting themselves with the broader historical, political and social context within which the research is conducted. Researchers might be concerned about critical reflexivity, but what exactly does this mean? What is the content of such critical reflection? Does it include reflection on one's own 'whiteness' (or heterosexuality, or maleness, or class position or absence of impairment)? Does it include reflection on whether and how these subjective identities might be significant to the way in which researchers interpret the lives of those they study?

The argument that those who conduct partisan research are more likely to be biased (see Hammersley, this volume), is, in my view mistaken. Making one's politics explicit is no more likely to introduce bias into one's analysis than declaring that one does *not* have a value position. What the latter position does is to mask the fact that research interpretations are arrived at via styles of reasoning and deduction which fit particular theories and particular world views. These in turn derive from one's life history or cultural experience as a member of an ethnic group: female or male; middle-class or heterosexual; non-disabled; or a combination of some or all of these.

What do we mean by neutrality?

The most relevant definitions of the term for our purposes are the following: *impartial; taking the middle position; not helping or supporting either of two opposing sides* (see Concise Oxford Dictionary; Chambers Dictionary; Universal Dictionary respectively).

The debate about values, and about researchers not being blank pages waiting for research 'findings' to fill the blanks, has been well rehearsed over the years. It is accepted that researchers bring their 'baggage' with them into the research process, but that every attempt is made, in Margaret Mead's words, 'to sweep one's mind clear of every presupposition' (cited in Walker 1986). Instead, the researcher's definitions and understandings should be guided by and adjusted in relation to the data collected. Through the research, one might learn new ways of 'seeing'. However, research does not necessarily alter previous theories, but can and often does reinforce what previous studies have found.

If we assume that most researchers have integrity and are concerned primarily with trying to uncover and to understand 'the problem', and will therefore conduct their study with the rigour that a self-respecting research community expects, then the question of neutrality must impinge most strongly at the point of analysis of the data. Presumably, according to proponents of objectivity and neutrality, one stands back from the data and employs methods of interpretation which do not 'help or support either of two opposing sides' (see Foster *et al.* 1996). The assumption here is that analysing research data is like umpiring a game of cricket – anyone looking at that same data would reach the same conclusions because 'the facts' are there to be seen and judged by a set of rules which apply to all players at all times, regardless of which side the umpires would in their heart of hearts like to see win the game. This is, in my view, an untenable position. It is untenable not only because research is, as already indicated, a political activity in which the researcher is heavily implicated, but also because it creates a hegemonic research community. Through this hegemony, not only are the rules of the game decided by an established elite, but alternative voices are likely to be excluded if they do not fit within predetermined criteria for what is deemed to be valid research. Those who consider that research should be no more than an exercise in 'naval-gazing' are likely to dismiss or find unconvincing the 'findings' of those who consider research which is done for the sole benefit of the researcher to be unethical. Such research takes information from or about already oppressed groups, and gives nothing back, a model which Lather (1986) refers to as the 'rape' model. The 'umpire' model of analysis discussed above thus creates an obvious difficulty for researchers who believe in using their research for social change. Unlike cricket, research into social inequalities is by its very nature about umpiring a game that is played on different and unequal levels. Whilst the (declared) partisan researcher would consider it necessary to take this inequality into account by examining the power relations that exist and exploring the effects of these differential power relations, the non-partisan researcher might choose to ignore this inequality and the inherent power relations and focus only on the rules (Connolly 1992). What this illustrates is not only that research is contested terrain, but also that neither position is or can be neutral.

It is, moreover, an error on the part of those who conclude that bias is an inevitable consequence of political commitment, to assume that partisan researchers have no interest in probing 'the truth', however unpleasant that may be. Indeed, social justice demands absolute integrity and a rigorous attitude and approach to one's research. How, otherwise, could one hope to understand 'the problem' and contribute to change? This does not, of course, mean that the dangers of bias are absent. But this is not the argument here. What is argued is that commitment to social justice does not make the research and the analysis any more biased than absence of commitment. It must be the dream of every black or minority parent living in the West to reach a stage when extensive research can reveal that there is no more racism in schools. Without racism as a complicating factor, it might make finding solutions to the problems faced by black children in schools that much easier. Mead comments that: 'The point of going into the field at all is to extend further what is already known, and so there is little value merely in identifying new versions of the familiar when we might instead, find something wholly new' (cited in Walker 1986: 208).

Racism: what is it and who decides?

It is important to ask whether 'what is already known' is accepted within the research and academic community as a valid position from which to start. Can one, for example, begin on the assumption that 'race' is a social construction and not a scientific or biological fact, or does one have to go back and establish this in every project, and how and where does one do this? More importantly, do the research and academic community accept work that has been internationally acknowledged and accepted as 'what is already known' and hence a valid position to start from? And if they do not, then on what basis do they reject that work?

Presumably the answer to the first question is 'yes'; one can begin on the basis that social groups are 'produced' in discourse as 'races' and that in societies where 'race' is an important axis of differential power, this will affect the life chances and opportunities of the less powerful 'races'. If this is indeed accepted, how is racism in its different forms *and as experienced by black people*, to be defined and who does the defining? This, then leads onto the second question raised above where we find that there is much less consensus of opinion. For instance, is the experience as defined by black people and taken on by antiracists more biased than the definition imposed by those who have never and never could have such an experience? Who decides this and by what right or authority? Was the decision by Peter Foster (1990a) (a major proponent of neutrality in research) to ignore the experience of racism as defined by black students in his study a neutral decision and if so, why? To what extent might his own identity as a white researcher, together with his rejection of how black students felt that racism affected them, have introduced bias into his findings? Furthermore, if white researchers do not accept the numerous findings of black and antiracist researchers, findings which resonate so powerfully with the experiences of black people, then from where do they derive their claims to neutrality?

Understanding ethnocentrism

I have at times been surprised and frustrated by responses to my own work. For example, in my research into the over-representation of black pupils (not including pupils of South Asian descent) in exclusions from schools, one of my earliest observations was that black pupils in Britain are a diverse group coming as they do from a range of different cultural, linguistic, social class and family backgrounds, including differences in gender. It was also clear from my observations and from interviews with teachers, parents and pupils, that black pupils presented diverse responses to particular phenomena, including schooling, and that there were similarities and overlaps in their behaviours and responses with their white and Asian counterparts of similar backgrounds, as indicated by interviews and teacher referral records. I had also deliberately chosen three schools that differed in their social and material circumstances, their social class intake, their location and the percentage of black students within them. Controlling therefore for these various factors of class, ethnicity, gender, location, numbers etc. (and bearing in mind that official government statistics had found this over-representation to be a national pattern (DFE 1992) and therefore not confined to the schools in my study) I concluded that the over-representation of black males as a group in exclusions from these schools must relate to factors outside this group and not inherent to it. This did not mean that there would be no exclusions but that there would be a random distribution of black pupils among those excluded, proportionate to their numbers in a particular school, as there were for pupils from white and Asian ethnic groups. In other words, it was unlikely that black pupils as a group would exhibit behaviour patterns and responses which were different from their white (working class) counterparts when responding to the ordinary everyday phenomena of schooling common to all pupils regardless of background. If any difference did emerge in the behaviour of black pupils as a group, compared to their white peers, then this can only be explained in relation to their differential treatment *as a group* by the school.

What then were these patterns? Interviews with over a 100 black pupils aged between 14 and 18 produced one clear pattern of response – that black (male) pupils received an unfair share of negative comments and reprimands from teachers, that white and Asian pupils received more help and encouragement, that black pupils were picked out for reprimand even when other ethnic groups were involved, and that they were given harsher punishment than their white and Asian peers for the same offences in these schools. This was confirmed by a study of referral forms for one year in one of the schools. The forms outlined the nature of the offence committed by students and the length of exclusion given. These forms revealed clear discrepancies between the length of exclusion given to some black students for the same – and sometimes *lesser* – offences than their white and Asian peers. They also experienced blatant racism from teachers in the form of racist comments and 'jokes'. These findings confirmed what many others before me had found in relation to the experiences of black pupils. This includes the findings of large-scale studies conducted in primary schools (Tizard *et al.* 1988) and in junior schools (Mortimore *et al.* 1988) where it was found that black pupils received more criticism and negative feedback than other groups. Such overwhelming evidence, suggested that black pupils were perceived in schools as one homogenous and undifferentiated group and that this was resulting in their being treated, *as a group*, differently from their white and Asian peers.

I was therefore interested in the ways in which black pupils were not only constructed, but 'produced' as a homogenous group in schools and how this impacted on their school experiences, in particular their experiences of exclusion. In drawing out the themes that emerged from my interviews, I divided teacher responses into three groups: those who saw black pupils as the problem; those who saw it as a combined problem of racism and pupil behaviour; and those who saw racism in the education system as the problem. My technique was to deconstruct teachers' discourses in order to understand the frameworks used by teachers for understanding pupil behaviour. It emerged that the teachers who saw the problem as mainly one of discrimination against black students were more likely to talk about black students as individuals and less likely to use stereotypes in their explanations of pupil behaviour. On the other hand, teachers who saw black students as being responsible for their over-representation in exclusions tended to talk about them as members of a racial group, and not as individual personalities. I thus concluded that stereotyping was indeed one way in which teachers made sense of the behaviours of black pupils. I decided to analyse closely these stereotypes in order to show how they might contribute to the problem of over-representation of black pupils in exclusions. One colleague's observation was that I had been unfair to subject some teachers' discourses to closer scrutiny than others. This means, presumably, that I had not been neutral in my approach. It is difficult to see, under the circumstances, what kind of neutrality was required. The problem that I thought necessary to investigate was one of stereotypes. The focus therefore was not on teachers who did not stereotype, but on those who did – regardless of the ethnicity of the teacher.

A useful outcome of this critique of my paper was that it reinforced the importance of being explicit and not leaving meanings embedded in the text, especially in as 'sensitive' an area as 'race'. However, another colleague suggested that I was focusing too much on teachers and not enough on the behaviour of pupils and that I should turn my attention to the possibility that black pupils *qua* black pupils do behave worse than their white and/or Asian peers. Given the diversity of black students, the implication therefore was that there must be something racial, or biological which makes black pupils, as a group, more prone to bad behaviour and therefore more deserving of exclusion. Indeed, this is precisely the underlying assumptions in the work of Peter Foster (1990a) discussed above, who suggested that black pupils, by virtue of their worse behaviour, were less deserving of places in the academic streams in the school in which he worked (see also Gillborn, this volume). We were, however, given no information as to why skin colour should be the criteria that marked these students out from their peers. There was no discussion of the cultures of these students, so it was impossible to tell from where this behaviour was coming. In my opinion, this was in part a product of Foster's superficial understanding of the history and politics of 'race', I would argue also that his whole theoretical orientation is rooted firmly in what Stanfield refers to as, 'folk notions' of racial differences (Stanfield 1993b: 4). I would go further to suggest that it was also due to a failure on Foster's part to reflect back in on himself and interrogate the possible role that his world view as a white person might play in his interpretation and analysis of 'race' (Connolly 1992; Gillborn 1995). Despite his numerous criticisms and dismissals of the work of antiracist researchers, the conclusions he drew in his own work, bearing in mind his rejection of the views of black pupils, could hardly be said to be based on a neutral analysis in the context of race relations in Britain (Connolly 1992).

Neutrality or white defensiveness?

As my story at the beginning of this chapter shows, self-reflection when one is in a position of (relative) power is by no means an easy thing to do, especially when one's actions are not necessarily motivated by racial prejudice. Christine Sleeter (a white professor of teacher education at the University of Wisconsin), writing about a two-year staff development programme on 'race' which she conducted for teachers, describes how, over that period, she 'saw them [white teachers] select information and teaching strategies to add to a framework for understanding race that they took for granted, which they had constructed over their lifetimes from their position as white people in a racist society' (Sleeter 1993: 168). She also comments that 'Whites so internalize their own power and taken-for-granted superiority that they resist self-questioning' (167). (See also Roman 1993; hooks 1984.)

I would agree with McCarthy and Crichlow that we need a more complex understanding of the contradictory interests and needs as well as the educational and political behaviour of minority groups, but also that 'much work needs to be done to understand and intervene in the ways in which whites are positioned and produced as "white", in the language, symbolic and material structures that dominate culture in the West' (McCarthy and Crichlow 1993: xix).

Black and antiracist researchers do, nevertheless, need to pay attention to the criticisms that are levelled against us if we are to produce sharper and more refined analyses. However, there is a sense of frustration on the part of black researchers when we can see that our work on 'race' is assessed from within frameworks which are ethnocentric in that they assume one 'correct' view of the world, and are blind to the subtle nuances of racism (Essed 1991). The expectation that experiences of racism must be observable (by anybody), measurable, and show intention if they are to qualify as racism only confirms the hegemonic nature of these requirements (see, for example, Hurrell 1995). This perspective ignores the complex nature of racism. As Kovel (1988: 54) states: 'No one behaves simply; he [*sic!*] is the amalgamated product of a host of historical, cultural and personal influences'.

An example of the different frameworks through which 'race' and racism are seen by white colleagues who have not acquired the necessary theoretical framework for understanding the different ways in which racism operates is recounted by Britzman *et al.* (1993: 191). They cite Patricia Williams, an African American legal scholar who wrote a critique of a law exam in which students had to argue a case based upon 'a decontextualized version of Shakespeare's *Othello*, in which Othello is described as a "Black militaristic African leader" who marries the "young white Desdemona" whom he then kills "in a fit of sexual rage" '. William's critique was that:

> The problem presents a defendant who is black, militaristic, unsophisticated, insecure, jealous, and sexually enraged. It reduces the facts to the very same racist generalizations and stereotypes this nation has used to subjugate black people since the first slave was brought from Africa. Moreover, it places an enormous burden on black students in particular who must assume, for the sake of answering this question, these things about themselves – that is the trauma of gratuitous generalization. The frame places blacks in the position of speaking against ourselves. It forces us to accept as 'truth' constructions that go to the heart of who we are.
>
> (Williams 1991: 82)

Williams' colleagues responded by asking why she couldn't be 'objective', and why she imposed her own personal agenda on something as 'innocent' as an exam. The student who complained about the question was labelled 'an activist'.

When our contributions are thus judged and dismissed from within an ethnocentric framework, it presents us with a real dilemma. On the one hand, we consider our work important and wish to disseminate it widely, and on the other we are conscious that in order to do so we have to work within disciplinary conventions in which the rules which govern procedure and validity are themselves non-representative and exclusionary. This is not to suggest that work on 'race' or other areas that deal with social justice issues should operate entirely by different sets of rules. We all need to be critical of, and reflect on the knowledge and information we produce and the methods by which we produce such knowledge. Feminists, for example, are more critical of or reject outright the supposed dichotomy between quantitative and qualitative studies (Siraj-Blatchford 1994; Jayarantne and Stewart 1995). My argument here is that we need to question whether decisions to accept or not accept the work of black and antiracist researchers are indeed based on neutral criteria, or are 'a defense mechanism exhibited by those who wish to not acknowledge the importance of the empirical findings or claims of these researchers' (Stanfield 1993b: 29).

Conclusion

My concern in this chapter has been to question the notion of neutrality in research analyses, and to suggest that what often passes for neutrality in social research is no more than a mask which hides taken for granted partisan notions of what constitutes 'good' research. It is partisan because it ignores the possibility of diverse systems of knowledge production and multiple interpretations of social phenomena. This diversity does not exclude the importance of agreeing that every researcher needs to be guided by ethical codes of conduct. I argued that our interpretations are underpinned by our life histories and our investment (whether or not acknowledged) in our personal and group identities. Neutrality in social justice research is therefore a myth, whether or not one declares one's value system. I would argue further that the myth of neutrality may well serve to hide processes which exclude from publication the work of black and antiracist researchers who write about sensitive (and emotive) issues around 'race' and ethnicity. As most gatekeepers in the West are white, it is necessary that we look at how 'whiteness' and 'blackness' are socially constructed and differentially positioned in discourses of 'race', in order to better understand the processes which exclude. At issue, as Aronowitz and Giroux contend, 'is the quest of diversity in ways of producing knowledge, and, more broadly, the validity of the distinction between legitimate intellectual knowledge and other kinds of knowledge' (Aronowitz and Giroux 1991: 17).

It is not enough, however, to *understand* the role of subjective identities in the production of knowledge, but for marginalized and subordinate groups to actively *assert* our place in this process and challenge the canon of received notions of what constitutes legitimacy in academic work. Feminists have largely succeeded in carving out a space in which their voices are heard and taken seriously, and this has reaped some rewards in relation to the contribution of feminist research in the education of girls. Research on 'race' and education cannot claim similar success; the level of awareness raised and the changes in practice implemented as a result have been more than an uphill struggle. It is as necessary as it has ever been that in researching 'race' and education, we keep the focus firmly on commitment to social justice.

2 | Partisanship and credibility: the case of antiracist educational research

Martyn Hammersley

partisan *n.***1.** a strong, esp. unreasoning, supporter of a party, cause, etc. **2.** *Mil.* a guerrilla in wartime. *adj.* **1.** of or characteristic of partisans. **2.** loyal to a particular cause, biased.

The Concise Oxford Dictionary, ninth edition

Introduction

In an article published shortly before his death, Barry Troyna argued the case for partisanship in research concerned with 'race' and education (Troyna 1995). In the course of his discussion he contrasted this approach with that which I and some colleagues had proposed (Hammersley 1993a, 1993b; Foster *et al.* 1996). Here, I want to explore one aspect of his argument, relating to the issue of credibility. The conclusions I come to are ones with which he would almost certainly have disagreed. His death deprives us of the kind of critical response that would undoubtedly have followed. But, in writing this chapter, inevitably, I have found myself anticipating what he might have said in reply. In this sense he lives on for me, and no doubt for others too.

Central to Troyna's argument was a reference to Howard Becker's much cited article 'Whose side are we on?' (Becker 1967), which he describes as 'one of the fullest and most public expressions' (Troyna 1995: 397) of the case for partisanship in research. In particular, he draws attention to Becker's concept of the hierarchy of credibility and its implications for educational research. This concept highlights the question of how researchers treat the accounts of informants, but it also raises more general issues about the relationship between research and other forms of discourse and practice.

Becker, credibility and partisanship

One of Becker's central themes is that within societies, organizations and local communities there is often an established hierarchy of credibility running alongside the power structure, so that it is widely assumed by members that those in power have 'the right to define the way things really are' (Becker 1967: 241), or at least that they have the most complete picture of what is going on. In this type of situation subordinates tend to be seen as having partial views, in both senses of that term.[1] Becker outlines two responses of sociologists to this credibility hierarchy, and their associated consequences. On the one hand, many accept it, adopting the point of view of superordinates, and can therefore be accused of bias *but usually are not*; on the other hand, a few adopt the viewpoint of subordinates, and they frequently *are* accused of bias. On this basis he claims that 'we can never avoid taking sides' (Becker 1967: 245). This argument derives, in large part, from Becker's experience of doing research in the sociology of deviance, where he and others were criticized because they presented the perspectives of deviants, and in so doing did not take for granted the dominant view of deviance as a social fact that is to be explained in terms of pathological causes.

Troyna, like many others, interprets Becker as dismissing mainstream research's 'avowed concern for "objectivity"', as arguing that researchers are forced to adopt either the perspective of the powerful or that of the less powerful (see also Mac an Ghaill 1991: 116), and as having answered the question he raised in the title of his article 'emphatically in favour of subordinate groups'. On this view, a researcher's political commitments should explicitly 'help to shape and direct all aspects of the research act'. Moreover, that act should be 'transformative': researchers should 'contribute towards social change in and through their research activities' (Troyna 1995: 397).

While Becker's article is not unambiguous, I think it can be shown that this is a fundamental misreading of it: that what Becker and Troyna mean by 'taking sides' differs. Becker is concerned with partisanship in two rather limited senses: that the researcher will have greater sympathy with some groups than with others, and will tend to accept their point of view; and that his or her work will very often be *seen as* partisan. However, Becker insists on the importance of seeking objective knowledge of the world, by allowing for potential biases. He comments: 'Whatever side we are on, we must use our techniques impartially enough that a belief to which we are especially sympathetic could be proved untrue' (Becker 1967: 246). His use of the word 'impartially' is significant here; and, in a response to criticism of his article for advocating a more substantial kind of partisanship, he emphasizes that he was not suggesting that 'objective research' is impossible or undesirable (Becker 1971: 13). Furthermore, in a paper focusing on radical sociology, co-authored with Horowitz, he insists that sociology and politics are distinct, and indeed that there will be conflicts between them in the demands they make on us. Becker and Horowitz write: 'the radical sociologist will . . . find that his scientific "conservativism" – in the sense of being unwilling to draw conclusions on the basis of insufficient evidence – creates tension with radical activists' (Becker and Horowitz 1972: 55).

For Becker, partisanship is something that researchers have thrust upon them, not least in the sense that they are always likely to be seen as taking sides. He does not argue that they should do their work in such a way as to support one 'side' rather than another; though he does believe that good sociology can have radical political consequences.

The significance of Troyna's appeal to Becker's article is, of course, that it seems to legitimate partisanship in ethnographic research. In recent years, considerable emphasis has been placed on the effectiveness of such research in documenting racism within schools (Troyna 1991a; Gillborn 1995: ch.3). At the same time, this work has been criticized on the grounds that its partisan character has resulted in bias (see, for example, Foster *et al.* 1996). Troyna uses Becker's apparent support for partisanship to counter this criticism. He argues that the methodological position of the critics is 'inherently conservative' because it does not challenge the credibility hierarchy in society, and the power structure which this sustains (Troyna 1995: 402). At the same time, he insists that 'partisan research' is not a contradiction in terms: he is not suggesting 'that research should be sacrificed entirely on the altar of value-laden and political convictions' (p. 399); and he claims that the attempt 'to improve and protect the status of . . . empirical data by triangulation and cognate procedures' (p. 404) is not incompatible with partisanship.

In my view, 'partisan research' (as interpreted by Troyna and many others, see Gitlin 1994) is indeed a contradiction in terms. To demonstrate this, in the remainder of this chapter I will look at how partisan researchers in the field of 'race' and education assess the credibility of the accounts of informants. I will do this by examining one of the studies that Troyna cites as a major contribution to this field, Mac an Ghaill's *Young, Gifted and Black* (1988). This is a book which has been widely praised, and I do not want to imply that it has no virtues. However, in my view it shows the dangers of researchers being partisan.

Using informants' accounts

Young, Gifted and Black is presented as an ethnographic study of the experience of black students at a sixth form college and a comprehensive school, both located in inner-city areas of the same English conurbation. It looks, first of all, at a group of female students, of Afro-Caribbean and Asian parentage, called the Black Sisters, who were attending 'Connolly' sixth form college, and who responded positively to education. Subsequent chapters focus on the teachers and on two groups of anti-school black male students (the Rasta Heads and the Warriors) at 'Kilby' comprehensive school. Mac an Ghaill relies heavily on accounts from students and teachers, and I want to look at how he employs these in the light of the issue of their credibility.

There are two quite different purposes for which we might elicit and use informants' accounts, relating to what can be called information analysis and perspective analysis. While the same data may be subjected to both forms of analysis, the requirements of each are different.[2] First, a researcher may use informants' accounts as a source of information about the world; in other words as a substitute for his or her own observations. This usage is particularly likely in the case of events in settings to which it has not been possible to negotiate access, events which are so rare that observing them is difficult, or events that occurred before the research began. Equally, informants' accounts can be used as a supplement to observational data, for the purposes of triangulation or for providing information about additional instances of some class of events that is of interest, only a few of which have been observed. Sometimes, too, researchers may rely on informants' experience of particular settings as a source of generalizations about what normally happens, about the typical orientations of actors involved in those settings, etc. In all of this, informants are being used as surrogate researchers, and we need to apply much the same assessment procedure to the information they supply as we do to researchers' own observational reports.

The second use of informants' accounts is as a source of data about the perspectives, beliefs, attitudes, intentions, motives etc. of the informants themselves. Here, what they say is employed as a basis for inferences about their subjective orientations, these often being assumed to be stable over time and to be general across members of the category or group to which the informant belongs. The task is to understand people's own rationales for why they think and behave the way that they do, though the aim may also be to capture less conscious aspects of their orientations, including the way in which these have been shaped by social circumstances. Thus, there is usually an emphasis on treating the meanings of the people concerned as intelligible, and even as rational; but there is also often a concern with explaining them in social terms. Here, methodological assessment is required of the inferences made by the researcher from informants' accounts to their subjective orientations, and of the explanations proposed for those orientations.

Mac an Ghaill uses data from informants for both these purposes. However, his treatment of students' and teachers' accounts is very different. While students' accounts are quoted throughout the study, those of teachers are largely confined to one chapter. Indeed, he reports that in the case of the sixth form college he did not investigate the teachers because he felt that he could transfer and apply the analysis of teachers' orientations that he had developed in relation to Kilby school (Mac an Ghaill 1988: 7). More than this, there is a striking difference in the predominant uses to which the accounts of these two categories of informant are put. Students' accounts are employed mainly as a source of information, notably about the incidence of racist practices within schools, and about their own modes of adaptation. The teachers' accounts, on the other hand, are used for the most part as a basis for analysing their perspectives, primarily in terms of the extent to which and ways in which these are racist.

This differential treatment can be illustrated by reference to one short section of the book. In his first chapter Mac an Ghaill reports that:

> The Black Sisters claimed that racism pervaded the three schools that they [had] attended. For them, the stratified streaming system was the most visible element of the racist processes in operation within their secondary

schools. In two schools with an Afro-Caribbean majority student population, Afro-Caribbean students were concentrated in the lower streams
and remedial departments. The division between the 'high-achieving'
Asian and white students and the 'low-achieving' Afro-Caribbeans was
further reinforced by the process of demotions to lower streams, with the
latter group being disproportionately selected. Both the Afro-Caribbean
and Asian young women recalled many Afro-Caribbeans of high ability
who were demoted during their secondary schooling.

(Mac an Ghaill 1988: 15)

In support of this, Mac an Ghaill quotes interview data where the students
make this point about demotion, and he notes that the Black Sisters 'frequently returned to the question of racist stereotypes, their origin and the
power of whites to implement them within particular social practices' (Mac an
Ghaill 1988: 16). He then quotes an extract from a discussion which ends with
the following student comments:

Judith: I don't know how all these stereotypes came about but I remember
reading, right, that racism. It really surprised me, you know, like it
surprised me that racism really started because the Europeans,
with all their humanitarian business, wanted to justify slavery and
indentured labour. How could they justify dealing with another
set of human beings in this way? By saying that they weren't
human and emphasizing all these negative aspects of it, and that's
how it grew up to the extent it is now. Europeans always wanted
to justify their actions somehow, with ethics an' all that sort of
thing.

Smita: And now they use different stereotypes to justify how they treat
blacks in school. And they use different ones to divide Asian and
West Indian kids in different streams.

(Mac an Ghaill 1988: 17)

Mac an Ghaill's commentary on this is as follows:

As Smita indicates, the young women were aware of the operation of the
system of racist stereotypes and its material consequences for black
students. However, [the Black Sisters] did not overtly challenge them as
they claimed the anti-school students did. Rather, here we see an example
of their mode of resistance within accommodation.

(Mac an Ghaill 1988: 17)

Having used the accounts of the Black Sisters to document racism in the
schools which they had attended before they came to the sixth form college,
and to describe their adaptation to racism, Mac an Ghaill turns his attention
to the question of racism in Connolly College itself:

The Black Sisters maintained that racism also structurally pervaded the
sixth form college. They argued that it was present at all times but became
most explicit on certain public occasions, such as college assemblies,
which were predominantly monocultural like most of the curriculum,

with its European, Christian focus. The young women recalled many incidents of racist practices. For example, when Judith came to the college to
be interviewed for admission she was advised to take two A-levels and an
O-level rather than three A-levels as she wished. Judith had attained five
O-level equivalent passes, four of which were grade 1 CSEs. Therefore,
according to the college's requirements, she was technically qualified to
take the course. Furthermore, she was better qualified than other white
middle-class students who were allowed to follow the course. Judith
declined the advice and after much discussion she was eventually permit-
ted to take three A-levels.

Mrs Williams, the teacher who carried out the interview, could not
recall the particular details concerning her assessment of Judith, but she
maintained that:

> If you look at the profiles of the West Indians who come here, you will
> see what I mean. They have exaggerated expectations of their own
> abilities. There are some strong candidates but most of them come
> with a couple of CSEs under their belts and expect to take traditional
> A-level courses. The coloured girls are the worst. One told me that she
> didn't want office work. They have no idea of our standards and the
> work involved.

Here we see the teacher's assumptions that inform her differential
response to black young women. Employing explicit racial and gender
stereotypes, she generalizes from particular black students' behaviour that
she has known to the social group as a whole.

(Mac an Ghaill 1988: 18)

There are several striking features of Mac an Ghaill's discussion here. First,
looking at his use of information analysis, the author apparently bases his
claims about 'the operation of a system of racist stereotypes and its material
consequences' in the schools that the Sisters came from solely on their retro-
spective accounts.[3] This is surprising given that what is being reported is a
controversial and complex explanatory claim to the effect that streaming in
all three schools involved discrimination on the basis of 'race' (Mac an Ghaill
1988: 15–16). When such a claim is made, we can reasonably expect some triangulation of data, for example in the way of observational reports of differential treatment and statistical information about the allocation of black and
white students to courses. In this case, neither kind of evidence is supplied.

Much the same problem arises with his discussion of racism in the sixth
form college. There is an *attempted* triangulation in relation to one of the
pieces of evidence offered here. Mac an Ghaill talks to the teacher who was
involved in processing Judith's application. But, given that she could not
remember the details, it is unclear why school records data were not reported,
in particular to show whether white girls were admitted to A-level courses with
less qualifications than Judith had. Of course, the records, even if available,
might well not resolve this matter since, given that Judith *was* in fact given
access to her third A-level course, what we need to know is whether equally or

less well-qualified white girls were automatically allocated to three A-level courses. Even then, in order for this to be conclusive evidence of discrimination against black students, it would need to be shown that this was a general pattern of discrimination across the cohort.[4]

The analysis in this extract is broadly representative of the way that students' accounts are treated throughout the book. Thus, in the later discussion of Afro-Caribbean and Asian anti-school subcultures at Kilby school, the author once again treats as valid the accounts of the students about teacher behaviour without corroborating evidence relating to the incidents reported. There is also generalized description which requires evidence but is not supported by any; for example, to the effect that 'many of the teachers at Kilby school had emerged from the working class and tended to identify more easily with white students' (Mac an Ghaill 1988: 93) or that 'teacher perception created a self-fulfilling prophecy' (p. 101). The discussion of the streaming system at Kilby school in Chapter 2 of *Young, Gifted and Black* lacks the detail one finds even in other studies of this kind (for example Wright 1986; Troyna 1991b, 1992). The same problem arises with the treatment of discrimination in the classroom. The best observational data provided is a report of a brief investigation of one teacher's responses to classroom deviance in a particular lesson, in which Afro-Caribbeans were over-represented and there was an instance of differential response by the teacher to the same behaviour on the part of an Asian and an Afro-Caribbean student. Even here, there is insufficient detail about the data, and it is probably inadequate for representing the teacher's routine practice; though it is important to note that the teacher accepted the validity of the analysis (Mac an Ghaill 1988: 66). Evidence is required for a representative sample of teachers, and as regards Afro-Caribbean in relation to both Asian and white students, in order to sustain Mac an Ghaill's arguments.

In short, in his treatment of students' accounts there is an apparent failure to allow for the threats to validity that arise in informational analysis. These include distortion as a result of reliance on memory, speculative interpretation and generalization, acquiescence and desirability response effects, bias etc. Also neglected are interpretative concerns about the way in which accounts are occasioned phenomena shaped by context. Instead, for the most part, Mac an Ghaill treats the students' reports of school processes as simple reflections of how the world is.

The section of the book summarized above is also representative of the very different way in which Mac an Ghaill treats teachers' accounts. Like the Black Sisters, the teacher who is quoted recounts her experience. However, where the experiential reports of the Black Sisters are apparently accepted at face value, Mac an Ghaill switches to perspective analysis in dealing with the teacher. Moreover, it is a kind of perspective analysis that makes little attempt to *understand* the point of view of the informant; rather, it employs what has been called 'the hermeneutics of suspicion' (Ricoeur 1970: 26–36). On the basis of what the teacher says in this brief quotation, Mac an Ghaill claims to identify the 'assumptions that inform her differential response to black young women'. And he asserts that these assumptions constitute stereotypes, in that she 'generalizes from particular black students' behaviour that she has known to the social group as a whole' (Mac an Ghaill 1988: 18). As a piece of ethnographic perspective analysis this is less than satisfactory. The meaning of the teacher's comments and their implications for her behaviour are 'read off' from what she says, without recourse to evidence from other contexts or to respondent validation. Moreover, there is an immediate move to a negative evaluation of her beliefs as false, along with an implicit moral condemnation of them. Even if one believes that evaluations can form a legitimate part of an ethnographic account, they require supporting argument.

In informational terms, Mac an Ghaill's treatment of this teacher's account is a mirror image of his treatment of the students' accounts: where the latter are accepted as valid with no provision of corroborative evidence, that of the teacher is rejected, again without evidence being provided. While there is no obvious reason why Afro-Caribbean students coming to the college would have exaggerated views of their own abilities compared to Asians and whites, it is not so implausible that it can be dismissed outright. Evidence is required, in whichever direction this argument is pursued.[5]

This treatment of teachers' accounts is characteristic of the whole book. In Chapter 2, which is devoted to 'teacher ideologies and practices', Mac an Ghaill categorizes the teachers' views in terms of three ideological types: 'old disciplinarians', 'liberals', and 'new realists'; with 'ideology' defined as 'a system of ideas which serves to legitimate vested interests' (Mac an Ghaill 1988: 160). His chapter is concerned with the development of these ideologies and their 'relationship to the dominant monocultural educational perspective within the school' (p. 37). Thus, he argues that while disciplinarians and new realists 'tend to be overtly involved in racist practices, the main liberal position serves to maintain a racially structured institution' (p. 37). Here too we have perspective analysis of a highly speculative and evaluative kind. And, once again, the falsity of the teachers' views is largely taken for granted, as also is the role of those views in structuring their behaviour and producing ethnic inequalities.

Inverting the credibility hierarchy?

There is a significant asymmetry, then, in the way that Mac an Ghaill treats the accounts of students and teachers. And this is at odds with what is generally taken to be good practice in ethnography. A central feature of that approach is recognition of diverse perspectives and of the need to understand these 'in their own terms'; plus an emphasis on the importance, for informational purposes, of using a range of types of informant and/or observational data to allow for the likely biases of particular perspectives (McCall and Simmons 1969).

At one point, Mac an Ghaill seems to commit himself to this approach. Citing Lacey, he argues that ethnographers should 'attempt to describe the social system from a number of participants' perspectives' (Mac an Ghaill 1988: 6). In practice, however, as I have shown, what he does is very different. He claims that his book 'pays due attention to the teachers' point of view' (p. 6), and appeals to the fact that he is a practising teacher. However, there is no automatic reason why one member of that profession would represent the views of others accurately; not least because she or he might be even more concerned with evaluating them than are many non-teachers. Moreover, it may be significant in this context that the Black Sisters are reported as saying that Mac an Ghaill is 'not like a "real" teacher' (p. 13). This was clearly to his credit from their point of view, but it might indicate a problem about his capacity to understand the perspectives of fellow teachers on the basis of common occupational membership. Moreover, his explanation of what giving 'due attention' to teachers' views means that it amounts to not blaming them for their racist beliefs and practices, treating these as the product of the constraints under which they work (p. 6). There is no recognition that *their* perspectives need to be understood ethnographically, just as much as do those of the students.

Indeed, Mac an Ghaill is quite open about his adoption of the black students' perspective. He reports how, in observing the anti-school Rasta Heads: 'focusing on the students' perspective of the meaning and purpose of school, I came to see the logic of their response as a survival strategy . . . as a legitimate mechanism opposed to the school's institutional authoritarianism and racism (Mac an Ghaill 1989: 177). However, within the ethnographic tradition, a distinction is usually drawn between understanding the 'logic' of a perspective and accepting its validity. Indeed, the more convincing one finds a perspective, the more difficult it sometimes is to gain ethnographic understanding of it. And, Mac an Ghaill subjects neither the students' nor the teachers' perspectives to the kind of explication that is required for this sort of understanding. Instead, both are simply *evaluated* in cognitive and moral terms; for the most part positively in the case of the students, and negatively in that of the teachers. And this is accompanied by an explanatory asymmetry: 'true' accounts are treated as reflections of the facts, 'false' ones are explained away as social products.[6]

What seems to be involved, then, is an inversion of the dominant credibility hierarchy. One way of viewing this is as a product of what Becker refers to as 'sentimentality' (Becker 1967: 246). He specifically warns against the danger of assuming that 'the underdog is always right and those in authority always wrong' (Becker 1964: 5). Moreover, he claims that 'This tendency has been particularly noticeable in studies of race relations, where the possibility that minority groups have some of the faults attributed to them by bigots is systematically slighted' (Becker 1964: 5). Mac an Ghaill's book seems to suffer from precisely this kind of sentimentality. Thus, while in discussing his approach to doing the research he lays great emphasis on triangulating data from different sources (Mac an Ghaill 1991: 109), this is not made evident in the text in such a way that readers can carry out their own assessments. Instead, the author's interpretations are simply presented as fact, accompanied by illustrative extracts from the data; the cognitive content of the latter being treated as either patently true or patently false.

However, Mac an Ghaill does not simply invert the official credibility hierarchy. In practice, he is selective in his validation of black students' accounts.

There are places where he subjects even these to negative evaluation. In the course of discussing Asian students' interpretations of racist attacks, he rightly draws attention to the significance of social class divisions within the Asian community. He contrasts the views of middle-class Asians, who saw these attacks as reflecting the attitudes of a minority of whites, with those of the anti-school working class students who 'offered a political explanation of racism that included an awareness of white imperialism in the past and the present' (Mac an Ghaill 1988: 121). The middle-class Asians are also portrayed as accepting 'the dominant teacher ideology' (p. 124), in believing that 'the Afro-Caribbean students were mainly disruptive and anti-authority' and that 'occupation and property ownership were more important than colour in determining their own relationship with white society' (p. 125). Mac an Ghaill also engages in evaluation of the views of some of the anti-school, working-class Asian Warriors, comparing these unfavourably with those of one of their number, Parminder, who was involved in the Communist Party and acted as Mac an Ghaill's research assistant. Parminder is described as helping 'to develop the Warriors' political consciousness'. This was necessary, Mac an Ghaill reports, because 'the dominant ideological response of the Warriors remained within a culturalist perspective' and 'their resistance to schooling was not informed by an organized political ideology' (p. 122).[7]

So, Mac an Ghaill does not simply adopt the perspective of black students but rather that of *some* black students, and even then selectively. In this respect, his approach resembles that of Willis (1977), who incorporates into his analysis the cultural 'penetrations' of white working class anti-school 'lads', but treats some aspects of their counter-culture as ideological, such as their sexism and racism. In the case of both authors this evaluation of students' perspectives is not based on evidence provided about the factual validity of their beliefs, in the manner of information analysis, but takes the form of judgement about the extent to which they correspond with what these authors regard as theoretically and politically correct.[8] In short, Mac an Ghaill, like Willis, engages in selective appropriation and 'translation' of the students' perspectives so as to support his own theoretical views, and also on the basis of what he takes to be the actual or likely political effects of those perspectives (for example in terms of promoting a united front on the part of 'black' students; see Mac an Ghaill 1988: 85).[9]

There is also the issue of reactivity. As with Willis, there are questions about the effect of Mac an Ghaill on his student informants. He emphasizes the closeness and informality of his relations with them; indeed he describes the research as collaborative. He comments:

> Most unexpectedly, the students identified with my Irish nationality, and this had major implications for my research . . . I had long conversations with the students on the effects of English imperialism on our respective countries of origin, and they showed a broadly sympathetic understanding of the Irish political situation . . . This shared political consciousness was developed explicitly with the Black Sisters.
>
> (Mac an Ghaill 1989: 183)

It is also of significance that some of the Sisters belonged to his sociology class, and he reports that they shared what they had learned with the others (Mac an Ghaill 1988: 13). All this raises questions about the extent to which the data Mac an Ghaill collected and presents were shaped by his own influence. Significant here is what Kevin, one of the Rasta Heads, said to him: '. . . You always proved to be on our side. You came to see how our lives really are and you explained things to us about our lives that made more sense than we could have thought of' (Mac an Ghaill 1991: 110). It seems that Mac an Ghaill may have played a major part in producing the 'credible' accounts supplied by his student informants.

In short, Mac an Ghaill uses informants' accounts to present his own theoretical and political views about the role of schools in reproducing racism. Where the accounts conform to those views they are treated as representing reality, where they do not they are portrayed as ideological or as insufficiently developed into an effective political orientation. Moreover, the student accounts he uses seem likely to have been strongly influenced by his views. And these features of his work are at odds with the usual requirements of ethnography, and with the commitment to objectivity indicated in Becker's (1967) article.

Conclusion

In this chapter I have provided a critique of Mac an Ghaill's book from an ethnographic point of view. Given that he labels his work as ethnographic, such critical assessment is obviously legitimate in principle. However, I do not believe that the failings I have identified derive from incompetence on Mac an Ghaill's part, or even from the constraints under which he was working as a teacher/researcher. Rather, they reflect his acceptance of a partisan or 'critical' approach to research. And, of course, from that point of view, these 'failings' appear in a different light. For example, his asymmetrical treatment of the accounts of black students and white teachers can be seen as following directly from standpoint epistemology, a central element in the critical research tradition. He comments at one point that 'inevitably a critical analysis, such as is presented here, emphasizes the teachers' negative responses' (Mac an Ghaill 1988: 6). His critique and selective appropriation of these accounts on the basis of a macro-social theory stems from the commitment to locate micro phenomena within a theoretical conception of the social totality; a commitment that is characteristic of 'critical' research. Similarly, what I identified as a problem of reactivity, as a vicious circle that produces bias, may be regarded as a virtuous circle from a political point of view: as contributing to the successful mobilization of black and other students against racism. Thus, Mac an Ghaill expresses the hope that: 'by adopting an analysis of racism developed by black activists and theorists . . . I have contributed positively to their political struggle' (Mac an Ghaill 1991: 115). And, despite doubts expressed by Troyna (1994c), he insists that his research empowered the students (Mac an Ghaill 1989: 188).

I have argued elsewhere that it is a fundamental error of 'critical' research to assume that it is possible to pursue both knowledge and practical political goals simultaneously. This relies on an Enlightenment myth about the essential harmony among values (see Hammersley 1997; also Hammersley 1992a: ch.6 and 1995: ch.2). Here, I have tried to demonstrate this same point through detailed discussion of a particular case. A critical approach undercuts the ethnographic commitment to employ informants' accounts both to understand their perspectives and to gain information about the world they experience. Instead, it involves 'giving voice' to some (to the extent that they have the 'correct' views) and subjecting others to ideology critique, as determined by the researcher's theoretical and political judgements.

Of course, Troyna and others argue that research cannot *avoid* being political. This is true in some senses of that term but false in others (Hammersley 1995: ch.6). In particular, it is not true that research is inevitably partisan, serving *consistently* (wittingly or unwittingly) the interests of some particular 'side'. The consequences of research are more uncertain, diverse and contingent than this. And the argument that research *should* be partisan in this sense relies on a simplistic sociological theory in which, fundamentally, there are only two sides – the oppressed and the oppressors. This is an idea that has been inherited, via Marx and Hegel, from early Protestant theology, which portrayed the universe as involving a battle between God and the Devil. While the forces at work have been secularized, the eschatological moral drama, in terms of which all of us must bear witness to which side we are on, has been retained, along with the evangelism it generates.

Contrary to what Troyna claims, as Mac an Ghaill's study shows, partisanship demands that political considerations override intellectual ones. The task becomes the subversion of the dominant credibility hierarchy, rather than that of discovering what is *justifiably* credible. And one of the consequences of this is to undermine the public credibility of social scientific research. A further consequence, ironically, is to render partisanship in research ultimately self-defeating, since it is parasitic on that credibility.

Notes

1 Partial in the sense of having incomplete information, and in the sense of being biased. From some points of view, notably those influenced by Hegel, these senses are two sides of the same coin.

2 This distinction conforms, broadly speaking, to McCall and Simmons' (1969: 4–5) contrast between the use of informants and of respondents. However, I will use the term 'informants' throughout to signal that it is not a matter of different types of *people* or *data* but different *uses* of data that are important. For further discussion see Hammersley and Atkinson (1995: 124–6).

3 He tells us that: 'much of the material for this study was collected from observation, informal conversations with the Black Sisters, their teachers at their secondary schools and at Connolly College, and with six of the young women's parents, and from recorded, semi-structured interviews' (Mac an Ghaill 1988: 13). However, the data he

quotes in this section on 'racism and secondary schooling' come entirely from the Black Sisters.

4 For a more detailed account of what is required to establish the operation of discrimination of this kind, see Foster *et al.* (1996: ch.4).

5 Moreover, it is worth noting that, contrary to what Mac an Ghaill claims, the teacher does not generalize 'to the social group as a whole'; she refers to 'the West Indians who come here [i.e., presumably, to Connolly College]' (Mac an Ghaill 1988: 18).

6 On this kind of explanatory asymmetry, see Bloor 1976.

7 It is not clear whether he is adopting a different definition of 'ideology' here to that quoted earlier. At one point Mac an Ghaill also evaluates the views of the Rasta Heads negatively, on the same grounds (Mac an Ghaill 1988: 108).

8 For this argument in relation to Willis, see Turner 1979 and Walker 1985.

9 There are also one or two places where he treats teachers' accounts as representing reality, when these are consistent with his own theoretical perspective.

3 | Racism and the politics of qualitative research: learning from controversy and critique

David Gillborn

Methodology is too important to be left to methodologists.

(Becker 1970: 3)

Introduction

Given the highly politicized nature of debates about 'race' and ethnicity it is not surprising that research in this field has repeatedly been the focus for controversies of one kind or another. In this chapter I examine one such controversy (in which I have been an active player); namely, an ongoing debate about qualitative research on 'race' and racism in school contexts.[1] My central aim in reviewing the arguments and counter-arguments is to explore the different ways in which *racism* is defined and deployed in these debates. Perhaps most importantly, I am also concerned with how racism operates *through* the work. That is, how qualitative research and critique might, itself, strengthen or defend particular stereotypes and ideologies that further marginalize and pathologize students of ethnic minority back-ground.[2] *Research, whatever its conscious aims and professed values, can be racist.* Such a charge is not to be made lightly and certainly should not be used as a simplistic means of rejecting criticism and avoiding further engage-ment in criticial interchanges. All research must be open to critical scrutiny; but so too must the critiques themselves. As I will show, a methodological project is currently being pursued in the United Kingdom that threatens to reduce sociology in general, and the sociology of education in particular, to the status of an anodyne, uncritical commentary that privileges the status quo and, in its basic assumptions and presentation of minority students, is fundamentally racist. The present controversy highlights important lessons for all those concerned with empirical research on 'race' and racism, not least in terms of the need to challenge taken for granted assumptions that might reproduce wider inequalities in the racial structuring of educational opportunities.

Qualitative research on racism in teacher/student interactions

There is now a growing body of qualitative work that addresses issues of 'race', ethnicity and education in the UK. A particularly significant development has been the publication of a series of ethnographic studies of multi-ethnic secondary schools. Research by Cecile Wright (1986), Máirtín Mac an Ghaill (1988), Peter Foster (1990a) and myself (Gillborn 1990) represented the first sustained attempts to chart the realities of life in secondary schools where 'race' and ethnicity were accorded a central place in the analyses. With the notable exception of Foster's work (to which I return shortly) these ethnographies share several common features. They:

- make extensive use of observational and interview data to explore the daily character of life in multi-ethnic comprehensive schools;
- focus on interactions between white teachers and minority students, especially as they relate to academic selection and matters of school discipline;
- chart students' progress in terms of survival and accommodation strategies within school contexts that are (whatever the institutions' rhetoric) experienced as hostile by many ethnic minority students.

Additionally, both Mac an Ghaill and I consciously address the significance of 'racism'. We go beyond individualistic analyses of personal 'prejudice' to examine how racism operates as a complex and multifaceted aspect of school life; one that links the wider structures of power in society with the minutia of classroom experience and control. This research has been complemented and extended by subsequent qualitative work in primary schools (Troyna and Hatcher 1992; Wright 1992a, 1992b; Connolly 1994, 1995b); as part of a wider study focusing on black young women (Mirza 1992); and new research on black young people's secondary school experiences (Sewell 1995; Nehaul 1996).[3]

All of these studies privilege qualitative data; most claim to be 'ethnographic'. Although they give different amounts of attention to their theoretical and methodological antecedents, they each give priority to understanding the dynamics of students' experiences via the analysis of multiple types of qualitative data (especially by observation and interview). They suggest that, even where well-intentioned white teachers are conscientious and committed to equality of opportunity as an ideal, they may nevertheless *act* in ways that unwittingly reproduce familiar racial stereotypes, generate conflict (especially with African Caribbean young men) and perpetuate existing inequalities of opportunity and achievement. As Mac an Ghaill notes:

There may be no conscious attempt to treat black youth in a different way to white youth, but the unintended teacher effects result in differential responses, which work against black youth . . . There was a tendency for Asian male students to be seen by the teachers as technically of 'high ability' and socially as conformist. Afro-Caribbean male students tended to be seen as having 'low ability' and potential discipline problems.

(Mac an Ghaill 1988: 3–4, 64)[4]

Teacher expectations can lead to inequitable treatment. Classroom observation, for example, has suggested that African Caribbean students are frequently singled out for criticism even where several students (of other ethnic backgrounds) share in the conduct (for examples see Gillborn 1990: 30–31; Wright 1992a: 16–19).

In my study of 'City Road Comprehensive' (Gillborn 1990), an inner city secondary school in the English Midlands,[5] I noted teachers' tendency to perceive a threat to their authority in many routine dealings with African Caribbean students. The vast majority of City Road teachers were genuinely committed to the ideals of equal opportunity, yet in practice they tended to generalize, seeing conflict with an African Caribbean student as indicative of a more deep-seated rejection of authority, typical of African Caribbeans *as a group*. This view is captured in the following quotation, for example, where a female teacher implies that while verbal abuse is not uncommon in City Road, only African Caribbean students are capable of physical assault: 'I've never been assaulted by a white kid. I've been thrown against a wall by a pupil and it was a black kid. I've been called a "Fucking slag" but I've only ever been *hit* by a black kid' (Gillborn 1990: 38).

African Caribbean students were seen to represent both a more frequent, and a more severe, challenge to teachers' authority. This 'myth' became an accepted (though largely unspoken) part of teachers' 'craft' knowledge – their idea of 'how it really is'. One of its consequences was that any sign of apparent disobedience by an African Caribbean student might be dealt with harshly so as to 'nip in the bud' any further problems. Additionally, actions that conveyed the students' sense of ethnicity – their identity as black young people – were often interpreted by teachers as a sign of aggression or the wrong 'attitude'. When teachers acted on these perceptions they increased the potential for further conflict, especially where students drew attention to what they saw as unfair treatment. Strikingly similar processes of labelling and increased teacher/student conflict have been documented by Cecile Wright and Paul Connolly in primary and middle school classrooms (Wright 1992a, 1992b; Connolly 1995b).

In contrast to this body of work, Peter Foster's study of a multi-ethnic school in the North of England ('Milltown High') challenges the view that racism is a subtle and widespread influence on the lives of minority students.

Peter Foster on 'Milltown High'

In his book, *Policy and Practice in Multicultural and Anti-Racist Education* (Foster 1990a) Peter Foster looks at the development of multicultural and antiracist education policy in a school. He also considers how students were differentiated into hierarchically set teaching groups and explicitly addresses the question of racism in the school. The most striking of Foster's conclusions is that 'ethnic minority students enjoyed equal opportunities with their white peers' (p. 174). Foster's work is almost unique as an ethnography of a British school where racial inequalities are not highlighted as a major issue despite the author having made 'race' a central problematic of the research (see Hurrell 1995).

The distinctiveness of Foster's conclusions was rapidly picked up by others in the field. David J. Smith and Sally Tomlinson (1989: 63), for example, noted the lack of 'racial antagonism' in Milltown High; a finding they contrasted with previous work on racial harassment but which coincided with their survey-based results (see Gillborn and Drew 1992; Troyna and Hatcher 1992). In a brief review of qualitative research on 'race' and schooling, Peter Woods also drew attention to the contrast with previous work. Rather than using Foster to question the accuracy of others, however, Woods sought an explanation in the nature of Foster's case:

> Why should this school be so different from those studied by Wright and others? Assuming the methodologies were comparable, there were some significant differences. Foster's school served a community with a long history of co-operation. It had a most liberal organization. Its staff had a high level of awareness about 'race', and were actually implementing an anti-racist programme. Above all, perhaps, it was most generously staffed . . .
>
> (Woods 1990a: 100)

Woods' points are well made and allow for the obvious possibility that (despite their contrasting conclusions) Foster and the other ethnographers of multi-ethnic schools have each accurately represented the realities of life in their chosen cases. Unfortunately, when Foster's account is scrutinized, it is difficult to sustain such a conclusion: Foster's failure critically to deconstruct teachers' racialized assumptions is especially significant.

A careful reading of Foster's book reveals a good deal of prima facie evidence of the racial structuring of educational opportunities in Milltown (see Connolly 1992; Nehaul 1996). One of the most obvious examples is the over-representation of African Caribbean males in low status teaching and examination groups. In the English department: '. . . a number of students who were defined as "bright enough" were ruled out because of their record of past behaviour. Interestingly these students were nearly all Afro/Caribbean boys, which perhaps accounts for the fact that there was only one Afro/Caribbean boy in the top English group in that year' (Foster 1990a: 143).

In science and humanities: 'The Science teachers then created their male class of "difficult" students, the majority of whom, in the 1985–6 fourth year, were Afro/Caribbean, and the Humanities department selected a "remedial" group of "those who need most help". Again the majority were Afro/Caribbean boys' (Foster 1990a: 144).

Despite an acknowledged 'tendency for Afro/Caribbean boys to be under-represented in high status groups' (Foster 1990a: 145), Foster finds no cause for concern. He notes Wright's (1986) work on the negative consequences of teachers' labelling black students as troublemakers but defends the process in Milltown High:

They [African Caribbean boys] did seem less likely to secure places in high status groups . . . often for behavioural reasons. However, such a criticism [as Wright's] is, in my view, unjustified. It seems to me that both academic ability and motivation (which is, I would think, most reliably indicated by past behaviour and work output) are important in deciding which students are likely to make best use of a place in a high status group, and this is what teachers must decide.

(Foster 1990a: 145)

In fact, at one point in his study, Foster does accept that their over-representation in low status groups may have exposed a greater proportion of African Caribbean young men to low teacher expectations: 'My rather tentative conclusion is that boys, especially Afro/Caribbean boys, were slightly disadvantaged . . .' (Foster 1990a: 147). Unfortunately, this 'slight' disadvantage falls from sight quite quickly; a few pages later a new chapter begins with the bold statement: 'There was no evidence that ethnic minority students were disadvantaged by the internal practices and procedures of Milltown High School' (p. 151).

Foster, therefore, recognizes that the distribution of African Caribbean young men was not equitable, but defends this on the basis that their 'past behaviour' did not suggest they would 'make best use of a place in a high status group' (Foster 1990a: 145). Because he does not provide typical examples of this 'past behaviour' the reader is unable to judge whether the issue was really as clear cut as Foster suggests, or may have included cases of the kind of racialized disciplinary control described by other researchers (see Gillborn and Gipps 1996).[6]

Foster's description of Milltown High – on the surface at least – confirms the patterns of racialized control and selection that have been highlighted by a succession of qualitative studies. What sets Foster apart is his conclusion that the processes were legitimate. Having reached this conclusion, Foster followed the publication of his book with a succession of articles that attempted 'to understand the discrepancy between his findings and those of other researchers in the field' (Hammersley 1993b: 430). In the following section I examine the development of this project.

A project of methodological criticism

Peter Foster, Roger Gomm and Martyn Hammersley recently passed judgement on years of sociological research on the school-based processes that might create, shape and reproduce systematic inequalities in educational opportunities and outcomes: 'In short, there is no convincing evidence currently available for any substantial role on the part of schools in generating inequalities in educational outcomes between social classes, genders, or ethnic groups' (Foster *et al.* 1996: 174). So it was that Barry Troyna's earlier description of their work was fully realized: 'They have taken on the mantle of 'methodological purists'. Their purpose is to explicate the allegedly dubious empirical grounds on which claims of racial inequality in education have been mounted' (Troyna 1993: 167).

Foster, Gomm and Hammersley's conclusion on the 'bogus scientific claims' of researchers in this field (Foster *et al.* 1996: 183), therefore, is in keeping with a line of critique that the three have pursued over several years. Research on 'race' and racism in schools provides an important, though not exclusive, focus for the group. Since 1990, Peter Foster has published a series of papers, each focusing on one or more qualitative studies that have claimed to produce evidence of racial injustice in educational settings. Foster's conclusion, *without exception*, is that the work fails to stand up to his scrutiny. Regarding Carrington and Wood (1983), for example, Foster suggests they 'have selectively interpreted much of their data in order to fit their case' (Foster 1990b: 341). Similarly my own work is dismissed as 'implausible' and my 'empirical claims, like those of Mac an Ghaill (1988), are unsubstantiated and unconvincing' (Foster 1992: 94). In one paper it is asserted that my analysis 'rested on only one example' (Foster 1993: 548).

These judgements are especially interesting because I consciously drew on a range of both qualitative and quantitative data. My study of City Road uses interview material (from conversations with teachers and students); observational notes and audio recordings of school life in a variety of contexts (such as classrooms, corridors and in the assembly hall); and data from school documents (such as students' personal record files and the school 'punishment books'). When drawing these different sources together I tried to be aware of potential queries or alternative explanations. In examining teachers' disproportionate criticism of African Caribbean young people, for example, I used data from my own observations, from sentence completion questionnaires, from school records and from interviews. In the latter case, I was careful to include the views of high achieving white students to establish that 'an awareness of teachers' frequent criticism and control of Afro-Caribbean pupils was not restricted to the Afro-Caribbean pupils themselves or to their more "disaffected" white peers' (Gillborn 1990: 32).[7]

Foster finds these data 'unconvincing'; others have found them a good deal more persuasive (see Marland 1990; Eggleston 1991; Tomlinson 1992; Klein 1993). The key point here is not whether there is a single 'correct' verdict on my, or anyone else's, research. Rather, it is vital to note that Foster's reading of others' work *always* finds evidence of teacher racism to be unconvincing. Typically he moves from a micro-level critique (say of a single piece of data, for which he will supply a possible alternative explanation) to a full-blown rejection of the research in its totality. Whatever the variety of data, Foster seems to find nothing of worth in these studies.

Foster has been joined in his critique by Martyn Hammersley and Roger Gomm (see Hammersley, this volume). Martyn Hammersley, of course, is a prominent and prolific writer on social science methodology. His recent work has addressed a series of concerns about the nature and validity of qualitative research (e.g. Hammersley 1990, 1991, 1992a) – part of what John Brewer (1994) terms 'the ethnographic critique of ethnography'. Work on 'race' and ethnicity plays little or no part in most of Hammersley's books: his writing here seems to have developed as an extension of his previous critiques (e.g. Hammersley 1992c) – notably echoing his objections to feminist methodology (Hammersley 1992b, 1994) – and as a response to those who have criticized Foster, a former student of his (Hammersley 1993b; Hammersley and Gomm 1993). Roger Gomm's involvement with this debate began with a critique of a quantitative paper, on the disadvantaged position of South Asian students in a school's system of setting and examination entry (Gomm 1993).

Taken as a whole, therefore, the work of Foster, Gomm and Hammersley amounts to a major project of methodological critique, culminating in the co-authored book, *Constructing Educational Inequality* (Foster *et al.* 1996). Although 'race' research does not provide their only focus, it is a prominent concern and their work cannot simply be dismissed. Of particular significance are the consequences of their position for the way that researchers conceptualize 'race' and racism in empirical research. In the next part of this chapter I explore these issues as they arise through the intended and unintended consequences of their work.[8]

Intended consequences of the methodological project

In this section I want to consider briefly the conscious aims and objectives of the 'methodological purists', as laid out in their own writings.

The pursuit of truth: plausibility and credibility

Throughout their various critiques, Foster, Gomm and Hammersley set out their central task as the pursuit of knowledge. Some postmodern critics would challenge the assumption that there is any 'objective' truth beyond the multiple readings (texts) produced by different actors (see Baudrillard 1983; Clifford and Marcus 1986). However, the 'purists' goal is in keeping with the approach taken by many of the writers whom they attack: most (including myself) have to date retained a vision of science and empirical enquiry underlain by what Norman Denzin describes critically as 'a "realist" conception of the social – there is an obdurate world out there' (Denzin 1992: 158).

Put simply, the methodological project's first intended goal is 'to subject empirical studies to critical scrutiny' as a necessary part of 'the aim of empirical research in education . . . to increase our knowledge of how the educational system works' (Foster 1991: 165). So far, so good. But a major problem emerges when this 'critical scrutiny' translates into a debate about whether a case is 'proven beyond reasonable doubt' (Foster 1990b; 1991). This suggests the possibility of identifying a critical mass of evidence, beyond which a case should be accepted as proven, but where anything less is rejected. Such an approach is 'authoritative, closed and certain' where a more helpful approach might seek to open up the complex and contingent nature of social processes (see Ball 1994).

In their attempt to find an authoritative guide to what constitutes proof 'beyond reasonable doubt', Foster, Gomm and Hammersley appeal to 'methodological common sense' (Hammersley 1993a: 339), but risk simply reifying one set of assumptions over another:

The problem of what constitutes adequate evidence for us to judge a claim valid is one that faces all of us once we abandon foundationalism. Elsewhere, I have outlined a proposed solution, suggesting that claims and evidence must be judged on the basis of two considerations: plausibility in relation to knowledge we currently take as beyond reasonable doubt, and credibility in relation to judgments about the likelihood of various sorts of error (Hammersley 1991, chs 3 and 4; 1992a, ch.4).

(Hammersley 1993a: 340)

According to this view disagreement about the plausibility and/or credibility of a study should be decided in relation to assumptions 'that we expect to be accepted as beyond reasonable doubt by other members of the research community' (Hammersley 1993b: 439). In practice Foster, Gomm and Hammersley tend to apply crude and absolutist notions of plausibility and credibility that reflect a view of the UK in general – and schools in particular – that fails to engage with critical theory. As Caroline Ramazanoglu notes (in her response to an attack on feminist methodology) Hammersley adopts a position that fails to problematize the question of 'who has the power to judge what is relevant': 'His sense of the superiority of reason over political commitment is to be validated in the good sense of scholarly colleagues. The way in which he takes his conception of rationality for granted allows him to justify his position in terms of his personal judgements . . .' (Ramazanoglu 1992: 208).

What seems plausible and credible to some, might appear to be wildly exaggerated, or even politically motivated propaganda, to others. *The criteria for plausibility and credibility cannot be divorced from the assumptions of the individual critic, whose views may reflect particular political, methodological, class-based, gendered and racialized assumptions* (see also Blair, this volume). Foster, Gomm and Hammersley, however, seem to assert their independence from such concerns, trusting an idealized community of academics to settle rationally any disputes that arise. Yet evidence of the weakness of such an approach is available in their own writings. For example, their faith in the wisdom of the academy does not extend to those members who disagree with them: Hammersley describes as 'suppression' the view of a journal referee who opposed the publication of 'Foster's dubious arguments' (Hammersley 1993b: 448).

The purists' position, especially their talk of 'proof', neglects the degree of uncertainty that characterizes *all* social science research. Qualitative data are always open to alternative explanations; the amount and type of evidence we produce may make our analyses more or less convincing, but there is no fixed line between proven and unproven: 'In the empirical sciences there is never compelling proof there is only plausible proof' (Becker cited in Verhoeven 1989: 145). And: 'no set of guidelines or conditions will ever be sufficient to rule out alternative explanations. At best an ethnographer (like all social scientists) can only persuade the reader to agree that the explanation is a plausible one, but not that it is the *only* plausible one' (Brewer 1994: 243, original emphasis).

The methodological critique, therefore, rests on a simplistic reading of the issues surrounding plausibility and 'proof' in the social sciences. By invoking a closed and inappropriate notion of 'proof', the critique becomes blind to the complexity of the situation.

The defence of teachers and 'what we know' about multi-ethnic schools

This much is clear: research on 'race' and ethnicity in education, like any other branch of science, must be open to critique. Foster, Gomm and Hammersley have every right to be critical of research. The main problem with their project lies in its persistent attempt not only to raise problems, but to go beyond this, to conclude that there is no good reason to believe that minority students are unfairly disadvantaged by school-based processes and the actions of teachers:

> We see our methodological assessment as having positive value in these ways. It has provided a defence against unjustified claims based on inadequate evidence which often, in our view, serve to victimise teachers. It has also made a contribution to the development of knowledge by clarifying what we know, beyond reasonable doubt, and what we do not know, about 'race' and in-school processes . . .
>
> (Foster 1993: 550)

The 'defence' of teachers, therefore, is given a central place in their methodological project. Yet this invokes a simplistic reading of previous research. Most of the work Foster and his colleagues criticize seeks to understand teachers' actions and perspectives as they are created and modified through multiple interactions in complex organizational settings. True, much of this work is critical, but none amounts to a blanket condemnation of teachers as a group. Teachers have led many antiracist initiatives and most writers assign them a crucial role in moving towards a more equitable education system (see Nixon 1985; Troyna and Hatcher 1992; Epstein 1993; Gillborn 1995). To portray critical research as 'victimization' risks constructing a dangerous dichotomy between work that is either *for* or *against* teachers. Such a position leaves little room for progress and assumes that teachers constitute a homogeneous group – a view that is contradicted by most qualitative research on teachers (see, for example, Sikes *et al.* 1985; Ball 1987; Woods 1990b; Gewirtz *et al.* 1995).

Peter Foster does not spell out 'what we know, beyond reasonable doubt, and what we do not know, about "race" and in-school processes' (Foster 1993: 550). Because of the nature of their project, the methodological critiques are mostly constructed in negative terms – questioning others' views rather than establishing any new insights. A reading of Foster's work, however, suggests a view of African Caribbean young people that echoes the new racist political discourse now dominant in British politics; a view that effectively defines ethnic minority young people in general, and black young men in particular, as outside the 'mainstream' and representing a potential threat to social order (see Foster 1992). In the following section I examine, in greater detail, the ways in which Foster, Gomm and Hammersley's methodological project may play an unintended role in defending and sustaining existing racial inequalities – it is in this respect that their 'scientific' project may have racist consequences.

Unintended consequences of the methodological project

This section deals with the unintended consequences of the methodological project. That is, consequences that may not be part of Foster, Gomm and Hammersley's conscious agenda (and may even conflict with their avowed aims) but arise as a result of their work. Their methodological project threatens critical research in the sociology of education; it denies the nature and extent of racism in schools, defends the status quo and, ultimately, reifies an uncritical and deeply un-sociological vision of science as an apolitical activity. Of crucial importance is the limited understanding of racism that informs the analysis. Even if we take an avowedly apolitical stance, research inevitably forces us to make decisions (e.g. about conceptual issues) which might unwittingly reproduce the very assumptions that shape existing inequalities.

Defining and seeing racism in schools

I have already considered Foster's research in light of the problems involved in identifying racism in school processes. Here I wish to return to that study as a means of exploring the methodological purists' understandings of what constitutes 'racism'. In revisiting Foster's work I am following the critics' own recommendations: having dismissed others' research, Foster, Gomm and Hammersley refer their readers to Foster's research as 'an attempt to handle informants' accounts about racist teachers in a more methodologically adequate manner' (Foster *et al.* 1996: 177).

In his study of Milltown High, Foster defines racism as: 'practices which restrict the chances of success of individuals from a particular racial or ethnic group, *and* which are based on, or legitimized by, some form of belief that this racial or ethnic group is inherently morally, culturally, or intellectually inferior' (Foster 1990a: 5, original emphasis). This definition enshrines a classic notion of racism that includes both (1) discriminatory action *and* (2) a 'racial inferiority/superiority couplet' (Mac an Ghaill 1988: 3). This is a crude and limited notion of racism: it defines out of existence the possibility of 'unintentional' or institutional racism, where individuals and organizations act in ways that are discriminatory in their effects, though not in intention (see Eggleston *et al.* 1986: 12–13; Gillborn 1990: 8–10; Klein 1993: 12–14). Subsequently, Foster has attempted to clarify the methodological purists' position on racism. He describes as 'grossly inaccurate' the suggestion that his research defined-out the possibility of institutional racism:

> I devoted a considerable amount of attention in my book to investigating school practices which might indirectly disadvantage ethnic minority students (see Foster 1990a: 6–8, 174–6) . . . The definition of racism used in my book has not underpinned our subsequent work; most of our concern has been with evidence about more indirect, institutional forms of discrimination.
>
> (Foster 1993: 549)

There are significant contradictions here: Foster denies that his book used a limited view of racism because he considered 'practices which might indirectly disadvantage ethnic minority students'. Yet Foster, Gomm and Hammersley's methodological project does *not* apply the 'definition of racism used in my book' because their focus has been 'indirect, institutional forms of discrimination'. It is also worth noting that when judging his own work Foster considers six pages (from a total of 190) to be 'a considerable amount of attention'. At best, therefore, there is confusion about the definition of racism that Foster and his colleagues are applying. This is particularly disturbing because, in Foster's empirical study, there is evidence that he granted his own understanding of racism priority over the views of his research subjects. When African Caribbean students accused teachers of racism, for example:

> When pressed further these boys found it difficult to specify exactly what they meant and to give examples of incidents which they felt showed 'prejudice' . . . Occasionally the hostility of Afro/Caribbean students was expressed using the vocabulary of 'racism', but such accusations rarely specified incidents that were racist in terms of the definition I have used.
> (Foster 1990a: 135, 136)

Accusations of racism, therefore, were not reflected back onto a critical examination of teacher/student interactions, but simply interpreted as a sign of the students' 'hostility'. This apparent disregard for students' perspectives is surprising. A useful approach would have been to clarify the kinds of incident that students perceived to be 'prejudiced' or 'racist' and to explore the consequences for teacher/student interaction. Unfortunately, Foster simply rejects the students' views as failing to meet *his* preferred definition.

It is regrettable that Foster, Gomm and Hammersley have failed to specify a definition of racism that they would accept as a basis for empirical research on 'indirect, institutional forms of discrimination' (Foster 1993: 549). If we knew the standard against which data were to be measured it might be easier to achieve broad consensus about what is 'plausible' and 'credible'. As it is, Foster's earliest understanding (racism = discriminatory action + a sense of racial superiority) remains the only definition to have been specified in their work. The sum of Foster, Gomm and Hammersley's methodological critiques is an inescapable (though implicit) conclusion about the extent of racism in schools. Since all existing evidence fails to meet their personal standards of plausibility and credibility, they effectively reduce the 'more indirect, institutional forms of discrimination' to nothing more than a theoretical possibility: 'They ['racial' inequities in within-school processes] may, of course, exist, but, as our work has demonstrated, this has not been convincingly established' (Foster 1993: 551).

In this way, the methodological project goes beyond its intended goal of '*clarifying* what we know, beyond reasonable doubt' (Foster 1993: 550, emphasis added). Despite their failure to specify the kinds of evidence they would accept regarding indirect or unintended racism, the critics feel secure in rejecting all existing attempts. Institutional racism is thus reduced to a speculative possibility: according to the purists, it *may* be out there but no research has found it (see also Hammersley and Gomm 1996: 19). The consequence is an implicit denial that racism exists as a fundamental characteristic of the lived experience of ethnic minority school students.

Sociology and the status quo

In view of a public perception that frequently links sociology with a fashionable, but ultimately superficial, brand of 1960s radicalism (see Bradbury 1975), it is easy to forget the discipline's conservative roots, often characterized by elitism and a central concern with order and stability (Hamilton 1992). This is a far cry from the critical perspective described by Mills (1959) and given centre-stage in much British sociology of education: 'The practice of sociology is criticism. It exists to criticize claims about the value of achievement and to question assumptions about the meaning of conduct . . . to examine, to question, to raise doubts about, to criticize the assumptions on which current policy, current theory and current practice are based' (Burns cited in Burgess 1986: 10). This does not mean that sociologists must blindly criticize for its own sake; rather, that a critical sociological perspective will tend to produce new insights that challenge taken for granted assumptions. Classic functionalism aside, whatever the particular school(s) of thought to which we adhere, we should surely be cautious about sociological work that presents the existing status quo as an equitable or natural state of affairs, since such arrangements usually emerge as anything but equitable in research that penetrates surface assumptions. This does not mean, of course, that factors such as social class, gender, sexuality and ethnicity will always be present with predictable consequences in every situation; it means that we should be sensitive to the ways they have operated elsewhere and how they might be figured (sometimes in novel and contradictory ways) in contemporary relations.

Perhaps most importantly, a consequence of Foster, Gomm and Hammersley's position is to *privilege* the status quo by granting current practices and assumptions a protected status until evidence can be produced that will convince them 'beyond reasonable doubt' that something is wrong:

> Drawing attention to the limitations of research studies in this area may serve to defend the school practices which were attacked, but if practices in the schools studied were equitable and fair (and the research studies concerned did not establish that they were not), then this seems reasonable (especially as the schools concerned have little opportunity to reply). Indeed, it seems unfair and unwise to criticise current practices unless there is reasonable evidence that such practices are deserving of criticism.
>
> (Foster 1993: 551)

The onus of 'proof' is, therefore, placed squarely on the shoulders of those who seek to question the current distribution of opportunities and rewards. According to Foster's position even where African Caribbean males are consistently over-represented in low status teaching groups (as they were in his own empirical study) schools should not feel compelled to change the practices that produce such a racially structured hierarchy.

The arguments here echo the debate concerning IQism and the 'null hypothesis' (Kamin 1974: 175–6). That is, in the absence of conclusive 'proof' there is a judgement to be made about the course of action with the least damaging potential. Hence, the most sensible approach to the nature/nurture debate about 'intelligence' is to assume no significant role for genetic heritability; if this belief is correct we avoid needlessly condemning countless young people to a second-class education and wasting incalculable human (and economic) potential. Alternatively, if the hypothesis is false we will have wasted resources on those who could not take full advantage. It is a value judgement that places possible human suffering and inequality against short term economic concerns. There is a parallel question concerning the extent of racism (overt, institutional or unintended) in schools. If we accept existing evidence as sufficient cause for concern and begin to question current practices then hypothetically we risk wasting time and energy trying to address inequalities that are not significantly influenced by schools. Alternatively, we can accept the status quo and risk knowingly perpetuating massive educational, social and economic inequalities.

Racism and sociological discourse

It is not necessary to accept the entire body of post-structural and postmodern theory to recognize the importance of discourse as part of the operation of power in society. An analysis of the political nature of discourse is especially relevant in the field of 'race' and ethnicity – where even the most basic categories are continually contested (see Bulmer 1986; Cross 1989; Mason 1995).

Foster, Gomm and Hammersley's critiques deploy a particular discourse of methodological purity that, like all discourse, 'limits the other ways in which the topic can be constructed' (Hall 1992b: 291). Notably they close down certain pedagogic, research and policy alternatives. This is clearest where Foster asserts the supremacy of 'basic societal and educational values' central to the operation of schools in 'liberal, democratic, industrial societies' (Foster 1992: 96). But it is also present, and potentially most powerful, as a thread that is woven throughout their discussion of possible ('more plausible') explanations for data that others interpret in terms of racism. Their analyses are presented as founded in academic neutrality – a concern simply to identify alternative possible explanations – yet their discursive effect is to construct minority students in terms of *difference*; they become a strange and threatening 'other' – the bearers of chaos and destruction (see Said 1978). In trying to account for conflict between white teachers and African Caribbean students, for example, Peter Foster suggests the 'social structural situation of Afro/Caribbean communities' as a major factor (Foster 1990b: 343). When challenged to defend this assertion, he is careful to reject the idea that school processes play *no* role, while simultaneously appealing to images of alienation and disorder that firmly locate the source of any conflict as lying outside the school:

There is also, of course, quite a lot of evidence which documents the general alienation of some Afro/Caribbean young people and their 'resistance' to aspects of mainstream British society (see, for example, Dhondy 1974; Hall *et al.* 1978; Pryce 1979; Scarman 1981; Cashmore and Troyna 1982). It seems a reasonable possibility that sometimes this alienation and resistance spills over into the school situation. My own experience of teaching in three multi-ethnic schools supports this . . . I think that there may be a general tendency for Afro/Caribbean students *on average* to be less well behaved in schools.

(Foster 1991: 168, original emphasis)

Foster returns to the same theme in a later critique:

If, for example, different cultural norms result in students from a certain group being more noisy, aggressive, inattentive, prone to classroom disruption, or disrespectful of others, then teachers surely cannot, and should not, be expected to accept such behaviour just because it is the product of different cultural norms.

I think there is a possibility that this may be the case with some of the cultural norms of certain Afro/Caribbean students – especially those associated with male, youth, subcultural forms.

(Foster 1992: 96)

Speculation about '*some* Afro/Caribbean young people', '*average*' differences in behaviour and '*certain* Afro/Caribbean students' is presented, therefore, as '*reasonable*' cause to reject critical analyses that view teachers as actively implicated in the racial structuring of educational opportunities. Foster's speculations about African Caribbean students echo popular images of minority communities in general, and African Caribbean young people in particular, as 'other' – as not really part of the nation; as outside 'mainstream British society' (Foster 1991: 168). This links directly with contemporary debates about national identity and the definition of belonging in multi-ethnic Britain. The new racist political discourse is here reworked using the language of scientific neutrality as a means of denying the political and social implications of the discourse (and the assumptions that sustain it). Hence, a strongly negative and stereotypical picture of African Caribbean young men is implied by Foster's conclusion on teacher/student interactions in 'Milltown High' and the explanations offered for the conflicts described by other researchers. Having supported the very stereotype that others have sought to expose and undermine, however, Foster and his colleagues are free to wallow in the reassuring belief that as scientists they have no responsibility for the consequences of their work. When defining a code for an idealized research community, their first 'norm' is that: 'The overriding concern of researchers is the truth of claims, not their political or practical implications' (Foster *et al.* 1996: 39).

As I have noted, Foster, Gomm and Hammersley's methodological project invokes an image of scientific neutrality that is explicitly depoliticized. This view cannot accept that science, rules of evidence, and judgements about 'plausibility/credibility' might, like schools themselves, be 'deeply implicated in forms of discourse, social relations, and webs of meaning that produce particular moral truths and values' (Giroux 1991: 507; see also Blair in this volume). In this way the discourse of methodological purism is implicated in the defence of the racist practices at the heart of this debate. Specifically, from a standpoint of professed academic neutrality, it is a discourse that emphasizes cultural difference and serves to pathologize minority students in general, and African Caribbean males in particular.

The political nature of research is a central problematic for those engaged in the field of 'race' and ethnicity in education. In the next section of this chapter, therefore, I will examine the version of politics that underlies the critiques of the methodological purists. Finally, I consider briefly some aspects of an emerging school of research that seeks explicitly to address issues of power and politics in research.

Politics and partisan research: from bias to critique

Politics, or more specifically the supposed political bias of some research, supplies a central and recurrent theme in the critiques proposed by Foster, Gomm and Hammersley: 'recently, especially under the influence of feminism and anti-racism, there has been increasing pressure to make educational research serve political ends. The result, in many cases, it seems to us, has been a distortion in the process of enquiry' (Hammersley and Gomm 1996: 20).

Introducing a collection of his writing entitled *The Politics of Social Research*, Hammersley proposes several key issues to be addressed, including 'the purposes of research in the field. Is the aim to generate knowledge about school processes or to serve a political cause?' (Hammersley 1995: xi). The question is therefore formulated in terms of an *either/or* choice: the two cannot seemingly be pursued in tandem. The three conclude their jointly authored book by arguing the following:

> research in this field has operated under a systematic deception: it is purportedly about educational inequality, which appears to be a purely factual matter, something about which science can in principle provide evidence; yet, inequalities have been treated as obvious inequities. So the effect has been to promote political views about the education system on the basis of a spurious appeal to science. In these various ways, the proper work of research has been seriously distorted, and the authority of social science has been abused.
>
> (Foster *et al.* 1996: 183)

Of special significance here is the way that the authors construct particular associations so that certain ideas become tainted while others are elevated in status: hence:

- Politics *is associated with* bias *which equals* deception.
- Science *is associated with* facts *which equals* trustworthy.

The methodological purists are keen to position themselves firmly in the 'scientific' camp: 'For me, the point of research is to produce knowledge, not to transform the world, or to achieve any other practical result' (Hammersley 1994: 293).

In this way a stark binary division is suggested: the imputation is that research which deliberately engages with the political character of knowledge is antithetical to good scholarly practice. In response to feminist critics, Hammersley discusses his perspective on this, making clear that he equates political motivation with illegitimate partiality in the research act. The argument is simple; if you are politically motivated, and hope to use research (directly or indirectly) toward political ends, the chances are that you will compromise your position as a scientist. On the question of 'important differences between research and political activity', Hammersley states:

> in political activity it is often not sensible to mention relevant information that could weaken one's case; and, on occasion, we may feel that deception and manipulation are justified. By contrast, such tactics are not reasonable in a research context. This is because the aim here is to discover, through empirical investigation and rational discussion, which conclusions are sound and which are not, and why.
>
> (Hammersley 1994: 294)

Hence, research and political activity are defined as mutually exclusive, with the avowedly non-political researcher placed firmly on the moral high ground. Interestingly, no consideration is given to the possibility that research might actually inform a political project. Politics (in this view of things) is defined as closed and resistant to 'truth'; this may accord with some people's view of organized party politics, but it is a narrow and derogatory image to attach to all political projects irrespective of their nature and scope. Hammersley (1993b) appeals to similar ideas when he portrays Foster's critics as *compelled* to reject academic rigour where it conflicts with their political stance. The result presents antiracism (and all who are identified with it) as irretrievably biased and closed to evidence.

Reflecting on problems in sociological writing, Peter Woods has warned against building a 'straw person', where 'in an attempt to highlight one's own argument and increase its purity and force, one may construct an apology of an opposing one which does not really exist' (Woods 1986: 184). Hammersley falls into this trap when, in his paper 'Research and "anti-racism": the case of Peter Foster and his critics', he judges it 'neither possible nor necessary' to 'reconstruct the actual views of Foster's critics'. Instead, he discusses 'what critics of this kind *could* say' (Hammersley 1993b: 430, original emphasis), deriving these arguments from a definition of antiracism 'in common usage' (no supporting references are offered). According to his view antiracism is a closed ideology that includes 'specific ideas about the nature, distribution, and origins of racism and about how it must be dealt with' (Hammersley 1993b: 446). Such a position, of course, would have no need of research since its devotee's would already 'know' both the problem and the solution. It is a position that contrasts with that of many prominent writers in the field but echoes familiar media and right-wing presentations of antiracism that 'still the voices of those, like myself, who tried to say that there was no body of thought called anti-racism, no orthodoxy or dogma, no manual of strategy and tactics, no demonology' (Sivanandan 1988: 147). Hammersley acknowledges that his description is an abstraction, but he doubts that this matters very much: 'It is also true, of course, that "anti-racists" differ about many issues, but for the purposes of my task in this paper these differences are probably not significant' (Hammersley 1993b: 446).

The methodological project is presented, therefore, as concerned purely with scientific rigour and truth. In contrast, those who seek to counter Foster and his colleagues' attacks are presented as politically motivated and consequently non-academic and not trustworthy. This position not only places Foster, Gomm and Hammersley on the moral high-ground, it also offers them further ammunition with which to attack the counter-arguments of their critics: since, in the purists' scheme of things, such researchers are *by definition* biased and untrustworthy, their criticisms can be discounted as ideologically motivated 'propagandising' (Hammersley and Gomm 1996: 19; see also Foster and Hammersley 1996; Hammersley, this volume).

In view of their representation of science as self-consciously detached from practical and political concerns, it is hardly surprising that Foster, Gomm and Hammersley have little time for the growing body of work on partisan research approaches, which they assert 'remove the traditional constraints on bias' and so have 'exacerbated' the decline in standards of sociological research (Hammersley and Gomm 1996: 19). There is insufficient space here for a detailed review and exploration of the many issues that partisan approaches raise for researchers concerned with ethnic and 'racial' considerations in education. However, it is perhaps worth noting some general points in relation to partisan approaches.

'Partisan' research encompasses a broad spectrum of approaches

There is no single blueprint for partisan research. Barry Troyna (1995) identified a range of approaches that he classified as broadly falling within this category, including 'conviction research' (Smith 1993), 'empowerment' (Troyna 1994c), 'anti-discriminatory practitioner research' (Broad 1994) and 'advocacy position' (Cameron *et al.* 1992). Troyna argued that among the general characteristics uniting such approaches is: 'the conviction that research takes place in social settings where power relations are stratified by class, "race", gender, age and other structural characteristics. It is argued that in this "unequal world", researchers have the potential to exacerbate and reinforce inequalities both *within* and beyond the research process' (Troyna 1995: 397, original emphasis).

Note that Troyna talks of researchers' *potential* to influence. In this way partisan research recognizes that the production of official knowledge through research may be a powerful tool in the reproduction or subversion of dominant stereotypes and assumptions (see Apple 1996).

'Partisan' is a poor descriptor for critical research

Arising from this first point, it is clear that the word 'partisan' is not a helpful label to adopt. *The Oxford English Dictionary*, for example, notes the strong negative associations that are often linked with the term: '*esp.* a devoted or zealous supporter; often in unfavourable sense: One who supports his [*sic*] party "through thick and thin"; a blind, prejudiced, unreasoning, or fanatical adherent'. This echoes Hammersley's description of antiracism as an ideology and does not seem an appropriate basis for research that seeks a wider audience as a credible perspective on pressing public concerns, such as differences in the school experiences and achievements of ethnic minority young people. The word 'critical' is somewhat overused already in social science, but may offer a better descriptor for general purposes. Such research is likely to challenge common-sense and starts with a concern for particular questions and inequalities. There is no necessary commitment, however, to reproducing any simple or predictable findings or recommendations – these remain an issue for empirical research.

Recognizing that research is political does not equate with falsifying data or suppressing findings

As I have shown, Foster, Gomm and Hammersley present a stark binary opposition between politics (as tainted and untrustworthy) and research (as objective and neutral). Partisan and critical researchers reject this opposition: their perspectives embody an awareness of the political character of all knowledge (see Ramazanoglu 1992; Banks 1993; Troyna 1995). This does not mean, however, that such researchers will by definition engage in falsifying data or suppressing 'unhelpful' findings as Hammersley suggests. They *may* do so, but so too do some people engaged in 'scientific' work supposedly controlled by the most rigorous checks (see, for example, Kamin 1974, 1981, 1995; Drew *et al.* 1995 on research into 'race' and IQ). In my view such falsification and suppression cannot be defended: in this I clearly agree with Foster, Gomm and Hammersley – where we disagree is first, in the degree of certainty that we have concerning different people's readiness consciously to engage in such practices, and second, in our belief in the ability of the academy to identify them without bias.

Good critical research is neither sentimental nor ideological

Howard Becker's paper 'Whose side are we on?' (Becker 1967) has frequently been misread as somehow advocating a kind of sentimental and quasi-political imperative on sociologists to side with 'the underdog'. Like most texts that are endlessly recycled through textbook references, however, the original repays close reading. Becker does not argue that sociologists should side with such groups as a matter of commitment or choice; he argues that a good sociologist is likely to end up at that position through having weighed their data and analysed it critically.

> it's using the view of the subordinate as a lever, a wedge, a way to find out things that you need to know to understand the organization fully. You are not accepting their point of view . . . you know, there are some terrible

people who are subordinates sometimes – politically speaking – it's not that they are such wonderful people. But they, after all, know more about certain things than the people above them . . . I systematically question as a routine matter whether the people who run any organization know anything about it. I don't say they don't, I just say it's a question . . . it's not that you do that for political motives you do it for scientific ones. But it has political consequence and the political consequence is almost invariably in the direction of anti-establishment.

(Becker, cited in Verhoeven 1989)

This links directly with my earlier arguments concerning the weight given to students' accounts in ethnographies of multi-ethnic schools and points to the importance of one of the basic requirements of critical qualitative research; that, where possible, the perspectives of a range of participants should be sought and included in the analysis. This is vital, not because of sentiment or politics, but rather because participants in 'subordinate' positions (for all they lack in formal training and institutional influence) sometimes understand more than their 'superiors'.

Conclusions

'What varieties of men and women now prevail in this society and in this period? And what varieties are coming to prevail? In what ways are they selected and formed, liberated and repressed, made sensitive and blunted?' (Mills 1959: 13). This is how C. Wright Mills formulated one of three 'kinds of questions the best social analysts have asked' (p. 13). Questions of power and social critique are central to the survival of sociology as a living and dynamic discipline: the imperative to question the taken for granted should not be sacrificed on the altar of methodological purism. Every piece of empirical work must, of course, be subject to critical scrutiny; this is one of the primary means of advancing sociological method and theory. This scrutiny, however, should itself remain true to the critical spirit of the sociological imagination: 'Avoid the fetishism of method and technique' (p. 246).

In this chapter I have explored some of the difficulties facing those who use qualitative techniques to research the role of 'race' and ethnicity in educational settings. I have focused on a controversy, concerning qualitative research on racism in schools, as a vehicle for examining wider issues arising from how researchers conceptualize racism and antiracism. How a researcher thinks about 'race' and ethnicity influences the design of their project, the kinds of data they gather, and the analyses they conduct. Some writers (myself included) have suggested that qualitative research, with its attention to multiple participant perspectives, social interaction and power within institutions, is more suited to the exploration of 'race' and racism in schools. A growing methodological project, however, calls this idea into question by critiquing existing qualitative research on 'race' and schooling.

Critiques by Peter Foster, Roger Gomm and Martyn Hammersley challenge the conclusions of several studies of multi-ethnic schools. They are especially damning of researchers who claim to identify school-based processes that disadvantage members of one or more ethnic minority groups. A prominent theme in these critiques, and in Foster's empirical work, has been the defence of teachers against accusations of racism (unintended and otherwise), especially in their disciplinary control and criticism of African Caribbean students. I have summarized the main characteristics of this methodological project and identified serious problems associated with it. I have argued that in their concern to scrutinize research on the racial structuring of educational processes, Foster, Gomm and Hammersley lose sight of the critical dimension that is central to sociological work. Their methodological project enshrines judgements about the plausibility and credibility of evidence as if they were apolitical matters of fact, rather than subject to particular perspectives which may embody class related, gendered and culturalist elements.

Such a position is not inevitable. Sociology has an impressive history of challenging the taken for granted; piercing institutional and professional facades; subverting common stereotypes and prejudices. Research that applies qualitative approaches to urban settings has produced some of the most striking examples of this strand in the sociological imagination. The work of the Chicago school, and the many studies following in its wake (including much British research) is replete with powerful insights into people's experiences and lived careers. Criticisms of this work as 'voyeurism' (Denzin 1992) or 'novelty hunting' (Hammersley 1992b) miss the point. These accounts produce new insights that undermine received wisdom about groups of people ('immigrants', 'mental patients', 'criminals', 'drug users' etc.) that are commonly constructed as outside the 'normal/moral' (frequently white/middle-class) world. In so doing, this work offers a possible subversion of dominant processes of labelling and social control.

There is an important balance to be struck. Foster, Gomm and Hammersley seek to enshrine a static and simplistic notion of science which offers little chance of critical sociological analysis. Alternatively, there is also a danger that, taken to extremes, postmodern and post-structuralist approaches may (despite their self-consciously radical posturing) also be incapable of addressing deeply-rooted structures of power and inequality:

> postmodernism has a tendency to democratize the notion of difference in a way that echoes a type of vapid liberal pluralism. There is in this discourse the danger of affirming difference simply as an end in itself without acknowledging how difference is formed, erased, and resuscitated within and despite asymmetrical relations of power. Lost here is any understanding of how difference is forged in both domination and opposition . . .
>
> (Aronowitz and Giroux 1991: 72)

There is a clear need for sound, critical research that recognizes, and engages with, the complexities of contemporary educational policy and practice. Such an approach may draw on 'partisan' approaches but will be more than a simple assertion of sectional interests or macro-political ideology.

Notes

1 This chapter builds on an earlier contribution to the debate, previously published in Gillborn (1995). Here, I have taken the opportunity to expand and update the discussion in view of subsequent publications and new additions to the research base.

2 There is, of course, no universally accepted means of identifying and naming the various social groups commonly constructed as 'racial' and/or ethnic minorities. I try to adopt categories that the people so labelled recognize and accept. For this reason, I use the term 'black' with reference to people of African Caribbean ethnic background but *not* for people of South Asian ethnicity. See Gillborn (1995: ch.1); Mason (1995); Modood (1992).

3 For a review of the principal research findings in this area see Gillborn and Gipps (1996).

4 Mac an Ghaill refers to 'people of Asian and Afro-Caribbean origin as black' so as to highlight their 'common experience of white racism in Britain' (Mac an Ghaill 1988: 156).

5 The pseudonym 'City Road' is wholly fictitious.

6 For a useful discussion of social class, gender and sexuality as factors in the social construction of 'normality' and disciplinary 'problems' see Carlen *et al.* (1992) and Gleeson (1992).

7 In the space available here I can do no more than sketch a reply to some of Foster's criticisms of my research. For those interested in the specifics of the debate, the best solution is to compare my analysis of life in City Road (Gillborn 1990, especially Chapters 2 and 3) with the parody presented in Foster's critiques (Foster 1992, 1993; see also Foster *et al.* 1996).

8 Although the classical sociological discussion of unintended consequences is provided by Merton (1963), the concept is not necessarily bound to functionalist analyses (Giddens 1984: 12).

4 | Silenced voices: life history as an approach to the study of South Asian women teachers

Anuradha Rakhit

Introduction

When I first experienced discrimination, victimization and marginality in teacher education and as a teacher in the 1970s, I had no idea that 20 years on I would be writing a PhD thesis about it. I knew that those personal experiences were social issues rather than signs of my 'personal inadequacy', but I certainly could not articulate them then. In this chapter I discuss how I have used life history methodology in my own doctoral research to explore the sociological significance of those experiences.

> The work of inquiry in which I am engaged proceeds by taking this experience of mine, this experience of other women . . . and asking how it is organized, how it is determined, what the social relations are which generate it.
>
> (Smith 1979: 135)

This chapter consists of four closely connected parts. First, I explore the autobiographical background to the research – how and why I came to undertake the project. Second, I review the available literature on the subject and set out some values of life history research focusing on why I decided to use that approach. Third, I discuss how I actually carried out the research, making strategic use of my own teaching experience. Finally, I share the emerging issues with the reader.

The background to the research: my intellectual autobiography

I begin with my life story, one which focuses on the ways in which my own modes of interpretation have been influenced by my personal relationships and lived experiences. I feel that the details of my biography will help readers to comprehend the importance of selecting the life history methodology which exploits the researcher's inevitable participation in the ensuing social milieu (Hammersley and Atkinson 1995). As Thomas (1995: 99) points out, 'an autobiography will add to reliable knowledge if it makes use of individual experience.' The main themes that emerge in this section will also be found running through other aspects of this chapter relating to the research itself.

I lived most of my formative life in India and carried the indelible stamp of my native language and culture. I came to the UK in 1966. Racial discrimination before the 1976 Race Relations Act was more blatant and quite dispiriting, far more so than today. From the very start, I felt not only alien to British society, but literally irritated by it because of its tendency to classify people into rigid, endogamous categories based on their physical appearance, irrespective of class and cultural characteristics. Far from gradually becoming assimilated, as the policy of assimilation would have me, I reacted against it. I realized that within this society 'race' has become a prominent criterion of social differentiation and considers 'us' categorically inferior. I became more alienated and much of my intellectual and academic life now is a product of that alienation.

Living in a predominantly white area of East Anglia, my colour, dress and language were oddities. I applied for some teaching jobs during 1970 and 1971 but did not find any because my qualification (BA in English Literature and Language) had not been awarded in the UK. So in 1971, I applied to do a Postgraduate Certificate of Education (PGCE) with English as my main subject, but was advised during my interview to study mathematics instead of English, being told: 'don't forget that you trying to teach English to our kids will be like carrying coal to Newcastle'. I was disappointed and hurt but still enrolled for a two-year PGCE in mathematics. Before the teaching practice our course tutor, who appeared very sympathetic, understanding and concerned, asked me whether I would mind going to the school wearing European clothes as I might face difficulties being accepted as I was. I found that attitude quite hard to accept and was bewildered, shattered and dumbfounded. I thought of leaving the course altogether. How was I going to instil in children a sense of pride and self-identity if I was not allowed to preserve it within myself? Issues of culture and identity began to acquire saliency in my mind and I started considering seriously the strategies which would facilitate cultural continuity.

> To wish to integrate with that which alienates and destroys you, rendering you less than a person, is madness. To accept the challenge to join it and change it from within, when it refuses to accept that you are there in your fullness and refuses to acknowledge the results of interaction between you and it, is double madness.
> (British Council of Churches Report 1976: 16)

The incident shook me, shaping my consciousness and experience of the world. Not wishing to be labelled as a 'trouble maker', I conformed. I felt the staff and the children accepted me at the school with some reservation. During my final teaching practice external examiners visited me. I felt uncomfortable and worried and was told by the head of the department that had I not been black the inspectors would not have come in. The old question of 'colour' had raised its ugly head again.

My first job was in a small secondary modern school. The headmaster in that school told me how he had changed his attitude towards immigrants since his only daughter married a Pakistani doctor. He was himself a 'Welsh foreigner' in insular East Anglia and I understood through him the psychological acceptance of roles. He made me realize my limitations and also helped me to laugh at English 'arrogance' and bigotry rather than being hurt and offended.

But the staffroom was a different matter. From the various comments the staff made I realized that they wanted me to become 'one of them'. I remember vividly during one Christmas fair how shocked they were to find out that I spoke to my children in my own language! Patronizing words wounded me deeply since all I wanted was to be left alone to do my job without feeling I was always being watched, assessed, measured and compared. It was hurtful and bewildering to see how some parents used their children as mouthpieces to express their prejudices. I still remember how each time the school said prayers for underdeveloped countries, the children would open an eye each and turn round to look at me.

During the fourth year of my teaching at that school, the head of the department was ill and I was in charge for a term and a half. The headmaster said that I would get some extra allowance, but the Advisor pointed out that I was not entitled to this as I did not have a degree in Mathematics! And so after a time I became disenchanted with teaching.

Fear born of uncertainty and disorientation took hold of me. I used to feel each day as if I was going into a boxing ring where any breach of my defences would put me flat on my back. I seemed to have been overtaken by a kind of illness, born of isolation and loss of identity. In the street I searched intensely for a black face, hoping that in finding one I would also satisfy an intense psychological need. In my heart there was a side where the whites lived with their words and insults and a black side where I lived with my wounds and my medicaments. The headmaster retired and I missed his genuine support.

I applied for several promoted positions in the Midlands area in multiethnic schools, hoping that I would be more readily accepted there, but did not get any interviews. At that time I was too naïve to really understand what goes on behind the scenes. I eventually got a job, not a promoted one, in an all girls comprehensive school in the Midlands, but it was not the type of school I preferred.

In that school I had little contact with teachers at the staffroom level as I found some members of staff used racist humour to make simple conversation. When I tried to challenge them, I was met with the response that I was oversensitive. One day within a month of my starting there, the headmistress, the head of the department and the advisor suddenly appeared in one of my lessons to observe me without any warning. I gathered later on that some of the parents had complained about my English pronunciation. What could I have done? I was painfully made aware of my skin colour, accent and foreign intonation. This sort of deeply undermining form of racism made me feel incredibly vulnerable and under siege in the school and in the community.

Within a term, a teacher on Scale 2 left and I applied for the post. I was called for the interview but was not given the scale point. The headmistress told me later on that she had to think about the image of the school and not just my ability. I was shocked then, but now I know that I am not the only one to face such discrimination:

> The legacy of acting on the perceived anxieties of white racist parents is . . . still very much alive in Ealing today . . . a black female teacher who was shortlisted for a Deputy Head's post was not appointed, and the reason stated by the Head to this teacher was that parents did not wish to have an Asian deputy, they expected pupils to be taught by white people.
> (London Borough of Ealing 1988: 60)

In my case the white teacher, who was appointed, had come out of training college only two years before, whereas I was actually doing the job! I realized that whatever I did, however effectively I taught, someone, somewhere, would not be convinced that I was able to do more, and I would always be at the bottom of the hierarchy. It was very depressing to me to be forced by colour to accept the status quo, especially when I saw colleagues much less qualified than I seeking and getting promotion. After about two terms that teacher left and I was given the scale point, but only temporarily.

Then I moved to a school with a multi-ethnic student intake, but soon realized how difficult it was to get any real support from the 'powers that be'. Within a year one senior member of the department was transferred. I was summoned to the headmaster's office and requested to take up the extra responsibilities my colleague had. I agreed, assuming naïvely that I would be getting his allowances as well. When I did not, I approached the headmaster, who pointed out that he had a hundred reasons why I should get it but his hands were tied and I should talk to the advisor. When I talked to the advisor I heard a different 'tale' – the decision for extra allowances lies with the headmaster! I was just shunted from the pillar to the post. It was obvious that no matter what I did I was not going to get the extra allowances!

Even a few years ago, when I was attending university while studying for a Master's degree, if ever I was late for any staff meeting or parents evening, I used to get remarks from some of my colleagues like : 'People should not study when they are working, they should either study or go to work'. I started considering such attitudes in greater depth than I had before and realized it was pointless to complain: racism is actually institutionalized in people. The problem of the 'them and us' stance is woven into the fabric of British society. It runs through the system – you do not have to get slapped across the face to realize it!

I have found it quite hard to write my own experiences partly because doing so released an avalanche of hidden feelings, emotions and sentiments which I tend not to bring to the surface. In writing this I have realized the depth of institutional bias and how much I have 'bled' inside. In schools we have had to face the child who would always test us, sometimes by ridiculing our accent;

parents who are suspicious; and teachers who are inhibited by our colour and are prejudiced. We have to become defensive and have had to fight for survival and dignity. Are we victims of prejudice and discrimination? Why is there no one giving us real support? I have moved deliberately between the singular and plural voices here in order to emphasize that much of what I have described are collective feelings and experiences. My intention to remain silent all these years was motivated by fear of being labelled a trouble-maker, but I started wondering whether my experience was 'unique'. This led me to want to try to understand my experience better and to try and discover whether similar experiences had befallen other Asian women teachers. In the next section I want to show how my unique autobiography, mediated by my pre-existing subjectivity and prior life experiences, has been central in shaping my research project.

> . . . my own experiences may have provided impetus for this project, but, in a more than reciprocal return, my study of the life histories of other teachers has given me an opportunity to reflect upon my own teaching, and to explore the social grounding of my own ideas.
>
> (Casey 1993: 9)

Why use a life history approach?

Women teachers' own understandings and interpretations of their experiences have been, until very recently, 'not only unrecorded, but actually silenced' (Popular Memory Group 1982: 210). A literature search on Asian teachers revealed only a small number of studies (Singh *et al.* 1988; Brar 1991; Ghuman 1995). Pat Sikes and her colleagues (1985) in their studies of teachers' careers included only one South Asian male respondent in their sample of 40 teachers and a brief reference was made about this teacher's experiences of racism within his school situation (pp. 87–8). My reading of the little that I could find on South Asian teachers' lives revealed that South Asian women teachers' experiences are still neglected and remain under-represented in research documents. I realized that if I wanted to understand the concerns, anxieties, hopes and aspirations of these teachers and tease out some of the salient issues and factors, I needed personal testimony. Hence the need for the life history approach which offers '. . . one respectable way of indulging our wish to have evidence from the lives of others that we are not alone in our difficulties, pains, pleasures and needs' (Measor and Sikes 1992: 210).

Life history is perhaps best defined as 'sociologically read biography' (Bertaux, cited in Measor and Sikes 1992: 210). One of the 'supreme' values of life history is its ability to take seriously 'the subjective factor in social life' (Blumer 1979: 81). Life history recognizes that lives are complex and all the 'ambiguities, nuances, changes and richness of lived experience' relate to each other (Beynon 1985: 164). By tracing the individual's life as it evolved over time, life history can show how individuals experience, create and make sense of the rules and roles of the social worlds they live in. As Goodson wrote, life history enables us to 'gain insights into individuals' coming to terms with imperatives in the social structure' (Goodson 1980: 74).

In 1981, Ivor Goodson wrote 'in understanding something so intensely personal as teaching it is critical we know about the person the teacher is' (Goodson 1981: 69). Teachers have their own 'idiosyncratic' biographies, hence a study of teachers calls for a study of them as individuals with their own personal and institutional life histories (Ball and Goodson 1985a; Beynon 1985; Sikes *et al.* 1985). So life history provided and continues to provide a way of getting to know more about the teacher as a person. As a member of the social group that I have studied, I have tried to give 'voice' to the 'marginalized' and 'vulnerable' individuals and have used a collaborative process by which we can come to an enhanced understanding of our lives and make sense of my own experience as a researcher within the social structure.

The strategic use of self in the research process

I now describe how I made strategic use of my 'insider status' in the actual process of carrying out the research. Rather than 'bracketing' my own experience for the purposes of the research, I self-consciously exploited it.

Sampling

In the UK the term 'South Asian' is used to refer to persons from India, Pakistan and Bangladesh in both the popular and academic discourse. This term is neither truly descriptive nor accurate. It relates more or less to people and their descendants coming from a certain geographical area and gives the impression that Asians are a homogeneous group sharing common characteristics. It thereby ignores differences in nationality, culture, religion, social class and language. The South Asian women teachers I worked with, whether they had migrated to the UK as wives or daughters, or had been born to and brought up by parents from the Asian sub-continent, were a very heterogeneous category of people with varying sets of social and cultural differences which affected the responses they were able to make to the educational or employment structures available to them in the UK. But I found that they all related to me well, mainly due to the specificity of our skin colour.

I started with my own networks of friends, and by using what has been called the 'snowball sampling' method (Coleman 1958), I was able very quickly to find a large enough sample. Of the 20 teachers I interviewed, 11 were not known to me prior to the interview. I made the initial contact by telephone and explained my aims and objectives. The telephone conversation allowed the teachers to ask questions and voice their doubts immediately. Complete confidentiality was assured to all of them. Almost every teacher I contacted by phone expressed interest in the study and needed little, if any, persuasion to agree to take part.

Based on my experience I drew up a list of some important hypothesized variables. This process is often called 'judgement sampling' (Burgess 1984b) or 'strategic sampling' (Thompson 1988). These variables were: to include teachers of both primary and secondary sectors; to include both 'first' and 'second' generation teachers; and to include teachers of different ages and at different stages of their careers. The term 'first generation' refers to those Asian teachers who were educated in their country of origin and may even have taught elsewhere before arriving in the UK in the 1960s and 1970s. Some of them had to take further training to improve their academic standing or to do in-service work. The term 'second generation' refers to those Asian teachers who had gained their academic and professional qualifications in the UK.

The biggest problem I encountered was deciding when to stop. By the end of the fieldwork period I had the names of quite a large number of teachers, each of whom would have fitted my criteria of variables. On a number of occasions my imagination was simply caught by something I was told about an individual teacher, and I decided to interview her as a result.

> One of the deepest lessons of oral history is the uniqueness, as well as the representativeness, of every life story. There are some so rare and vivid that they demand recording, whatever the plan.
>
> (Thompson 1988: 131)

The research interview

The data for this research was collected through unstructured face-to-face in-depth interviews. The interviews took place in a variety of settings, including respondents' homes, teachers' centres, respondents' schools and my house. The interviews, which occurred over several sittings and lasted between one and a half to four hours, were taped, with the teacher's permission. Several teachers spoke bilingually and enjoyed their conversations as they could switch languages according to the topic under discussion. 'Conversation' is actually a better description of these sessions than 'interview'. One-to-one conversation has a number of advantages: it is easier to manage; issues can be kept relatively confidential; and analysis is more straightforward in that only one person's set of responses are gathered at any one time. However, observational field notes, like the interviewees' facial expressions, gestures, tone of voice, and other non-verbalized social interactions were all noted very carefully. Often these details proved as important as the interview itself. For example, one teacher stood up and paced back and forth while describing an unpleasant incident in the playground. As she walked from one corner to the other, looking and pointing to the garden outside, it became clear that she had relived this moment many times. In another instance, while describing a sexual harassment incident, the teacher kept on covering her face with both hands as if she was ashamed to be seen. Sometimes conversations at the beginning or end of meetings yielded very rich data, as interviewees' perceptions of reality were expressed as feelings, thoughts and beliefs.

The fact that became quite clear was that the teachers felt very comfortable talking to me, not simply because of shared gender, but also because of shared colour and experiences. Like myself, the majority of my interviewees felt that they: experienced 'passive' racism as a result of a lack of support from white colleagues; endured a denial of their human dignities when they were humiliated by petty harassment by colleagues, parents and even students; had problems having their qualifications recognized (first generation teachers); and had to go through more interviews than white applicants to gain any promotion. As soon as it was established that we had shared experiences and a shared vocabulary for discussing them, the teachers seemed to open up to talk about their 'negative' experiences quite boldly. Greed (1990: 147) stated 'I have already lived what I am researching', and that feeling played an important role in establishing my relationship with the teachers. I also found that the strategy of self-disclosure (i.e. as the teachers talked about their experiences, I imparted details about my own) helped me to gain access to more personal areas of data as I moved from the status of stranger to friend (Lather 1986). According to Bertaux (1981: 20), data gathered in this way will then 'become a mutually shared knowledge, rooted in the inter-subjectivity of the inter-action'. Some researchers have claimed that self-disclosure carries ethical safeguards by diminishing 'the distance between "taker" and "giver" of the life history' (Measor and Sikes 1992: 215) and argue there should be 'no intimacy without reciprocity' (Oakley 1981: 49). But Hammersley discusses what often happens: 'What is involved in the process of self disclosure is the presentation of those aspects of one's self and life that provide a bridge for building relationships with participants, and the suppression of those which constitute a possible barrier' (Hammersley, cited in Goodson 1992: 215).

Some researchers argue that self-disclosure strategies are 'ethically dubious', because 'while we talked about the importance of relationships it nevertheless seems that we viewed them as exploitable, they could be sacrificed for the pursuit of data' (Measor and Sikes 1992: 216). But my familiarity with everyday life at school and its routine and vocabulary meant that I was able 'to avoid meaningless and irrelevant questions, and to probe sensitive areas with greater ease' (Riemer 1977: 474), which also helped to establish a certain level of 'in-built, face-level trust' (p. 474) between myself and the teachers.

I was particularly careful to point out to the teachers that my primary relationship with them was for research purposes and not for more general purposes of friendship. Lynda Measor also discussed the importance of 'staying bland' (cited in Burgess 1984b: 24) as she encountered difficulties when some of her views were known in a school where she was doing research (Measor and Sikes 1992: 216). But, in practice, I found it difficult to adopt the role of 'marginal native' (Freilich 1977) as I was not only interviewing teachers who shared experiences, beliefs, values and friends with me, but I was also researching *myself* and my experiences. I am not sure what the teachers wanted from me in return, as I did not ask them at the time of the interviews, but I am positive that being 'listened to' counted a lot for some of them, and I found that almost all the interviews proceeded smoothly, much like long, intense conversations. Some interviewees wanted me to go back and talk to them again. I did this in seven cases, but after about three or four sessions in each case, I felt that I had to stop as the relationships were becoming too involved. However, having established intense, passionate connections with many of the interviewees, I often left interviews with invitations to make social calls in the future, and our membership of a local black teachers' group made it possible for some of us to meet informally afterwards.

I was frequently asked for my opinions and experiences (as were Oakley 1981; Finch 1993). Sharing a similar identity with these women, I was able to answer fully and honestly with an insider's awareness of the complexity of our experiences. Sometimes I had to listen to the injustices they had encountered and talk to them at great length to provide some sort of support. To some extent this jeopardized the research as a great amount of time was spent counselling rather than interviewing. Measor and Sikes have observed:

> One of the issues that emerged was the way that some of our respondents took advantage of the counselling potential of the interviewing sessions. There were some limited points of comparison with a Rogerian style of counselling, in that we listened, reflected back, asked questions which encouraged people to reflect on their actions and did not pass judgement . . . there is a responsibility there . . . it is a basic human responsibility to other people. We should not initiate situations that we are not prepared to see through to their potential conclusion.
>
> (Measor and Sikes 1992: 226)

I am convinced that my counselling role added to the richness of the interview material as we shared our own memories of fear, humiliation, confusion, unhappiness, dissatisfaction and the dynamics of intercultural encounters in the teaching profession. The interviews covered our training, our problems of obtaining teaching jobs in Britain, our subsequent experiences of teaching, difficulties we encountered in career advancement, the attitudes of our white colleagues, parents and pupils as well as our analysis and comments on a range of educational policy matters. The perceptions of both first and second generation teachers were compared. Sometimes the divergence or similarity of our opinions and experiences became a topic of discussion in itself and the interviews typically became dialogic. For example, one of my interviewees emphatically replied that she had not experienced any discrimination as an Asian woman. She had become a deputy head in a special school after nine years of teaching. Nevertheless she expressed that being the only Asian teacher in special education had acted as a spur for her, making the comment: 'I am as surprised as anyone to be where I am'.

Most, if not all, of my interviewees had the same interest in and relation to our situation. Some of them appeared to be equally involved in the main objective of the research and we spent hours mulling over findings and hunches. Throughout the five years of my fieldwork I continually asked the teachers directly about my latest ideas and theories and incorporated their feedback into my evolving analysis. The final analysis I developed draws heavily on the theoretical contributions of the teachers I interviewed and to this end I believe that I have conducted a 'collective' piece of research.

Important issues

The education system has changed rapidly in recent years. New service contracts are imposed and with the introduction of the Education Reform Act and the National Curriculum, the whole context in which we work in education has been thrown into turmoil. And yet, sadly, so much remains the same. Our life histories reveal that racial and sexual struggles inside the education system in the UK still remain unchanged. The Swann Report (DES 1985), the Commission for Racial Equality (CRE) (1988) survey, *Ealing's Dilemma* (London Borough of Ealing 1988) and the MacDonald *et al.* (1989) enquiry were all concerned with the position of ethnic minority teachers within the British education system.

It is remarkable that the experiences of the teachers I interviewed resonated so closely with my own life history outlined earlier. My study has shown that despite our superficial acceptance by British people, we still feel that we live in a relatively hostile, negative environment, where our culture, languages and religious values are of passing interest or curiosity value to the indigenous population. We are either invisible, incapable, savage or exotic. Our narratives are full of memories of racial challenges in college and teaching jobs. The following extracts portray some of the similarities of our experiences. One teacher (second generation) recalled her experiences after receiving a college degree and finding employment:

> When I qualified, I applied for numerous teaching jobs but did not get any
> . . . After about two terms, I had a temporary job for a term. Again I was
> unemployed for another term, then I got an interview. The irony is that
> during the interview I was asked why I have not still 'passed' my proba-
> tionary year! Before I could even answer, the other white teacher who was
> also interviewing me with the headmaster, asked 'which Asian language
> can you offer?' I tried to point out that I was not qualified to teach any
> language, I am a science teacher, but he did not even let me finish my sen-
> tence! Anyway I did not get that job.

From her perspective, racism played a central role in her case. As a general rule, we continue to feel undervalued, that our skills and expertise go unacknowledged, and that our contributions are marginalized. Skin colour is seen and constructed as a significant determining factor resulting in differential treatment. Another teacher (first generation) ruminated: 'My degree wasn't good enough, it wasn't anything. I was told that I had to start from scratch . . . I felt really put off'.

Like myself, the teachers also felt that their careers were stunted and their expertise was continually questioned, particularly when applying for a promoted post. For another teacher (second generation) determined to get a promotion, challenging authority made her feel highly conspicuous and very vulnerable:

> When I applied for the permanent supply team (Scale 3), twelve of us were
> shortlisted for the first interview . . . Out of those twelve, six of us were

selected for the second interview, but I did not get the job. Then after a few months I saw one teacher coming to our school as a supply teacher who was amongst the first twelve candidates but not the final six. That really hurt me because I realized that I must have been a better candidate to make the final six whereas she had not. But she was recruited whereas I had been rejected . . . It was really difficult for me when she came to our school. I made a complaint but was told by the advisor that perhaps my presence, my 'blackness' may not be so valued in certain all-white schools, they may not be ready for me, their attitudes may be negative. It really demoralized me. What can I do ? If there is something lacking in me, I can do something about it, but I cannot change the colour of my skin.

Many of my interviewees were often regarded as 'experts' in ethnic minority cultures and burdened with the responsibility for the multicultural curriculum which led to marginalization and sometimes endangered their chances of promotion. Another teacher (second generation) explained:

Being the only Asian teacher in the school, I had to do a lot of extra work like organizing religious assemblies, arranging multicultural evenings, liaising with parents, translating newsletters and school reports and so on. The other teachers used to come to me for advice regarding Asian pupils as if I have 'given birth' to every Asian child! . . . After about four years I applied for a scaled post in the school. I was not even called for an interview. Although I had at least two major areas of responsibility, I did not get the scaled post . . . The appointee was awarded the scale point for the specific responsibilities I was doing.

Another teacher (second generation) defended herself against the psychological abuse of her white colleagues:

Frustrated in my aspirations and constantly undermined by other staff I felt that I did not have the status to carry out my duties effectively, I thought I would resign. I began to wonder whether they were trying to demoralize me and get me to leave the school . . . But I was convinced that I could do the job and I continued working. I never accepted defeat.

I was struck by the similarities of my determination and resilience with the other Asian women teachers. Although many had clearly experienced overt as well as covert racial and in some cases sexual discrimination in their careers, they were determined to challenge the oppression and move forward. We adopted a range of similar methods as coping strategies, like setting up and maintaining a black women's group, having close ties with the communities in which we lived, having a clear commitment to challenging racism and sexism, and developing a mutually supportive way towards this end. Nonetheless I agree with the teachers that for these oppressive experiences to be radically altered our own defiance needs to be supported on a collective level. Like myself, the teachers did not 'see themselves as individuals striving for academic achievement; within the institutions of education, they are interpolated as, and choose to present themselves as, representatives of and for their people' (Casey 1993: 124). By researching and documenting our experiences, predicaments and requirements, I feel that it is possible to offer important insights and provide a progressive platform through which we can not only understand the extra burden that racist sexist behaviour puts on us, but also help to overcome it.

Conclusion

The best way to write a conclusion to this chapter is to share with the reader what I have learned both from conducting life history research and from the process of writing the chapter. My work has confirmed for me the importance of continuing to conduct life history research in education to explore the specifically gendered and racialized experiences of black women. 'We weren't just individuals; we were really part of that whole movement' (Casey 1993: 152). Life histories have the potential for 'facilitating reflection upon the experience of society' (Quicke 1988: 92) by eliciting the way in which a personal life can be penetrated by the social and the political.

While doing life history research on teachers as a teacher is full of practical and ethical dilemmas and problems, my study has shown that it is possible to overcome these problems by genuine collaboration. For example, when some teachers treated the interview sessions as counselling sessions, I tried to involve them in the research process so that they felt that it was a collective enterprise. Similarly, as I met most of them informally and socially, we were able to maintain an ongoing dialogue. I also returned the processed accounts 'to the informant for appraisal and to check the accuracy of the data' (Woods 1986: 83) and discussed their feedback with them at great length.

I have tried to conduct a truly collective piece of research whereby I incorporated their ideas, theories and interpretations in the final analysis. An increased understanding of the lives of black women teachers may teach us ways to make significant progress toward eliminating racism, sexism and other forms of oppression in order to create different school atmospheres from those that currently exist. To conclude, I can but advocate that life history method is a 'two-way' process where the researcher and the researched learn from each other.

Acknowledgements

I am indebted to Pat Sikes and Paul Connolly for their constructive comments on earlier drafts of this chapter. My special thanks to all the teachers who participated in this collaborative work for their time and friendship, without whom this study would not have been possible.

5 | 'Caught in the crossfire': reflections of a black female ethnographer

Cecile Wright

Introduction

With the growth of qualitative research has come an acceptance that the researcher is unable to investigate a setting without in some way affecting it or 'contaminating it' (Hammersley and Atkinson 1995). This is in contrast to the conventional research approach, which seeks to distance the researcher from the content of the study in pursuit of research objectivity. Accounts from other ethnographers have clearly demonstrated that undertaking ethnographic research is essentially as much a social process as it is a technical measure (see, for example, Burgess 1984a, 1984b; Ball 1985).

In recent years, feminist researchers have made a considerable contribution to the debates on the social dimension of research. The literature on feminist methodology has provided, for instance, a number of illuminating accounts of the place of both the 'personal' and the relational within the research process. In particular, writers have highlighted issues concerning how researchers structure relationships with respondents in the setting: power relations – especially the contradiction between the differential power status of researcher and researched; and political and ethical matters and responsibility in the research process (see, for example, Oakley 1981; Warren 1988; Stanley and Wise 1990; Reinharz 1992; Mama 1995). Yet, while there is this growing and much welcomed critical reflection on the research process from a variety of perspectives, there is still work to be done in examining how the ethnic origin of the researcher impacts upon the research process and influences the relations developed with the 'researched', especially when the researcher is black (notable exceptions, however, are Bhavnani 1990; Phoenix 1994a; Mama 1995).

In this chapter I attempt to explore how being a black female influenced my position within the research field. More specifically I want to outline how I inevitably came to be 'caught in the crossfire' of relations between teachers and black students. It will be shown that on the one hand, many of the African-Caribbean students would identify with me as a black woman and would look to me for support during conflicts with their teachers within the classroom. However, on the other hand, the teachers would see me primarily as an adult and an ally within the classroom during these times of conflict, with my black identity offering a further resource that they would expect me to use to relate to, and help them control, the black students. Following a brief introduction to the background to my own research, I will examine how this tension manifests itself within the formal context of the classroom and within the more informal settings of the staffroom and school corridors respectively.

The research context: black children's schooling

Over the last 20 years there has been a great deal of both academic and popular interest in questions concerning the academic achievement of black children. Although parental aspirations and support for their children have always been shown to be high (see Tomlinson 1984; Brah and Minhas 1985), nonetheless, the ability or willingness of British schools to assist black children, particularly of African-Caribbean background, to achieve their academic potential has been seriously questioned. In essence, African-Caribbean students (especially boys) have been found to be disadvantaged at all levels of their school career (see, for example, Gilborn and Gipps 1996).

The last two decades have also witnessed concerted attempts to advance explanations for the disadvantage experienced by black students within the British education system. The viewpoint which predominated in the 1970s and early 1980s with respect to this situation falls essentially within a culturalist paradigm. That is to say that white, middle-class male mainstream researchers saw black students' educational disadvantage in terms of 'cultural deficit'. The crux of this viewpoint was that black students' educational disadvantage was a consequence of their inability to adapt to the school environment. Thus black students' adaptation to school was considered to be hindered by features within their own culture, such as family structures, 'way of life' and so on (see Driver 1977 and Banks and Lynch 1986, for explanations of the culturalist approach). In effect, black children were seen as a problem within the British education system. Not surprisingly, I remained extremely sceptical of the culturalist argument. This scepticism which arose from, for instance, my own ethnicity, being of African-Caribbean background, and as such I was well aware of the considerably high value which black parents place on education and the support which they showed for their children's education. Indeed, the literature shows that the prospect of a good education for their children was one of the motivating factors which led to black parents migrating from their country of origin in the 1950s, 1960s and 1970s to the UK (see, for example, Tomlinson 1984; Brah and Minhas 1985). My voluntary work with black children and their parents at a local voluntary 'Supplementary/Saturday School'[1] in the 1970s and 1980s, set up by black parents with the intention of both supporting their children's education and remedying the disadvantage faced by their children within the British education system, also shows this. Finally, there were my undergraduate studies which introduced me to (at the time) a small number of research accounts of 'life inside' school, emanating from the 'new sociology of education' agenda (see, for example, Hargreaves 1967 and Lacey 1970). All this provided the essential backdrop against which my interest in the relationship between students' ethnic origin and their experience and achievement within the British educational system came about.

The experiences cited above provided me with a perspective with which to assess the adequacy of (what was then) existing research accounts and theoretical perspectives of black children's disadvantage within British schools. I was thus particularly interested in problematizing the role of the school itself in reducing the life chances and prospects of black children and found the work of David Hargreaves (1967) and Colin Lacey (1970), which showed how school organization could contribute to differentiation, extremely useful. Their work provided a framework from which to both construct the research problem, and an effective means by which to select the most appropriate research methods to use. Furthermore, my reading of the work of Clarricoates (1980) and Stanworth (1983) helped me gain an insight into the fundamentally gendered nature of schooling, as did Sharp and Green (1975) and Willis (1977) with regard to social class. I was intrigued, but not surprised, by the lack of attempt to get 'inside' multi-ethnic schools; to study at first hand the process which might lead to black children being disadvantaged in the education system.

My research interest was thus an attempt to fill this void. Within the last 15 years I have conducted two ethnographic studies. The first was undertaken in two multi-ethnic secondary schools (1982–4) and the second in four primary schools (1988–90) (Wright 1986, 1988, 1990, 1992b). Both studies were particularly keen to monitor and document the experiences of black students, their interaction with their white peers, and their teachers. This was achieved through a combination of ethnographic techniques, using formal interviews with staff, students and parents, in conjunction with classroom observation and around-school observation (i.e. playground, lunchtime and so on).

As already indicated, my choice of research methods was influenced by the richness and the quality of the data that ethnographic methods can provide. Moreover, it also seemed to provide the best instruments with which to develop a more comprehensive insight into the processes and practices which combine to disadvantage black children within the British education system. The following discussion is concerned with some of the complexities, difficulties, contradictions and dilemmas arising from the fieldwork stage of my research. It thus focuses on the nature of the contradictory relationships which developed between myself as the researcher and the (predominantly white) teachers and African-Caribbean students, drawing primarily on the fieldwork within the secondary schools studied.

In my role as a researcher I entered the two secondary schools which formed part of my study in the early 1980s as a 23-year-old black female. Thus I shared a racial identity with some of the research respondents (i.e. the black students and the black teachers) and a position of difference in relation to other students and teachers. I will explore the impact of my racial identity on the research context and the contradictory nature of my relationships with teachers and black students in relation to my observation of participants in two main contexts: the formal setting of the classroom and the informal settings of the staffroom and corridors within the schools.

The classroom setting

During my time in the classroom, I adopted the role of non-participant observer. A strategy which I intentionally adopted as a means of minimizing my impact on the normal classroom proceedings and also in an attempt to encourage a degree of detachment, which was considered necessary for a thorough appraisal of the data gathered. However, from the outset, there was a sense (as will be seen from the accounts below) in which I was almost invariably drawn into classroom proceedings, albeit unintentionally.

In the classroom, I attempted to be unobtrusive in my positioning. This was achieved through sitting at the back of the classroom while always ensuring that I could see the faces of most students in the class. I tape recorded all of the lessons observed (having gained permission from the teachers), using a small, unobtrusive tape recorder, which for the most part seemed to have been ignored by both teachers and students. My positioning within the classroom made it easy for the students to ignore or forget my presence momentarily. Indeed, this strategy worked particularly well with the white students. The teachers, however, found it more difficult to ignore my presence in the classroom. This was partly due to the fact that my sitting position meant that I was in their direct line of sight for much of the time. On occasion, having given the students targets to perform a teacher would sometimes come across to my desk to converse with me. This made it extremely difficult to write fieldnotes, particularly as some teachers sought to read them.

Moreover, there were instances in the classroom where teachers explicitly drew attention to my presence. This generally happened when the teachers were involved in serious confrontations or clashes with an African-Caribbean student or groups of African-Caribbean students. During these clashes the teachers frequently appealed to me verbally or non-verbally for support (a request I suspected that had more to do with me being black rather than being another adult in the classroom). When this occurred there were expressions of intense resentment and confusion on the faces of the black students with whom, as will be seen below, I had built up a good relationship within the more informal settings within the school. Any attempt by their teacher to enlist my help was therefore seen by them as a way of trying to undermine this relationship. It was the overtly confrontational nature of these situations and the inevitable logic of 'taking sides' that left me with a definite sense of being 'caught in the crossfire'. My response was to try and regain my neutral position, which was being compromised by the teachers' endeavours to draw me 'on side', by not responding and sitting impassively while keeping the tape recorder running. This, however, made the teachers a little uneasy and caused embarrassment. Presumably, during conflictual situations like these where relations become polarized and an 'us and them' mentality emerges, my decision to remain neutral and not 'join the teacher's side' was interpreted by them either as a demonstration of my disagreement with their actions and/or of my support for the African-Caribbean students.

These feelings on the part of the teachers were perhaps exacerbated by some of the teachers' perceptions of the purpose of my research. As the following teacher from Upton school[2] indicated, the fact that I was African-Caribbean may have added to the polarized thinking discussed above, where I was seen as being primarily interested in the African-Caribbean students' welfare:

> I think on the whole they felt that because you were black, because you were doing some research, it was obvious that you were just looking at the way they were treating black kids, or that's the impression that I got from people who talked about what you were doing. 'Oh! Cecile's looking at the way we're teaching black kids and what we're teaching and how they are set in school'.

This sense of 'threat' at my presence was also witnessed by a black teacher in one of the schools who explained:

> They [white teachers] teach the community as a whole. They think that they are the sovereign thing in the classroom. If anybody treads in that area, they feel threatened. In this school, because the majority of the kids are black, the white teacher, when he [sic] feels a researcher, especially a black researcher, coming into his [sic] area where he is not confident that whatever he is doing right, feels threatened. And the conclusions you can draw yourself.

Extraordinarily, despite this obvious unease and discomfort that I suspect teachers felt with my presence in the classroom all the time or some of the time, this was never communicated explicitly to me nor, to my knowledge, had teachers refused to have me in their lessons. However, while not expressed overtly, such feelings of unease and discomfort at my presence were experienced by some. As one teacher commented:

> No teacher complained about you going into their classroom. However, there were some teachers who felt that although you weren't actually saying anything, they felt the interference, as they would have felt the interference from anyone, particularly as it was a sensitive area.

Significantly, as will be seen below, such feelings also found expression in a number of indirect ways in the more informal settings of the school, particularly the staffroom.

My presence in the classroom similarly elicited responses from the students. These responses varied according to their ethnic origin. The stark difference was between the white students and the African-Caribbean students. The white students' initial responses were of curiosity and considerable interest in my presence (which was partly influenced by the knowledge that the lessons were being taped). They were eager to find out the purpose of my visit to the school and why I was visiting their classroom. Interestingly, some of the white students became convinced that I was in the classroom to assist the African-Caribbean students. However, the white students' interest in my presence in the classroom waned within a few weeks of the study. These students ignored me most of the time, but would fairly often check to see my response when a member of the class was involved in a serious clash with the teacher. Occasionally a white student would initiate humorous comments at the teacher's expense and would then look around frequently for my response. Moreover, they were eager to express openly in the classroom any observed changes in the teacher's behaviour which they considered to be a consequence of my presence. Thus, teachers were frequently subjected to comments such as: 'You're only helping us 'cause she's here, why don't you act normal?'

The African Caribbean students, although initially appearing a little reticent and awkward with my presence in the classroom, at the same time showed delight in my presence. Indeed, some of the African Caribbean students insisted on either sitting next to me or in close proximity, and would frequently ask me to assist them with their class work. Furthermore, in my presence they were eager to project themselves as being academically able, hardworking and conscientious. Indeed this response on behalf of the African-Caribbean students could be interpreted in terms of them finding an adult in school that they could finally relate to and who would listen to them and take them seriously. This is certainly the view of one teacher who also, interestingly, touches upon the sense of 'threat' felt by some teachers from African-Caribbean students:

> Some of the kids felt that's what you were doing as well. The [black] children were slightly flattered that someone had come in to look at them, they were interested and they were anxious that you should talk to them, about anything. For some of them, particularly when you first arrived, it gave them a chance to voice some of their own anxieties, complaints, feelings of disillusionment, etc. for the first time, to somebody they felt might be sympathetic to them as a group of people. Up until that point, particularly with the first lot of 5th years that you dealt with, which included the Simms twins [African Caribbean girls] and so on, I think that they felt that they were very much alone, and to a certain extent some teachers ignored both their good behaviour and their misbehaviour because they felt that as a group [of African-Caribbean students] they were threatening.

Overall then, several teachers appeared to feel slightly threatened by my relationship with the African-Caribbean students and, in a similar vein to the students' perceptions of the teachers, remarked on what they observed to have been noticeable changes in some of the African Caribbean students' behaviour and attitude to work, which the teachers felt was directly related to my presence in the classroom. As one teacher stated: 'Since you started visiting this class I've noticed a change in the black children's attitude to work, particularly Steven; he has produced some really good work'.

Quoting from my field notes, the following extract would appear to give further support to the teachers' observations:

In one of the lessons observed, I was seated across the room from a group of four African-Caribbean boys, who sat discussing in loud voices the class exercise set, whilst the rest of the class worked individually and quietly. The teacher, who stood at his desk at the front of the classroom, glared at them disapprovingly. The boys, noticing the teacher's expression, looked across at me. On seeing that I was observing them they ceased their conversations and for the remainder of the lesson they worked quietly, periodically looking across at me to check my response. At the end of the lesson the teacher commented to me on this scenario: 'You get more out of them than I can. Possibly because you're black. They usually take exception to a white honky[3] telling them off because they feel that I may be picking on them whereas with you they know that you're likely to act fairly.

Interestingly, the African-Caribbean students in their comments seemed to imply an observed change in the teacher's behaviour towards them as a result of my presence in the lesson. They commented particularly on the greater interest that they felt the teachers appeared to take in their work. The following exchanges, from a lesson observed, illustrate this point:

Teacher: [talking to a group of African-Caribbean students] When you have finished that exercise bring your books out to the front to be marked.

Ken: [African-Caribbean boy looking at the teacher with an exaggerated look of surprise] You don't usually mark our books like that.

The teacher, looking embarrassed, walked over to Ken's desk and spoke to him, in a low voice, at the same time ensuring that his conversation with Ken was not audible to me. During the conversation Ken kept looking over in my direction.

It is evident from the dialogue cited that I undoubtedly had some impact on the participants in the class observed. Also it would appear that the most sustaining impact was on the teachers and the African-Caribbean students. The most direct example of this were the attempts by teachers to draw me into the conflicts that would arise between them and African-Caribbean students and the intense anger and resentment that would arise in response to this from the African-Caribbean students. However, as seen above, my mere presence in the classroom and my general position of being 'caught between' – being seen as an adult/teacher on the one hand and an African-Caribbean on the other – meant that *both* teachers *and* African-Caribbean students would appeal to me via claims that my presence was forcing the 'other side' to adapt their behaviour and act more reasonably.

Informal settings

These overt conflicts and underlying tensions also tended to spill out into the informal settings of the staffroom and the corridors. During my own field-work, both of these was subjected to prolonged observation. It is noteworthy that in assessing the impact of the researcher on these settings it is important that we take cognizance of the fact that the network of relationships within a naturalistic research setting will invariably reflect a continuum between the formal setting of the classroom, for instance, and the informal settings, and vice versa. This point is borne out by ethnographic accounts of the function of staffroom talk, for instance. These accounts have shown how teachers use staffroom talk as a resource for assessing and evaluating their encounters and subjective judgement of students in the classroom (Hargreaves *et al.* 1975; Hammersley 1980; Wright 1988).

Staffroom

The staffroom provided the best opportunity for observing most teachers in an informal setting. I spent part of most breaktimes and lunchtimes in the staffroom. When I did not have a class to observe I returned to the staffroom where often there would be teachers undertaking preparatory work. At the early stage of my staffroom observation I conversed mainly with those teachers I was acquainted with through observing their classes.

In the staffroom I took care to alternate my location and acquaintances so as not to be seen to prefer the company of any group or individual. I made every effort to participate in conversations in order to build up a sense of rapport and shared humanity and to make my relationship appear less asymmetrical. The purpose of this participation was to make me less intrusive than I would have been if I had been consistently uncommunicative. I gave some attention to my non-verbal communications and also made an effort, as in the classroom, to keep my facial expressions reflecting interest but not approval or disapproval. I never volunteered comments on controversial or school-related topics. I replied to questions with other questions or carefully chosen bland statements.

The teachers who were not part of my classroom study frequently asked me about the nature of my research. This interest was often followed by their expressed opinions on the value of research generally, and notably these opinions often appeared contradictory. On the one hand, they were very dismissive and cynical about all research, and there were comments about the relevance of academic research. On the other hand, they occasionally suggested that research ought to be done on 'the school and some of its students', inferring that the institution and some of its consumers were beyond normal comprehension at times.

My research and my ethnicity were used by the occasional teacher as topics of staffroom humour. Humorous comments came both from teachers I was acquainted with through observing their classes and from teachers who were familiar with me through being in the staffroom. These comments, which were generally made in my presence, were also made with a view to command an audience. The following three extracts that occurred in the staffroom illustrate this.

Extract one

Mr Martin:	[shouted over to me] Are you still going into teachers' classrooms and intruding into their private affairs? A special staff meeting was called about what you were up to, at which members of staff expressed their anxieties of having you in their class, intruding into their private affairs.
Mr Vine:	[sat next to Mr Martin laughing] Yes, we know what you're up to.
Miss Simpson:	[seated next to me] Ignore them, they're pulling your leg.

Extract two

One of the teachers whose classroom I had observed jokingly said to me, in the presence of his colleague: 'When is this research going to be published, so that I can go and consult my solicitor?'

Extract three

I had been wearing my hair plaited and put back in a ponytail. One of the male teachers, having noticed my hairstyle, remarked loudly: 'Hey, what's this? [*pointing to my hair*] All you need now is a bone through your nose and lip base and you'd look like a real Zulu Queen.'

Some teachers present laughed at this remark, but others looked at him disapprovingly. Reflected in these remarks, I suspect, is an indication of the threat which I evidently posed for some of the teachers, particularly the white male teachers. It was a threat, presumably, that had its most immediate source in the conflictual relations they experienced in the classroom with African-Caribbean students and what they interpreted as, on the one hand, my unwillingness to support them during such encounters and, on the other, the interest and pleasure that the African-Caribbean students took in my presence. Not surprisingly, I therefore found the staffroom extremely stressful and uncomfortable. This state was partly accentuated by the staffroom comments from teachers of the nature quoted above. Moreover, there is a sense in which I felt that the white male teachers' comments appeared more generally to be exacting revenge on a black person who did not in their eyes occupy the normalized position of 'race' and gender, thus evoking in them a sense of discomfort and vulnerability. This confirmed Kum Kum Bhavnani's (1990) observations of the inversion of the usual balance of power which occurs when the researcher is a black woman and the respondents are white. However, I would argue also that the respondents retributive comments reflect a shift in the balance of power from the researcher to the researched.

School corridors

The African-Caribbean students were the main student group observed in the corridor and around the school during breaktime and lunchtimes. At breaktime many of the African-Caribbean student cohorts, together with

African-Caribbean students not formally part of the research, socialized around the corridors as a large mono-ethnic group. Observation of these students' corridor activities and experiences engendered a rather interesting reciprocal relationship *via-à-vis* the researcher and the participants. The African-Caribbean students mutually accorded me their full attention. In fact, they were eager to include me into their group. They gained extreme pleasure from conversing with me on a variety of issues (some of which assumed a common Jamaican heritage) including their school experience. Furthermore, they were determined to exclude non African-Caribbeans from the group and the discussions. One way in which they achieved this was to converse with each other including myself in their own dialect – that is, Jamaican patois. Such situations therefore provided the main process through which the African-Caribbean students came to identify with me and regard me as 'one of them'.

African-Caribbean students grouping in the corridor at breaktime frequently attracted the attention of the teacher or teachers on break duty. The teacher often responded to this situation by interrogatively ushering the group out of the corridor. The African-Caribbean students in turn generally responded to the teacher's request by hurling derogatory remarks at the teacher in Jamaican patois. This act was then followed by laughter from other students. As with the situations in the classroom discussed earlier, my association with the African-Caribbean students in the corridor would often exacerbate the unease and embarrassment felt by the teacher having to deal with the situation.

One such scenario which occurred in my presence involved the deputy head-teacher at one of the schools who was on lunchtime duty. After the incident the deputy headteacher invited me to her office to discuss it and share with me what she perceived to be a general problem in the school concerning the African-Caribbean students' behaviour and their use of Patois. As she remarked:

Deputy head: I suppose I lack the confidence to ask the black students why they speak in patois. I know they talk to you in patois and in the presence of teachers.

CW: Yes, they do.

Deputy head: You understand it, but the teachers don't, you see. So immediately what they have done, they have made a state-ment about race to you, haven't they? If I'm here and you're there and there is a group of black lads and they talk to you in patois . . . I mean they're saying to you – look we're black, she's white. That's the feeling that is prevailing in the school when it happens. To me that's a very serious problem.

This uneasiness felt by the deputy headmistress was also picked up by other members of staff. As one teacher explained:

I certainly think certain people in senior positions have felt that they were under scrutiny and that they didn't want to be scrutinized in this way. And whether the fact that you have got an African-Caribbean background

also bristled them up the wrong way, I should imagine it did. Their prejudice showed immediately. Mrs Crane [the deputy headmistress] came to
me one day and said: 'Who is that young lady you talk to?' I told her that
you had been in school a long while.

Conclusions

My research, focused over the last ten years, has been in the area of 'race' and
education. Of particular importance have been questions concerning the academic achievement of black children within the British educational system. It
was felt that for this research agenda, ethnographic methods seemed to provide the best tools with which to develop a more comprehensive insight into
the area of 'race' and schooling, particularly in relation to the processes and
practices which combine to disadvantage black children.

One of the major concerns of researchers adopting qualitative techniques in
the research field is the issue of the research process itself. In this chapter, I
have explored the relationship between the researcher and researched within
the research process, focusing specifically on the ways in which the intersection of the 'race' position of the researcher and researched can impact on participants and respondents in the research setting. These issues were examined
here in the context of two years of ethnographic fieldwork undertaken in two
multi-ethnic secondary schools.

Thus, attempts were made to delineate the texture and nuances of social
relationships in the research process for both researcher and researched. In
particular, as a black researcher researching relations between (predominantly white) teachers and African-Caribbean students, this chapter has
shown just how complex and contradictory the relations can be that develop
within the research setting. In my own case there was a definite sense in
which I was 'caught in the crossfire' with various attempts to either directly
draw me into the confrontations among teachers and students or, indirectly,
to implicate my presence as the main reason for what was perceived by
teachers to be a change of behaviour among the African-Caribbean students
and vice versa. Overall, the discussion above clearly indicates that 'race' positions, and in turn the power positions they entail, do enter into the fieldwork situation but they do not do so in any unidimensional or essential way
(Phoenix 1994a).

Notes

1 The 1970s and 1980s saw a proliferation of Saturday or supplementary schools in parts
of the UK with a large enough black population. They were set up by parents or community groups. The schools were held outside mainstream school hours, normally on
a Saturday, hence the name 'Saturday school'. The main aims of the school were to
motivate children to succeed in the mainstream and to enhance basic skills while
giving the students some knowledge of their own history and achievements, almost

wholly ignored in the mainstream curriculum. The teaching was normally undertaken by both parents and qualified teachers.

2 All names of places and people in this study have been altered to maintain confidentiality.

3 'Honky' is a racial term of abuse often directed at a white person.

6 | 'Same voices, same lives?': revisiting black feminist standpoint epistemology

Mehreen Mirza

I am a Black woman/
I am the colour of hope.
(Asian Women Writers' Collective 1990: ix)

Introduction

In this chapter I discuss some of the ethical and methodological dilemmas I faced as a British South Asian woman[1] conducting research on other South Asian females, as part of my doctoral research. They were dilemmas that arose from attempting to translate seemingly 'lofty and intimidating' (Scanlon 1993) epistemological principles into practice, in effect conducting 'research as praxis' (Lather 1986), such that there is no division between theory and practice.

In particular, my concern in this chapter is to outline the key principles of Black feminist standpoint epistemology that informed my research and the problems I faced in trying to translate those epistemological principles into practice. I consider the issue of 'matching', whereby there is some attempt at symmetry between researcher and researched on the basis of such personal characteristics as shared gender and 'race', which it is anticipated will facilitate the research process. I also consider the process of 'placing' whereby the interviewee and interviewer locate each other within wider social structures through an assessment of their personal characteristics, such as class, 'race', ethnicity and gender. This issue is significant as it can have a direct effect upon the developing relationship between the two. In conclusion, I re-evaluate Black feminist standpoint epistemology in light of my own experiences.

Black feminist standpoint epistemology

Research by its very nature is inherently political; it is about the nature of power as well as access to power (Ben-Tovim *et al.* 1986; Connolly 1993; Seiber 1993). The academy has been dominated by White middle-class and/or male researchers, whose political values and commitments have influenced social research, leading it to be predominately Eurocentric, bourgeois and patriarchal in its agenda (Lawrence 1982; Harvey 1990; Marshall 1994; Blair, this volume). This agenda has been informed primarily by the dominant groups, such that the 'marginal', the 'powerless' and the 'oppressed'[2] have been the excessive object of study. The convergence between 'racist ideologies and the theories of "race/ethnic" relations sociology' (Lawrence 1982: 95) has resulted in some researchers focusing not on the 'State and its functionaries' (Goldberg 1992) or even on 'racial' inequality and the racist nature and the structure of the social system but on the Black[3] communities themselves. These communities have therefore been constructed as problematic *vis-à-vis* the White middle-class 'norm' (Lawrence 1982; Phoenix 1987; Troyna, this volume). The significance is that South Asian females in the British context, by virtue of their ethnicity/'race' and gender, can be conceived of as 'powerless', 'oppressed' and 'marginal' in relation to the dominant groups. Indeed, Black women and girls are often excluded from studies which seek to understand 'normal' women, and only come into focus when the research shifts to considering devalued groups, reproducing many cultural and racial stereotypes. For instance, South Asian women have often come into view around the issue of 'arranged marriages' and young African-Caribbean women come into focus as assumed problematic 'teenage mothers' (Lawrence 1982; Brah and Minhas 1985; Phoenix 1994a, 1994b). Further, young South Asian women tend to be seen as 'caught between two cultures' struggling to deal with the alleged freedom of the 'host' society and the traditional, authoritarian nature of their parents culture (Parmar 1981; Lawrence 1982).[4] Thus South Asian girls/women are often made invisible or are constructed as 'other' in research, as well as 'dehumanized' and 'pathologized' in the research process.

In seeking to overcome the dominance of the Eurocentric, patriarchal and bourgeois agendas of previous approaches, many have pursued feminist[5] and/or antiracist[6] epistemological and methodological approaches to research. However it is argued that feminist methodology, while rejecting patriarchal assumptions in social science research has reproduced racist assumptions (Marshall 1994) and antiracist research has often neglected issues of gender (Christian 1989).[7] Thus Black (and White) feminists are increasingly seeking a methodology which is able to address the interlocking nature of oppression based on 'race', class and gender (Carby 1982; Parmar 1982; Mama 1989; Collins 1990; Harding 1991; Ball 1992; Neal, this volume). What is crucial in determining the epistemological and methodological approach is that it should avoid the assumption that research is apolitical, value-free and scientific which is often characterized as the 'view from nowhere' conventional stance of White western epistemology (Harding 1991: 311).

This concern leads to a consideration of Black feminist standpoint epistemology[8] which stems from the desire to understand the position of Black women and their experience of double subjectivity.[9] Collins (1990) argues that this double consciousness/subjectivity can be viewed as 'outsider within status'. That is, the ability to be both inside and outside of that which they research, such that they understand both. Indeed it enables a process of self-actualization whereby the Black woman as researcher or researched is an 'active subject', thus counteracting the trend for them to be pathologized and dehumanized in academic research.

Collins (1991: 37) outlines four assumptions which underpin Black feminist epistemology: first, that the content of thought (in terms of structure and theme) cannot be separated from the historical and material conditions which shape the lives it produces. Thus Black feminist standpoint can only be produced by Black women. Second, there is an assumption that Black women as a group will share certain commonalties. However, third, there are diversities between Black women on the basis of class, region, age, and sexual orientation. Finally, there is a recognition that even though a Black woman's standpoint might exist, it may not be apparent to all Black women.

Beyond these assumptions, Black feminist standpoint proposes that Black women should undertake 'self-definition' in order to reject externally created stereotypical images, and 'self-valuation' in order to construct 'authentic Black female images' (Collins 1990). Self-definition and self-valuation overcome the dehumanizing and objectification process of being viewed as 'other'. In addition it acknowledges the interlocking nature of 'race', gender and class oppression, that is '. . . unlike White women, they have no illusions that their Whiteness will negate female subordination, and unlike Black men, they cannot use a questionable appeal to manhood to neutralize the stigma of being Black' (Collins 1991: 41). By engaging in the multiple nature of oppression and the larger matrix of domination, individuals are able to see that '. . . oppression is complex and contradictory such that no one is ever either oppressor/oppressed' (Collins 1990: 229), but may be '. . . an oppressor, a member of an oppressed group, or simultaneously oppressor and oppressed' (Collins 1990: 225). Black feminist standpoint epistemology also recognizes that culture is not static but is created and modified through material conditions.

In relation to my own research, these assumptions led to a particular set of principles by which to conduct anti-oppressive research; that is, an overt and political commitment to the researched, as well as a commitment to doing non-hierarchical, reciprocal, negotiated, emancipatory and subjective research which would be both about the South Asian women, for the South Asian women, and conducted from within the South Asian women's perspectives, such that it prioritizes the participant's needs, over and above that of the need to collect data.

My own doctoral research is an exploratory piece of work with the general aim of examining South Asian girls' and women's experiences of education in 'non-traditional' areas[10], in a variety of settings, including schools, further education and higher education establishments in the north west of England. The research sought to gain an insight into their experiences and hence does not claim to provide data which is representative or transferable to other situations. In order to obtain as broad a range of experiences as possible, the research focused on Year 9 and 11 students in school; A-level and BTEC students at further education colleges; and sub-degree, first degree and post-graduate students at higher education institutions, studying non-traditional subject areas.

A range of methods were employed, which included questionnaires and interviews. However the predominant method was that of interviewing, which ranged from the structured to the unstructured. In total 75 interviews were conducted.

I chose to pursue a qualitative research methodology in order to explore the girls' and women's lives from their own perspectives (Brah and Shaw 1992). I felt that the interview technique would best allow social processes to be examined and questions of 'how' and 'why' to be answered. Thus the methodology would provide an informal environment which would encourage the women to discuss 'their experiences, beliefs and values, and the social meaning they attach to a given phenomenon' (Brah and Shaw 1992: 53). This was especially important as I sought to explore sensitive issues such as sexism, racism and culture, as well as the area of 'non-traditional subjects', which can be difficult. Interviewing enables respondents to move beyond answering the questions asked, to raising other issues and concerns which the researcher may not have considered or seen as relevant, thus providing 'considerable opportunity for respondents to control the interview and hence to dictate the content and form of the data' (Brannen 1988: 555). All but one of the interviews were tape recorded, with the permission of the respondents, as the verbal accounts were ultimately the only source of data and thus had to be accurate.

Putting principles into practice

Having outlined the main features of Black feminist standpoint epistemology and my methodological approach, I now want to discuss the methodological and ethical dilemmas I confronted when seeking to implement some of the principles advocated by a black feminist standpoint epistemological approach. I shall be especially addressing my attempts to adopt those principles in the interview situation.

Access to a sample population

Gaining access was problematic, both in relation to schools and institutions of further and higher education (see Mirza 1995), and also in relation to the South Asian women themselves. Thus my desire for a systematic representative sample fell by the wayside. In the end I pursued an 'opportunistic' snowball sampling approach, which was obviously self-selecting. Finding the 'opportunities' was difficult, and began to cause me considerable concern.

Often research is of marginal importance to the researched, who therefore decide on making alternative, perhaps better, use of their time. It is suspected that the particular group of students that I wished to interview could see no obvious benefit. The use of 'traditional' techniques, especially evoking the name of the university and the university's interest, may not be – and was not – successful as it appeared to have different connotations for these South Asian women. Thus we need to avoid assuming that 'institutions which give us status and credibility in the eyes of White women will necessarily do so in the eyes of Black women' (Edwards 1990: 485). In addition, some of the issues I was seeking to cover (such as non-traditional subject areas and equal opportunities) were not felt to be important by the respondents and it was almost impossible to make the areas seem important to them as my position as a young, female researcher carried no status. Rather, the South Asian women were concerned about the research process, confidentiality and the motivations of the research: why was I doing this, who was funding it, who would the report be written for, what angle was I coming from? They also wanted to know what was the purpose of all these questions. Their wariness was understandable.

In addition, the nature of the community itself hinders access; for instance Bhopal comments that:

> Asian women are a very difficult group to study and gain easy access to, some of whom belong to very close knit groups who have and portray a very strong sense of belonging and security in which their cultural identity is reinforced as essential to the well-being of the society, the culture and the individuals. Outsiders who do not identify with the group will be viewed with suspicion and seen as a threat to which they may·disturb/affect the pattern of harmony that exists in the community. Members of the community will question what it is the outsiders want and how they may affect the daily lives of the individuals who live in the community.
>
> (Bhopal 1994: 4)

Importantly I had no wider links with the South Asian community in the north west. I had moved there in order to work and study. In seeking to do the research and make contact with the respondents I felt as though I was being 'parachuted in' (Jeffers, cited in Brar 1992) which also led to difficulties (discussed below).

Appearance

Presentation of self is crucial in research, and affects both the process of negotiation to obtain potential respondents, and the actual interview process itself. Much of the discussion on the nature of impression management, in particular the nature of appearance (dress and physical appearance) focuses on the issue as it arises when interviewing men (see Neal, this volume). However it became a dilemma for me even though the main focus of my research was women.

My dilemma was that I needed to dress for three separate audiences: the potential respondents and subsequent interviewees, the educational gatekeepers and educational staff (especially in school settings) and for my employers. Each had distinct requirements, but it was critical that I should get it right. Dress, especially in relation to girl students in schools was crucial in 'gaining access to people . . . and ultimately getting their trust . . . [and] gaining acceptance from the girls' (Measor 1985: 61) and it ultimately determines the data obtained. In order to meet with the educational gatekeepers, to gain access to the educational establishments (especially schools) and to look as though I belonged there, I needed to present an image that was in keeping with that of a teacher: that is, fairly smart, conservative and respectable. On the other hand, to fit in with the students I needed something less formal that would enable me to gain access to their world and achieve some level of rapport in order to conduct the research, and which importantly would not cause offence or upset their sensibilities. For my employers, fairly casual wear was acceptable. My dilemma arose as I was often required to meet with all three on the same day. It was a dilemma most acute in the field. I needed to wear 'teacher-like' clothes in order to gain access to the schools, and appear at the very least like I was a 'bona fide' researcher (Smart, cited in Neal 1995b: 524), while still appearing suitable to meet the respondents.

I decided that a smart pair of trousers and blouse would do. However, in the actual interviewing situation it became apparent that my garb and the amount of make-up I wore was not acceptable, as the respondents commented negatively upon them. They would have found a more 'traditional' South Asian form of dress more acceptable (such as a *shalwar kameez*), as they commented: 'My parents wouldn't let me wear that' and 'That outfit is indecent'. However, a traditional form of dress would not have given me access to the school in quite the same way, as one gatekeeper commented: 'You're not like the students here. You're so western. You're like one of us'. My compromise suited no one. Others, such as Green *et al.* (1993) have resolved the problem by carrying a change of clothing. However as I did not have my own means of transport at the time, it was impossible to juggle a bag full of alternative clothing, a tape recorder, interview schedules, purse, personal alarm and so on.

As someone who has had cropped hair for a number of years, I realized that my hair might well cause a problem, and that I might not be seen as 'acceptable' by the South Asian girls and women I sought to interview. Thus I grew it as long as I could, but the length of my hair was still not acceptable. It drew attention to me in a negative way, for being 'different' (indeed of all the interviewees I met, only two had short hair). It was commented upon negatively: 'Asian girls aren't allowed/supposed to have short hair'. Or I was questioned thus:

Respondent: Did your mum and dad not mind you cutting your hair?
MM: No. Would you want your hair cut?
Respondent: Well I was asking my mum if I could get a perm and she goes, 'Well you ask your dad and you take your dad to the hairdresser' and that means 'No, your dad would never let you. Your dad'll never say yeah'.

I feel that these types of comments seriously affected the level of rapport I was able to achieve with the students (discussed below).

Placing

'Placing' refers to the ways in which the personal characteristics of the researcher and the researched such as, but not exclusively, class, 'race'/

ethnicity, and gender, assist the researched in locating the researcher within wider social structures (and vice versa). This is significant as it can have a direct effect upon the developing relationship between the two. Issues of 'identity' are thus crucial to 'placing'. I became aware that in order to cope with all the different people I was required to deal with, I was developing 'shifting identities', not only through my mode of dress but through my actual behaviour. Lois Weis (1992: 50) notes that: 'The fact that people define us in certain ways does have an effect on us, whether positive or negative. It is therefore important that researchers know who they are, before entering the field because others will define you as they see fit'. Further, she argues that 'One is what others define you to be in these settings and this definition is likely to be more removed from one's "real" self the further removed from one's original culture when doing fieldwork' (p. 50). Adelman echoes this, when he suggests that in order to overcome misrepresentation, the researcher should be a competent member of the culture he or she is writing about (Adelman 1985: 43). The development of my shifting and multiple identities made me uncomfortable, especially as the realization made me question whether I was a competent member of the South Asian community, as well as to ask myself 'who am I'?

This raises further issues. At the start of the research, there was an underlying assumption that as a woman of South Asian origin I would be able to make contacts within the South Asian community simply because I was South Asian. In other words, the particular combination of my gender and 'race' could be used as a passport into the community. However, as already indicated, this was not quite so simple. Here I will be discussing further the issue of 'matching of interviewer and interviewee' and the issue of 'placing' by interviewees of the interviewer, as the two are closely intertwined.

Finch (1984) discusses the critical need for placing to occur when women interview women. She argues that: 'One's identity as a woman therefore provides the entrée into the interview situation . . . the interviewer has to be prepared to expose herself to being "placed" as a woman and to establish that she is willing to be treated accordingly' (Finch 1984: 79–80). She goes on to say that: 'Once these identifications are made, it does indeed seem the easiest thing in the world to get women to talk to you' (p. 80). Finch found that because the women perceived her to be 'one of them' (p. 79) they 'became warm and eager to talk' (p. 79). The critical category for placing is gender, followed by particularistic others such as marital status. I assumed that my critical categories would be a shared gender and shared 'race'.

As I went into the field to obtain a sample and subsequently began interviewing, I realized that a superficial placing on the basis of shared gender is simply not enough, especially where one is seeking to 'create shared meanings' (Reissman 1987: 183). Indeed these factors, together with my social class, age and background became increasingly significant, which led to a dynamic situation of 'shifting similarities and differences and hence shifting sympathies' (Phoenix 1994a: 58). In focusing on the similarities between myself and the respondents, in order to conduct ethically and methodologically honest research which would provide 'good' data, I found that the differences between us became greater, to a point where a respondent felt it necessary to ask: 'You are Asian, aren't you?'. We were, in effect, 'circling' one another: we seemed to be wary of each other, seeking to determine how 'Asian' or 'other' we were, in particular were we South Asian 'enough' (see Song and Parker 1995: 248). Thus, in the field same sex and same 'race' interviewing was proving to be problematic.

Much of the discussion between the respondents and myself which suggested 'non-placing' occurred before and after the 'formal interview' when the tape recorder was switched off. Nevertheless, it is possible to surmise a number of reasons why I was not placed, including, for example, the fact that I was not from the north west of England. This was significant in two ways. First, I was frequently asked who I was related to in the area, to which I would respond, no one, as far as I was aware. This seemed to give the respondents the impression that I was detached from the community, since the remark attracted comments like: 'Don't your parents mind?' Second, it is increasingly recognized that the way people, including South Asian girls and women, experience their ethnicity is in part dependent on their location (Bhachu 1991). The South Asian community in the north west is fairly working-class and conservative in nature (Ali 1992), which does not quite reflect my experience of coming from a large conurbation. For instance one respondent commented: 'I mean in the north I think people are still very . . . well I'm talking about my experience that is, well it's a bit of a closed community thing. It's restricted . . . but if you go further down south the family becomes more western . . . they're totally different to what we are like. Very'.

Moreover, I lived on my own, which was uncommon and socially disapproved of by 'the community', as indicated by the respondent who suggested that if she were to do the same: 'They wouldn't mix with my dad . . . they wouldn't exactly come up to me and say, "You're like this you're like that". They'd probably smile in front of my face, but when it comes to talking to my dad, they'd probably look down on him because Asians are supposed to respect their parents. Anyway, you wouldn't do that kind of stuff'.

Additionally, I was still relatively young. My professional status as a researcher, associated with a university, carried very little weight. I was thus perceived of as 'statusless'.

Obviously I was not disrupting their community as an anthropologist might do, but I was disrupting their understanding of what a South Asian woman ought to be and the kind of work that she should do. The girls and women I wished to approach, and subsequently interview, were wary of me and were not prepared to be interviewed in their homes because, I suspect, I was seen as a 'threat' as I could not be 'placed' within their or their family's understanding of the social world. This was summed up for me by one interviewee who said: 'My mother-in-law would not like you'. On enquiry, it transpired, this meant that I would be seen as a 'threat' because I would be considered 'abnormal/deviant' within their social circle. My perceived 'deviancy' was due to my marital status, appearance and demeanour, and the fact that I was doing the research implied that I could not be 'one of them'.

Despite our mutual desire to place one another, our inability to do so successfully often meant that during interviews the respondents would defend themselves as though my very presence was an implicit criticism of their lives and their social world. This caused me much discomfort and ethical concern when women would excuse their religious beliefs, for instance, when they needed to go to pray, as though they felt they were not quite right. This process of placing created me as 'other' as opposed to 'marginal' (which I had prepared for, and accepted). Being perceived of as 'other' by the wider society is something that I have come to accept; to be constructed as 'other' within what one assumes to be one's own culture and society is something else entirely.

In discussions about the career roles that South Asian women and girls could take, we would discuss the then current soap opera 'Family Pride'. Regardless of its merits or demerits as a soap, it had several female characters in professional roles. The respondents saw these roles as totally unrealistic, and inapplicable to their own lives, and consigned them to the realms of fantasy. When I challenged this by saying that surely I was not fantasy, it was again emphasized that maybe where I came from that was possible, but not for them. I was being positioned in relation to my perceived cultural identity. That is, the interviewees used me in order to claim difference or commonality (Song and Parker 1995). Again I was the 'other'. (I hasten to add that there were cases of successful placing, but these also involved a shared 'culture', class, lifestyle, aspirations and expectations as well as gender and race.)

The advantage of not being placed were that: 'Such "placings" and assumptions may be particularistic, but they can also give researchers pointers to the ways in which groups of people construct and make sense of their lives in circumstances other than the interview itself' (Edwards 1993: 195). Further, respondents would often say in response to a question: 'Well *you* probably don't know this, but Asians . . .', or 'In *our* culture . . .'. Thus I felt that I had achieved the 'insider/outsider' position I had sought, although perhaps more of the outsider than the insider. It enabled me to get more 'objective' data, where assumptions were not made. Thus I disrupted any sense of the familiar and played the role of 'the stranger within' (Collins 1990). Indeed I felt that it was positive because it has been reported that Black people will not necessarily 'talk openly about their experiences and opinions' with other Black people, especially researchers (Rhodes 1994: 551).

A further negative aspect, over and above lack of rapport and access to a sample population, was that the personal cost was high. It raised questions such as: Who was I? What was I? Why didn't I belong? This always made me feel uncomfortable as it made me wonder how respondents perceived me – an 'honorary' White person? The notion was disturbing.

Self-disclosure and reciprocity: more principles in practice

The spirit of equality involves the use of self-disclosure and reciprocity as it overcomes inhibitions on the part of the interviewee and places the researcher and researched on a par. Finch argues that this is possible because there is a cultural affinity between women interviewers and the women they are interviewing because they 'share a subordinate structural position by virtue of their gender' (Finch 1984: 76). Edwards argues that the effects of self-disclosure can be, first, to allow research 'rules' to be broken; and second, to promote the sense of identification the women looked for with the researcher: 'All the women indicated at least some feelings or experiences that we shared' (Edwards 1993: 192). Finally, it enables women to make links between shared experiences and to create a sense of solidarity with those in the same situation.

Earlier discussions highlighted the value of 'self-disclosure'. I would attempt to do this at opportune moments before, during and after the interview in trying to establish a conversational style. However, it became apparent that this was not always welcome as it interrupted the women's own flow of thought. Moreover, self-disclosure on my part to enable rapport actually caused further distance. That is, I became more 'alien' and 'unplaceable'. Information about myself, and my opinion on numerous subjects was often sought, and I initially provided as honest an answer as I could. However this would often cause surprise and elicited further questions, until, probing further into my background in an attempt to explain and explore my response, the respondents would say: 'Ah, that explains it [my peculiar opinion]' and we were able to carry on. Becoming an interviewee became an uncomfortable position because of the continual challenges to my identity as discussed earlier, and I began to develop an increasingly 'uneasy and ironic adoption of a traditional, "malestream" academic persona, presenting myself as neutral, rational and objective . . .' (Neal 1995b: 524). This could be seen as unethical and the antithesis of good feminist praxis (Ball 1992). However I consider it a realistic response to the 'messiness' of real research; I felt that, like the respondents, I had a right to present a public account of myself and maintain some privacy.

Seeking to do more than just respond to questions, as an attempt at reciprocity in order to 'pay back' the respondents for their time and information, proved problematic and generated further dilemmas. For instance, the respondents did not express any interest in reciprocity and appeared to want nothing from me. Indeed they would often say: 'Why? What for? That's silly! There's no need, you need my help and I'm happy to give it you'. In effect it was a *favour* to me, a complete stranger. The occasional expression of reciprocity took the form of straightforward requests in exchange for their time and information, such as asking advice on the best type of video camera to purchase or the nearest Asian woman photography club, or on negotiating the tricky world of GCSE and A-level options, or completing UCAS forms – in other words, the respondents were utilizing 'my expertise'. For others, there was no such obvious service I could offer. Some of the respondents, flatteringly, credited me with more power than I had in requesting that I set up a course for South Asian women in the subject areas that they were interested in. My response that I could only recommend it as a policy option was met with disappointment.

Other respondents caused me considerable concern in the manner in which they sought 'pay-back'. For instance, I was perceived as a suitable person to intervene on behalf of a respondent in a marriage proposal that was sought. I was not prepared to do this, as I felt that this was inappropriate, but the respondent felt that I should, because she thought I could 'help'. Another respondent, a year after an interview, called to say that she had not passed all her A levels and was keen to do a law degree, and insisted that I use my contacts to ensure her a place on a suitable course. I could not possibly do this, but again it was expected that I would, in return for the information provided.

Respondents were not the only ones to see me in this way. Gatekeepers often shared their perception of me as a professional South Asian woman. For instance, one gatekeeper sought my aid in intervening between the school and a set of parents who were refusing to let their daughters come to school. It was felt that I could persuade the parents to return their daughters to school. The school expected this in return for having allowed access to the school. I declined as best I could, without appearing unhelpful and endangering my own continued access to the school.

I wanted to pursue interviews in a spirit of reciprocity, but this often proved self-deluding in the case of this research, because the researcher constructs the research problem, constructs the questions, seeks the relationship with respondents and ultimately determines what happens to the material created. Ultimately: 'What is in it for them is never what is in it for you. Even if they were interested it is usually not for the *knowledge* of it' (Glucksmann 1994: 154, original emphasis).

The research study, like many others, produced some very harrowing accounts of experiences that some of the South Asian girls and women interviewed were experiencing, or had experienced. I recognized that, despite my good intentions, I was not really in a position to 'help' and did as Brannen suggests, remaining 'silent yet empathetic [which] is hard and yet it may be all that the individual can offer in the circumstances' (1988: 560). I was not, after all, a trained counsellor. Despite the reciprocal approach, it did not feel appropriate to intervene in circumstances where I, as an outsider, perceived the respondents circumstances to be oppressive, but the respondents did not. The effects of such revelations were disturbing to me, but may have been far more traumatic for the respondent, such that after an interview 'the subject may be left with her emotional life in pieces and no one to help put them back together' (Edwards 1993: 192–3), a situation which has been described by Clark and Haldane as the 'scientific equivalent of slash and burn agriculture' (Clark and Haldane, cited in Edwards 1993: 192–3). Is it ethically acceptable to have done this?

Returning to standpoint epistemology

The above discussion has shown that one of the key elements of standpoint epistemological praxis, 'matching' and the attendant element, 'placing' are problematic. In addition, McLennan (1995) and Holmwood (1995) argue that the ontological and epistemological foundations of standpoint epistemology, and its claims to separate identity, are less than secure.[11] The requirement for symmetry between researcher and researched is questioned by others. Connolly (1996b) for instance, argues that the logic of the perspective cannot be maintained when it is recognized that the researcher and the researched possess multiple identities; for instance, no one is ever *just* a woman or *just* Black or *just* working-class, but actually possess fluid, multi-layered social identities. Connolly (1996b) provides us with some very pertinent examples of the dilemmas that can arise if we pursue standpoint epistemology to its problematic conclusion. For instance he poses the question 'who would be best able to research Black women – a White woman or a Black man?' (Connolly 1996b: 191). In other words, which aspect of the Black woman's identity would be most significant here – her 'race' or her 'gender'? He suggests that some might argue that the White woman was best placed to do the research because of their shared experiences as women, but on the other hand the Black man might be best placed to do the research because of their shared experiences of racism. However, if we consider that a Black woman has a multi-layered social identity, and that her total experience is much more complex, then the issue cannot be reduced to such simplistic symmetry, where White people can only ever study White institutions and structures while Black people can only ever study Black communities.[12]

Much more significantly for me, it has been argued that Black feminist standpoint has developed from a very particularistic African American experience which has been extrapolated to apply to all African women, both on the African continent and in the diaspora (see Zack-Williams 1995); later it was extrapolated to apply to all 'women of color' (Song 1995). The criticism is that this application of an African American perspective unwittingly provides a blanket perspective on the experiences of women of colour as this approach tends to ignore the specificity of other black women's experiences. It homogenises 'women of color', when we know that they do not constitute a homogenous group. (This becomes more problematic when we remember that White feminists have been similarly criticized for homogenizing the experience of all women.) The difficulty with terminology and frameworks developed in the North American context is that they become difficult to apply elsewhere. For instance, Song argues that the terms 'Black' women and 'women of color' are problematic because: 'these categories have contested memberships and boundaries and do not identify the distinctive experiences of ethnic migrant women or the disparate colonial (and slave) histories associated with specific groups . . . This is not to deny some of the concrete similarities and connections between diverse groups of non-white women' (Song 1995: 286).

If this approach is so problematic, why did I continue to apply it to my research? I recognized the need to be cautious about applying frameworks which had been developed elsewhere and which were rooted specifically in the African American tradition, however they did provide a vital point of reference for research into the lives of Asian and African Caribbean women in Britain (Graham 1991). Additionally, the value of Black feminist standpoint lies in the fact that it contextualizes Black women's lives by being historically and culturally specific about their experiences (Song 1995). In particular, Afro-centric feminist standpoints have been invaluable in theorizing the realities of

Black women's lives and how their lives are linked with alternative ways of 'knowing' (Collins 1990).

Moreover, I valued this approach as I felt that it would enable me (and the women I sought to study), to move beyond being constructed by the European colonizers gaze. As a South Asian woman researcher I was in the double position of being a member of the White western academy which traditionally oppresses and marginalizes through racism the communities from which I come. This leads to the difficulties of trying to 'both step out of and also draw on, one's subjective awareness of the social, economic and political subordination of one's community' (Marshall 1994: 109). Ultimately the value of these alternative epistemologies are twofold: they are able to challenge the process by which the powerful seek to legitimate their knowledge claims while they also effectively problematize all prior knowledge and claims validated as 'true'.

Conclusions

The aim of this chapter has been to explore the complexities of attempting to operationalize an anti-oppressive approach to research; in particular putting Black feminist standpoint epistemological and methodological principles into practice in a particular context. In focusing my gaze upon the South Asian girls and women, I sought to provide a means by which they could present their 'voices' in places and circumstances where they might not otherwise be heard. I sought to present these 'voices' in a manner which did not pathologize or reify them. I wanted to ensure that in making visible and recording the experiences of this group, I did not fall into the trap of 'informing the powerful about an oppressed group' (Stacey 1988). This is significant in relation to Black women whose relationship with the state is often one of oppression (Carby 1982; Parmar 1982; Mama 1989). Hence my desire to pursue an approach that would challenge existing perceptions, and address the priorities of Black women, so that the research could be used to improve the position of Black women in Britain (Marshall 1994). Further, I recognize that when viewed by the state, I am one of the researched and so I acknowledge 'my subordination as a Black woman whilst recognising my privileged position in relation to other women in regard to class, sexuality, age and ability. Like other feminists I share the common dilemma of reconciling my personal life and my political goals' (Marshall 1994: 122–3).

I have sought to illustrate how problematic research praxis can be, even in a 'best case' situation where the researched and researcher are 'matched' on the basis of 'race' and gender. My experience indicates that 'placing' and successful reciprocal relationships are dependent upon much more than an assumed symmetry based upon a shared gender and 'race' (as Connolly 1996b suggests). This experience demonstrated the complex nature of identity so that 'many dimensions of sameness and difference can be operating at any given moment. And where two people may claim commonality on one dimension, they may fall apart on another' (Song and Parker 1995: 246).

The 'failure' in achieving reciprocity and rapport on the basis of 'matching' also demonstrates the danger of creating a 'false-equality' trap (Gelsthorpe 1992) where none exists. This is all the more pertinent in a situation where as South Asian women our identities are constantly in flux and are multi-layered, and based upon a host of structures of which gender and 'race' are but two. Our identities are therefore continually (re)negotiated and (re)invented.

The value of conducting research on the basis of 'insider/outsider' is great; even if in my case I was ultimately more 'outsider' than 'insider'. Indeed, the role of the 'stranger' is a valid and valuable one (Collins 1990; Cotterill 1992) and should not be dismissed. This recognition leads me to continually question and deconstruct notions of what it means to be an 'insider' and 'outsider', because such dichotomies are unable to successfully capture the multi-layered subjectivities of South Asian women. This enables me to move away from boxing myself, and the researched, into one subject position and/or identity and to recognize that:

> We . . . sometimes include(s), other times exclude(s) me. You and I are close, we intertwine; you may stand on the other side of the hill once in a while, but you may also be me, while remaining what you are and what I am not. The differences made between entities comprehended as absolute presences – hence the notion of pure origin and true self – are an outgrowth of a dualistic system of thought peculiar to the Occident . . .
> (Minh-ha 1989: 90)

Thus it enables me to question and deconstruct the concept 'South Asian female', in order to overcome essentialist perspectives of South Asian womanhood.

Having shared some of my stories from the field and some of the 'learning' that I have undergone when trying to utilize an anti-oppressive methodological approach, where now? Despite the difficulties experienced, I maintain a commitment to '. . . an anti-racist socialist feminist understanding of the sources of oppression' (Ball 1992: 12), with its attendant principles (as discussed earlier). But, in a similar vein to Wheatley (1994a: 412), I would place this anti-oppressive approach within a framework which she refers to as a 'flexibility of mind' which assumes neither false unity nor consensus (1994a: 412). It is a form of 'eclecticism' which argues that the methodological approach should be 'contexually contingent' and should 'respect the variegated versions of feminist [and other anti-oppressive] intellectual practices and politics' (Wheatley 1994b: 422). In conclusion then, such an approach would allow me to present my own voice as well as the voice of the researched. This approach would enable me and the researched to construct our identities as South Asian women in Britain not: ' "in relation to", "in opposition", "as reversal of", or "as a corrective" . . . *but in and for themselves*. Such a narrative thwarts that binary hierarchy of centre and margin: the margin refuses its place as "Other" ' (Parmar 1990: 101, original emphasis). This approach would enable me to address the ever changing kaleidoscope known as South Asian womanhood.

Acknowledgements

I would like to thank a number of people who have been supportive to me in the writing of this chapter: Barry Troyna, Sarah Neal, Ken Phillips and especially Paul Connolly.

This is a revised version of a paper presented at the British Educational Research Association Annual Conference (Mirza 1994). I would like to thank all those present for their stimulating and valuable comments.

Notes

1 The term 'South Asian' is used to refer to those who define their heritage and/or ethnic origins as from the South Asian sub-continent, which incorporates Bangladesh, India and Pakistan, and includes East African Asians. This does not mean that the differences between and within each group based on, for instance, class, caste and religion, are not recognized. The term is merely used for convenience.

The term 'woman' is problematic as it is often used in an universalistic fashion, where the assumption is that womankind is White, middle-class, able-bodied, heterosexual, educated, and of the first world (Carby 1982; Parmar 1982; Harding 1986, 1991; Phoenix 1987; Stanley and Wise 1990; Graham 1991). The concept 'woman', and experience of being a woman, is and must be 'ontologically fractured and complex' (Stanley and Wise 1990: 22). Experiences of oppression do not equal 'same experience' (Stanley and Wise 1990; Kishwar 1994).

2 Following Neal (1995b) I would argue that the concepts 'marginal' and 'powerless' are problematic as they are both vague in meaning and have distinct overtones of victim passivity, thus denying the groups that they are applied to any 'agency' in resisting the circumstances in which they find themselves. I argue that the lack of alternative concepts ensures their continued use here.

3 'Black' refers here, and throughout the paper, to those of South Asian and/or African/Caribbean/American origin. In other words, all those who come under the rubric 'people of color'. I recognize the limitations of these terms and I do not use the term 'black' to negate difference nor to imply homogeneity. I recognize that these terms are contested. These reservations apply equally to the term 'White'.

4 Indeed these concerns can be seen in the titles of various studies conducted: 'The Second Generation . . . Punjabi or English' (Thompson, cited in Lawrence 1982: 122) and *The Silent Cry: Second Generation Bradford Muslim Women Speak* (Mirza 1989). See Parmar (1981) for a fuller discussion.

5 Although the concept 'feminism' is used, it is recognized to be problematic. Feminism is assumed to be 'open' and 'generic' yet it is often implicitly White in its concerns and focus (Stanley and Wise 1993; Kishwar 1994).

There is no one feminist methodology or epistemological approach, just as there is no one feminism (see Griffiths 1995). There are, however, amongst many advocates of feminist methodology the following shared assumptions. It should address women's lives and experience in their own terms, that is it should be grounded; it should promote an interactional methodology in order to end the exploitation of women as research objects; and finally, the researcher is central to the research and her feelings should be central to the process. (See, for example, Oakley 1981; Du Bois 1983; Duelli Klein 1983; Finch 1984; Harding 1986, 1987, 1991; Herbert 1993;

Stanley and Wise 1993, for more detailed discussions of the nature and complexity of feminist epistemology and methodology, than I am able to provide here.)

6 See Harvey 1990; Ball 1991; Connolly 1993; Troyna and Carrington 1989 for more detailed discussions of antiracist epistemological and methodological concerns than I am able to provide here.

7 Antiracist and feminist research differ from one another in focus, but they are often placed together, as in this research, because of their 'shared rejection of objective, apolitical, scientific research' (Neal 1995b: 519).

8 See Harding 1986 and 1991 for detailed discussions of feminist standpoint epistemology.

9 Du Bois argues that Black women have 'double consciousness', which refers to the way in which: 'We are in and of our society but in important ways also not "of" it . . . We are observer and observed, subject and object, knower and known' (Du Bois 1983: 111–12).

10 'Non-traditional' subject areas are those academic disciplines and related career areas that are considered 'non-traditional' for females in western Europe and North America, such as architecture.

11 See Hammersley (1992b) for further criticisms of standpoint epistemology than I am able to discuss here.

12 See Brar (1992) and Connolly (1996b) for useful discussions around the issue of 'symmetry' between researcher and researched when researching 'Black' people and their communities.

7 | 'The whites of my eyes, nose, ears . . .': a reflexive account of 'whiteness' in race-related research

Barry Troyna

> . . . the question 'what is going on here' cannot be answered without reference to the agent's own understanding of what she is doing.
> (Cameron *et al.* 1992: 11)

Introduction: 'We Whites'

The emergence of postmodernist frames of analysis in 'race' and ethnic relations studies has animated the discourse of the 'politics of identity'. The appearance in 1995 of a new journal, *Social Identities: a journal for the study of race, nation and culture* is testimony to this development. As David Theo Goldberg and Abebe Zegeye make clear in their inaugural editorial note, the journal is committed to furnishing 'an insistent inter- and trans-disciplinary as well as inter- and transnational focal point for theorizing issues at the interface of social identities' (Goldberg and Zegeye 1995: 3). This is emblematic of the 'politics of identity' which eschews all forms of fixity and essentialism and is intolerant of what Bob Connell refers to as 'categoricalism': that is, when the categories of 'race', class and gender are 'presumed to be biological and the relationship between them a collective or standardized one' (Connell 1987: 56).

As an integral feature of the 'politics of identity', the social and political construction of 'whiteness' occupies an unprecedented salience in contemporary social science writings on 'race'. The imperative seems to be 'making whiteness visible and challenging the use of whiteness as the normative referent or standard in studies of ethnicity' (Socialist Review Collective 1994: 7). This goes beyond the vignettes of white racism captured in the work of, say,

David Wellman in *Portraits of White Racism* (1977) inasmuch as it demands an exploration of the ambiguities and contradictions associated with the racialization of white subjectivity. Analyses along these lines are now beginning to feature in the configuration of 'race' and ethnic relations studies of the 1990s. Ruth Frankenberg's (1993) research into the ways in which white women differentially construct, signify and appraise the significance of their whiteness in a racially stratified society and Bob Blauner's essay detailing the status of whiteness as a 'racial term' (Blauner 1994: 27) are exemplary of this trend in the USA. There are parallel developments in the UK. The publication of *Murder in the Playground* (Macdonald *et al.* 1989), which represented a defining moment in the history of antiracist education in Britain, revealed how 'whiteness' had been peripheralized, often ignored, in antiracist conceptions of educational reform. The issues addressed by this report, and particularly its leftist critique of 'orthodox antiracism', which, it alleged, constituted 'whites' as an omnipresent enemy, helped to clear the stage for a range of new theoretical inquiries into the articulation between 'whiteness' and antiracist discourses. These have included the writings of Alastair Bonnett, who, among others, laments what he sees as homogenous and essentialist conceptions of whiteness within the genre of antiracist studies (Bonnett 1991). Bonnett argues for more nuanced and effective conceptualizations of this racialized identity within antiracist discourses. Writing in the same vein, Mary Maynard (1994) has also drawn attention to the need for 'whiteness' to be recognized as a racialized identity which she argues needs to be 'deconstructed'. She goes on to say that: 'White people are not racialized in the way that black people are and "race" is seen to be a problem for the latter and not for the former. Such a stance leads to the proliferation of discrete studies of a wide variety of experiences, but makes no effective challenge to the categories or frameworks within which they are discussed' (p. 17). These theoretical and empirical interventions have served to demonstrate that – to borrow Leslie Roman's declarative statement – 'White is a Color!' (Roman 1993).

In this chapter I want to make a modest contribution to this area of enquiry by offering a reflexive account of 'being white'. Specifically, as a white, male, academic who has been involved in a range of race-related research studies since the mid-1970s, I want to try and appraise the significance of my racialized identity in these contexts.

There are then two parts to this story. First, I want to look rather more closely at the ways in which 'whiteness' within race-related research discourses has been addressed in the literature. I will then proceed to consider the articulation between my whiteness and two research projects in educational settings with which I have been associated. The first, carried out as a graduate student in the 1970s, explored the cultural politics of youths of African Caribbean origin in Britain. The second is slightly different in so far as it was neither conceived nor carried out by me. It was a life history project involving teachers of ethnic minority background in Canada, conducted in the mid-1990s. I was invited by the co-director of the project to provide critical readings of the data already produced by the research and, following the publication of my critique of deracialized discourses on the sociology of teachers and the teaching profession (Troyna 1994a), to act as a 'critical friend' to the research team.

I hope that my representation of these accounts of my involvement in these studies is not seen as self-indulgence, an exercise in 'vanity ethnography' (Maynard 1993) or a gratuitous display of a series of 'heroic tales' (Lee 1993). Unfortunately, these are often characteristic of many reflexive narratives (see Patai 1994; Troyna 1994b, forthcoming for critiques). Neither is the chapter intended to be an autobiographical account of how and why I became involved in this field of study. Accounts framed in this way are available elsewhere (see, for example, Stanfield 1993a). Rather, this chapter is designed to examine reflexively and critically the political, theoretical and practical issues which have confronted me, as a white male researcher, in 'race' and ethnic relations studies. In this regard the chapter may be seen as a response to James Scheurich's call for the need for 'We Whites' to: 'study and report how being White effects our thinking, our behaviours, our attitudes, and our decisions from the micro, personal level to the macro, social level . . . We need to become aware of our racial positionality as it affects our intellectual products and then infuse this reflexivity into those products (Scheurich 1993: 9).

The 'Insider Perspective'

Although interest in the status of 'whiteness' has assumed a particular shape and cadence within the 'politics of identity', questions about the role of white researchers in race-related studies have, of course, been a vigorous, contentious and enduring theme in social science and political discourses. In particular, the spotlight has shone on the perspectives which white researchers have brought to the construction, operation and dissemination of educational and social research in this field of enquiry. As Bruce Carrington and I have argued before (Troyna and Carrington 1989) scepticism about white researchers in this context has tended to be structured around three distinct but related themes. First, the interactional politics of interviewing. Generally, this refers to the impact of categorical identities on the production of data. Specifically, it draws attention to those instances in which a white researcher interviews or administers tests to black respondents. The second concern focuses on the ability (and commitment) of white researchers to interpret accurately and with empathy the data elicited from black respondents. The third concern is that the focus of the (white) researchers' gaze on the black communities is misconceived and an anathema to antiracist goals. Each of these criticisms articulates with an overarching concern, namely, the role of white researchers as 'ombudsmen', to use Alvin Gouldner's phrase (1975). Here, questions have been raised about the relationship between information elicited by white researchers, especially within policy-oriented studies, and its use by the state in the maintenance and reproduction of racial inequality and oppression. I want to briefly consider these critiques.

Challenges to what is often termed 'cross-racial' interviewing are based largely on the assumption that some respondent accounts are more authentic and, as a corollary, intrinsically superior, than others and that these more 'genuine' and 'accurate' accounts are more likely to be elicited if there is symmetry between the ethnicity of the interviewer and respondent. It follows that the production of research data from black respondents is likely to be inhibited, distorted and inferior unless 'racial matching' is achieved, precisely because of the unequal power relationship between interviewer and respondent and/or by radical differences in their life experiences and cultural frames of reference. Those who argue for symmetry, then, are committed to the pre-eminence of the 'insider perspective' as a research strategy; this is seen as the most effective means of getting to the heart of the respondent's views on a range of issues, especially those of a contentious nature such as 'race'. As Penny Rhodes suggests:

> The issue is not simply that black people may be inhibited in their communications to a white interviewer or that these communications will be passed through a white cultural filter, but there are dimensions to black experience invisible to the white interviewer/investigator who possesses neither the language nor the cultural equipment either to elicit or understand that experience.
>
> (Rhodes 1994: 549)

Concern about symmetry transcends the so-called quantitative and qualitative divide and applies in equal measure to findings produced under experimental conditions and in natural settings. Whatever the context, it is important to point out that these doubts are based on a positivist conception of the status of research 'evidence' and of who is best placed to produce such knowledge.

In both the UK and USA 'race-of-interviewer' effects have been a long-standing concern especially for social psychologists who have been interested in setting up, interpreting and reviewing their own and others' studies of racial attitudes (see Schaeffer 1980). Not surprisingly, this debate has spilled over into cognate areas such as studies of children's racial attitudes as expressed under experimental conditions and in response to structured interview or questionnaire items (Davey 1983; Milner 1983; Aboud 1988). It remains the case that interpretations of these effects are inconsistent and limited. However, in distilling the main trends in the literature, Frances Aboud concludes on a pragmatic note, suggesting that because the 'cross-ethnic situation is not the usual place for discussing one's prejudices' it would be preferable to use an interviewer from 'the child's own family or family ethnic group because these are the people to whom children usually express their feelings' (Aboud 1988: 88).

Reservations about the absence of symmetry in interviews carried out by qualitative researchers in natural settings also hinge upon the authenticity, validity and reliability of the data produced. However, in this discourse, caveats are informed more explicitly by sociological considerations about power as it operates within the interactional politics of the research relationship. Here, questions are raised not only about the data produced and how they are interpreted but about the rationale for and the orientation of the research enterprise, *per se*.

Concern about white researchers 'studying down' (Harding 1987) in the racialized power structure has figured prominently in critiques of race-related research by black academics and activists. In the USA, for instance, the research of white social scientists in the 1960s, including the reports produced by James Coleman and Daniel Moynihan, prompted savage critiques from writers such as Andrew Billingsley (1970) and Joyce Ladner (1975) on the grounds that these studies legitimated a scenario in which African Americans were portrayed as playing an active role in the generation and maintenance of racial inequality. It was in this context that Ladner proclaimed *The Death of White Sociology* (1975) in which she denounced mainstream sociological studies for being reflective of the ideology of the wider society which has 'excluded the totality of Black existence from its major theories, except inso-far as it has *deviated* from the so-called norms' (Ladner 1975: xxiii, original emphasis). Nearly 20 years later, in her exposition of what she perceived as the central characteristics of American literature, the African American writer, Toni Morrison, echoed Ladner's criticisms and noted that the time had come to: 'avert the critical gaze from the racial object to the racial subject; from the described and the imagined to the describers and imaginers; from the servers to the served' (Morrison 1992: 90).

John Stanfield suggests that the advent of cultural studies and 'the re-emer-gence of academic ethnic studies' in the USA in the 1980s and 1990s have given momentum to the distrust which 'people of colour' have of the involve-ment of white researchers in this area (Stanfield 1994: 167). Interestingly, he reckons that one of the strategies used by white researchers to placate these anxieties is to frame their interventions in terms of an 'emancipatory' and 'empowering' discourse – a (disturbing) pattern which is also found in a grow-ing number of empirical studies into 'race' and ethnic relations outside the USA (see Gore 1993; Troyna 1994c).

The UK has witnessed similar critiques of white hegemony in the concep-tion, interpretation and application of research into 'race'. The initial incar-nation of the Institute of Race Relations (IRR), which had been set up in 1952, probably constituted the target for the first coherent and sustained criticism along these lines. Its understanding of objectivity in research, tied to its com-mitment to the preservation of capitalism, was challenged in the early 1970s by academics and activists such as Sivanandan and Robin Jenkins. They and their allies saw the IRR as a 'prestigious white body' dominated by a board of directors whose political, ideological and research agenda rested on a per-nicious and misleading representation of 'the problem' in analyses of race relations in the UK. As Jenny Bourne remarked, it was disagreement over this issue which animated the struggle for control of the IRR (Bourne 1980: 339). The ensuing 'palace revolution' presaged a transformation in which 'a white racist world in a white racist IRR became a black anti-racist Institute in a white racist world' (Mullard 1985: 195).

By the 1980s the claim that white (liberal and radical) researchers help to legitimate and reproduce a paradigm of 'race relations' which both distorts and misunderstands the experiences of black communities in the diaspora reached fever pitch. It was understandable that this indictment was often framed in an assertive and confrontational manner. Arguably, the most cele-brated of these critiques was mounted by members of the reconstituted IRR in the house journal *Race and Class*, and by participants in the 'Race and Politics' group at the Centre for Contemporary Cultural Studies (CCCS) at Birmingham University. These critiques were based on two central convictions. First, that white theorists were working within a paradigm of race relations which was based on the 'host/guest' dualism and geared towards assimilationist goals. Second, that their work had pathologized black citizens by helping to authenticate common-sense racist conceptions and imagery of those communities. In her appraisal of what she saw as the main impulses of this research Jenny Bourne of the IRR called for a reconstituted research agenda in which: 'It was not black people who should be examined, but white society; it was not a question of educating blacks and whites for integration, but of fighting institutional racism; it was not race relations that was the field of study but racism' (Bourne 1980: 339).

Bourne went on to claim that the commitment of (white) 'race relations' theorists to policy-oriented research was equally insidious and politically maladroit. In this and other respects, the IRR challenge to what was seen as the hegemonic status of the sociology of race relations paradigm bore a close resemblance to the critiques prepared by the CCCS. In their book *The Empire Strikes Back* (1982), CCCS members also argued that by bringing data about the daily lives of the black communities in Britain into the public eye, policy-oriented researchers were, wittingly or otherwise, colluding with the racist state. Errol Lawrence, one of the contributors to the book, maintained that: 'In a situation where state racism has intensified, it is disingenuous for policy-oriented researchers to expect that their racist and patriarchal conceptualizations of black people will not be of interest to state institutions which oppress black people' (Lawrence 1982: 134).

Questions about the politics and ethics of the sociology of race relations paradigm continued to be raised throughout the 1980s. Indeed, it is interesting to note that even with the emergence of postmodernist theorizing and its rejection of identities – ethnic, class and gender – as fixed and static, attacks on white researchers *qua* white researchers have not dissolved entirely with the passage of time.

Consider, for instance, the introductory chapter to *Inside Babylon*, published in 1993. There the editors, Winston James and Clive Harris, follow a well-trodden path in identifying the work of Ken Little, Sheila Patterson and John Rex as contributing to and providing social science's benediction to the tradition of ' "race relations" assimilationism' (Harris and James 1993: 1). However legitimate these critiques may be the authors then proceed to argue that researchers continue to focus on the degree of 'strangeness' among the black communities and the extent of 'adaptation' which they have to secure before becoming fully-fledged members of the community. They echo earlier claims in their insistence that researchers tend to be careerist, opportunistic and 'part of the system of power which blocks, prohibits and invalidates that knowledge and responsibility for consciousness' (p. 2). Coming dangerously close to essentialist theorizing they also assert that 'a whole scholarship has been dyed not only in the colour of the researcher's skin, but in the colour of their imagination' (p. 2).

What is striking about these critiques is that many are reliant on homogenizing tendencies, over-generalizations and totalizing principles. There is also a tendency to degenerate into psychological and individualistic reductionism; a logic, that is, based on essentialist arguments which pay insufficient attention to heterogeneity and conflict within identities. Their effect on the development of research might be seen to be equally corrosive because they are founded on an argument which privileges what Maynard calls 'the circumstances of the particular' (Maynard 1994: 18). As a result it is possible to find some white researchers contriving a credibility for themselves in their determination to show empathy with black experiences of racism.

An example of a white researcher becoming 'colour struck' can be found in Kathleen Casey's (1993) life histories of women teachers in the USA. Casey informs her readers that while she was confident of eliciting narratives from nuns and from women teachers of Jewish backgrounds (although she is neither a nun nor Jewish), 'I was troubled by the fear that I would not be told or could not understand the life stories [of African-American women teachers] because I am white' (Casey 1993: 107). However, Casey notes that this anxiety was assuaged during the course of the research partly because her interpretations were authenticated by African American women academics but also because her life story tellers found out that she had a black daughter and therefore 'knew something of the black cultural repertoire' (p. 109).

Once again, we can see how this reasoning presumes that the ethnic identity of the researchers, in and of itself, can provide a privileged access to 'truth'. However, this ignores the fact that the multiple identities of the interviewer intrude on the research process so that outsider/insider status is confirmed and achieved in a variety of ways. It also rests on the dubious belief in what Avtar Brah calls the 'authenticity of personal experience' (Brah 1992: 136). John Gabriel uncovers the flaw in this line of argument when he writes that:

> there is no single, authentic perspective that goes with being black or, for that matter, with being a woman, lesbian or gay, or indeed being white . . . Taken to its extreme, the idea of a single, authentic perspective born out of being black or a woman would also make both writing and reading and teaching and learning redundant, since those who already possessed the necessary experiential credentials would have nothing more to learn while the rest would be precluded from writing and learning simply by dint of who they were.
>
> (Gabriel 1994: 4)

I have argued in this first part of this chapter that attempts to isolate the effects of the ethnicity of researchers – or, more accurately, their skin colour – in considerations of the efficacy, authenticity and credibility of 'race' and ethnic relations research are at best partial and, in many instances, misplaced. It is now being recognized that researchers bring multiple identities to the research process and in complex ways these are constantly being negotiated in the course of interviews in ways which might attenuate or strengthen the insider/outsider status of the researcher. Michelle Foster, an African American life history researcher confirms this. Recollecting her relationships with black American teachers who recounted stories of their lives and practices, Foster notes that although she shared with them the same ethnic identity there were 'other characteristics which separated me from individual narratives making me an insider and outsider in ways that were intricate and intertwined'. She continues: 'I was a northerner when I interviewed southerners, an urban resident when I interviewed rural residents, a younger person when I conversed with older teachers, a woman when I interviewed men' (Foster 1994: 143).

I am arguing that it is in this context that we can begin to understand and locate how white researchers are positioned in the interactional politics and dynamics of research. I want to use these insights to enhance an understanding of my own position in two race-related studies.

Researching 'race'

'Stir it up'

In 1975 I embarked on a research project which was intended to explore empirically the cultural politics of teenage boys of African Caribbean origin in Britain (Troyna 1978). Specifically, my interest was in what ways, if any, their musical preferences articulated with their commitment to their ethnic identity and perspectives as young blacks in Britain. The study was multi-disciplinary and drew on a range of theoretical sources from the fields of 'race' and ethnic relations, cultural studies and the sociology of the media. But I was probably inspired most directly by the work of Graham Murdock and his associates (Murdock and McCron 1973; Murdock and Phelps 1973). His studies of white adolescent boys had indicated ways in which musical tastes may signify and confirm group and sub-cultural identities.

The research was based largely on interviews conducted in four schools with over 40 boys of African Caribbean origin who were around 15 years old. The schools were based in two urban areas which I knew well. I had been born and brought up in one of the areas and had attended one of the sample schools less than six years earlier. The second area was where I currently lived and studied. On the face of it, the boys seemed willing to cooperate in the project and were interested in the sorts of themes and issues I wanted to discuss. These included: school life; friendship groups; relationships with parents; leisure activities; reggae; the Rastafari movement and various issues associated with being young, black and male in 1970s Britain. Of course, having noted that the students seemed happy to talk to me about these matters Denscombe and Aubrook's concerns about school students' 'willingness' to participate in research being 'contextually specific' warrants serious consideration. As they have put it:

> In the school context, young people are something of a captive audience. They rarely feel at liberty to say 'no' to requests for involvement in research. Despite the researchers' intentions that participation should be fully voluntary . . . the fact that the research is conducted in *school time* and *in class* encourages the students to regard it as a piece of 'schoolwork' and, as such, it is *assumed* by students that they are under some tacit obligation to [cooperate in the research].
> (Denscombe and Aubrook 1992: 129, original emphasis)

Whether the students saw the research as another piece of 'schoolwork' is a matter for conjecture. At the time I took their willingness to participate as indicative of their enthusiasm to discuss matters rarely broached in their everyday school lives. Perhaps this was naive. It is certainly feasible to assume that institutional pressures on the one hand, combined with situational constraints on choice on the other, provided a context which was heavily inscribed by differential power relations. In this setting student acquiescence to white male authority figures could well have revealed overenthusiastic cooperation in determining their choice.

The interview data suggested that a typology of what I called 'life styles' could be developed for analytical purposes. These provided clues about the boys' different perspectives on Britain, their group and sub-cultural identification and the extent to which these were signified by music preferences. The titles of the categories, 'Mainstreamer', 'Rejector' and 'Compromiser', seemed to me to bear testimony to the different orientations, or 'life styles', which the boys had adopted. They were intended to demonstrate that, contrary to conventional wisdom, young boys of African Caribbean origin in Britain did not constitute an homogenous group either with regard to the way they viewed the salience of their ethnicity or to their perceptions, interpretations and adaptations to everyday life (Troyna 1979).

To what extent did my ethnic identity impinge upon the formulation, execution and dissemination of this research? To begin with, it is important to point out that the research was heavily criticized (see, for example, CCCS 1982; Gutzmore 1983) along with other contemporary ethnographies of the African Caribbean communities in Britain (for example, Cashmore 1979; Pryce 1979) for the following reasons, in particular. First, the decision to 'study down'; second, the inability of a 'cultural stranger' to understand and interpret the experiences of the youths; third, because of the generation of analytical tools and concepts which were allegedly ethnocentric and served to caricature the communities.

We have already seen that the issue of 'studying down' is a long-standing and controversial matter in this area of enquiry. Certainly, it can be said to help reinforce and reproduce an insidious trend in race-related research (see Morrison 1992). As Maynard notes: 'when questions of "race" are raised this usually means focusing on black peoples, its victims, who are thereby constructed as "the problem" ' (Maynard 1994: 21). By focusing on the black communities, this research along with others which 'study down' could be said to have been consolidating white hegemony by naturalizing it. However, the *focus* of the researcher's gaze is not the whole story. Equally important are the conceptual and theoretical tools which help to make sense of the research. That is to say, much of the research criticized by the CCCS, IRR and others tended to foreground the cultures and identities of ethnic minority communities and, in doing so, provided stereotyped and decontextualized accounts of these cultures. As Solomos and Back have argued, studying the experiences of ethnic minority communities is not necessarily antagonistic to antiracist goals. As they note, to ignore the perspectives of members of these communities 'would be comparable to studying slavery by speaking only to the slave masters' (Solomos and Back 1995: 13). What is important is the need to place those experiences in an analytical frame which centralizes the broader processes that come to impact and help shape those experiences.

This leads directly into the other criticisms of the research. Again, we have already rehearsed some of the arguments associated with the role of the 'cultural stranger' and their ability to interpret appropriately the experiences and linguistic codes of respondents. It is possible that my 'whiteness' did impact upon the nature and extent of what the boys shared with me about their experiences and how I interpreted those experiences. Nonetheless, as Lynn Davies points out in relation to similar debates in the cognate area of gender studies, this is irresolvable because it 'is impossible to state with any certainty . . . the specific effect of gender on any research relationship; all one can ask for again is that it might be borne in mind in planning and execution' (Davies 1985: 87). In other words, the researcher must be reflexive at all stages of the research process. Furthermore, my shared experience and knowledge of the schools, neighbourhoods, local facilities, music and associated regalia, and of course my age and maleness – in other words, other salient features of my identity – helped to establish my 'insider' status and facilitated a rapport with the youths within the research context which might not have been achieved by other researchers.

The third criticism was based on the argument that, as a white researcher, I had generated a classificatory system which helped to reproduce and legitimate an ethnocentric perspective on the black communities. This implied that in my determination to reveal the youths' understanding of and responses to life in Britain, including racism as one of its dominant norms and values, I had scrutinized, categorized and labelled the boys *in relation* to the white society. It is difficult to challenge this criticism. Let me explain.

It will be recalled that the categories, 'Mainstreamer', 'Rejector' and 'Compromiser', were intended to typify 'ideal types' representing the boys' perspectives. What is most striking about these categories is that they not only objectified black youth but that the labels took on an ethnocentric flavour by expressing differences in the way the boys were committed to being 'like us'. They were arranged along a continuum in which assimilation ('Mainstreamers') and separatism ('Rejectors') constituted the polar positions. It is also the case that these categories lent themselves to co-option by an ethnophobic discourse which, at the time of the study (mid-late 1970s) was in full flow. A series of confrontations between young black youths and the police at the 1976 Notting Hill Carnival had heightened the 'moral panic' associated with young men of African Caribbean origin. This articulated with media and public perceptions of the youths' alleged involvement in 'mugging' and strengthened the criminalization of young black males – especially those approximating to the 'Rejectors' life style. As Stuart Hall and his colleagues have pointed out, these youths were characterized as a threat to the stability, cohesion and moral authority of the state (Hall *et al.* 1978). Unwittingly, then, my study could be interpreted as consolidating the 'we/they' binary opposition and the perception of black youths as 'the other', as 'the enemy within', as the source of the problems. Such concerns are not misplaced. As we saw earlier, Errol Lawrence's comments about policy-oriented research draw attention to this danger (Lawrence 1982) and it is disingenuous for social scientists not to recognize and take account of their wider functional and ideological role within the state. As David Goldberg writes: 'Ideologically the State often invokes expedient analyses and the results of social science, whether by collaboration or appropriation, to legitimise State pursuits and to rationalise established relations of power and domination' (Goldberg 1992: 519).

'Once upon a time . . .'

In 1992, researchers from the Universities of Toronto and Western Ontario received funding for a project to explore the development of professional identities of a sample of 'racial/ethnocultural' minority teachers in Canada. The REMTEL study (Racial/Ethnocultural Minory Teachers' Lives), as they called it, drew on the conceptual and methodological traditions of life history for its theoretical scaffolding. This was intended to shed light on the relationships between teachers' individual stories and the structural and social features that frame personal and professional development. The data from the study derived from extensive semi-structured interviews. These occurred over several sittings, lasted up to 12 hours and covered issues such as: the teachers' childhoods and experiences as school students; the decision to become a teacher; their teacher education courses and career histories; and their lives in school and other settings. The sample comprised teachers of ethnic minority origin who had either migrated to Canada as children and remained in the country or those who had been born, brought up, sometimes even taught elsewhere and had settled in Canada during their adult lives.

The benefits of life history and cognate biographical approaches to research are often expressed in terms of 'empowerment', 'enfranchisement' and 'giving voice' to individuals and groups whose particular words, experiences and problems have traditionally been silenced by research. More broadly, the methodology is said to enable 'silenced' groups to reclaim their histories through stories, narratives and oral histories. It has been commended by Stephen Ball and Ivor Goodson as a method for 'opening up for study the sealed boxes' (Ball and Goodson 1985b: 13), within which relatively powerless groups live and survive. Shulamit Reinharz suggests, for instance, that biographical work articulates closely with the imperatives of feminist research precisely because 'it draws women out of obscurity, repairs the historical record and provides an opportunity for the woman reader to write and identify with the subject' (Reinharz 1992: 126). Michelle Foster argues a similar case. Reflecting on her use of life history in her study of black teachers Foster asserts that the methodology provided the opportunity for 'black teachers to speak for themselves, to call forth their own stories of resistance and survival, and to recognize their perseverance and unacknowledged victories' (Foster 1994: 156).

My role was to act as a 'critical friend' to the REMTEL project. This invitation stemmed largely from the project team's reading of a recent paper in which I had critiqued the way sociologists had 'deracialized' the everyday world of teachers (Troyna 1994a). By this I meant that writers had ignored or underplayed the significance of racism in the way they had interpreted and presented sociological understandings of teachers' career experiences and the teaching profession. The critique also questioned whether research such as the REMTEL project, which placed the experiences of black teachers centre-stage, constituted an effective intellectual challenge to deracialized studies. My argument was that by concentrating exclusively on ethnic minority teachers such studies run the risk of 'ethnicism' (Mullard 1986) which is not only theoretically unhelpful but also has the potential to strengthen the 'otherness' of these teachers. In this respect I was especially aware of the seductive properties of what Richard Dyer calls 'Images of' studies:

> 'Images of' studies have looked at groups defined as oppressed, marginal or subordinate – women, the working class, ethnic and other minorities (e.g. lesbians and gay men, disabled people, the elderly). The impulse for such work lies in the sense that how such groups are represented is part of the process of their oppression, marginalisation or subordination. The range and fertility of such work has put those groups themselves centre-stage in both analytical and campaigning activity, and highlighted the issue of representation in politics. It has, however, had one serious drawback, long recognised in debates about women's studies. Looking, with such passion and single-mindedness, at non-dominant groups has had the effect of reproducing the sense of oddness, differentness, exceptionality of these groups, the feeling that they are departures from the norm. Meanwhile the norm has carried on as if it is the natural, inevitable, ordinary way of being human.
>
> (Dyer 1988: 44)

The potential of 'Images of' studies to reinforce the differential status of groups perceived to be racially different is exacerbated by the close articulation between these studies and the multicultural discourse. That is, a discourse which celebrates cultural diversity and difference at the expense of an analysis of power relationships between groups categorized along racial lines.

It seemed to me that the best way to enact the role of 'critical friend' was to engage in an 'interview conversation' with my host and co-director of the project, Ivor Goodson, about life history and its application in studies of 'race' and ethnic relations (Sikes *et al.* 1996). In the course of the 'conversation' I told Goodson that my reservations about the study centred on the following methodological issues. First, the emphasis on life stories could encourage readers to view socio-political issues in individualistic terms. Second, researchers often commit 'symbolic violence' to the life-story teller by taking the story, representing it in the written text and, while advancing their own career and academic standing, do little to 'empower' the life-story teller, despite their claims to the contrary. Finally, while 'Images of' studies might obviate the problem of 'globalizing' – that is, when the experiences of white teachers are presumed to represent those of all teachers, irrespective of their ethnicity – they run the risk of consolidating hegemonic definitions of normality and 'otherness'. In sum, life history analyses have the potential to generate analytical tools and concepts that are ethnocentric and dismissive of those wider social processes, such as racism, which impact upon the experiences of the life-story teller.

Although rarely acknowledged as such, I argued that these problematic issues were inherent and particularly pronounced within this genre of research and writ large in the formulation and operation of the REMTEL study with white researchers snooping into and revealing the lives of black people (see also Foster and Seitz 1985). I argued with Goodson that this relationship assumed an even more insidious flavour in life history research because of the nature and purpose of the method and of the (contrived) intimacy between the researcher and life-story teller (Sikes *et al.* 1996). For these reasons I found my involvement in the REMTEL study, at least as a potential interviewer or interpreter of life scripts, slightly uncomfortable and politically questionable.

Conclusion

Despite the inexorable rise in the number of social and educational researchers willing to write exposés of their research activities, the methodological value of reflexive accounts of the research process remains open to question. Researchers such as Stephen Ball are convinced that reflexivity should be *de rigeur* for all ethnographers. For him it should be: 'the requirement for methodological rigour that every ethnography be accompanied by a *research biography*, that is a reflexive account of the conduct of the research which, by drawing on fieldnotes and reflections, recounts the processes, problems, choices and errors which describe the fieldwork upon which the substantive account is based' (Ball 1990: 170, original emphasis).

In contrast Dephne Patai is impatient with the 'hectoring quality' of extant writings on methodology and is adamant that researchers should now put behind them the 'sensitivity training, guilt-tripping and reflexiveness of the past few decades' (Patai 1994: 68). A few lines later in the article she asks the rather provocative and rhetorical question: 'Does all this self-reflexivity produce better research?' (p. 69). My own view on reflexivity in social and educational research has been elaborated upon elsewhere (Troyna 1994b; forthcoming). Briefly, I have argued that accounts of research grounded in this approach are partial and selective; they no more 'tell it like it is' than conventional research method textbooks. Against this, I do agree with those writers who suggest that researchers' willingness to be reflexive provides one of the ways in which they might distinguish their practice from, say, journalism, political rhetoric or other ways of describing and interpreting the world. According to this view, it is only through being reflexive and committed to self-disclosure – by making one's value positions explicit – that the validity of the research can properly be assessed.

Whatever the view on this genre of writing it is slightly surprising that such accounts are few and far between in studies of 'race' and ethnic relations within educational settings. Lois Weis' reflections on her research in the multicultural environment of a community college in the USA is exceptional in this regard (Weis 1992). One of the objectives of this chapter has been to redress this imbalance and to construct a reflexive case study based on an analysis of how the varied and complex ways in which my social identities, especially those relating to my ethnicity and gender, have interacted with any antiracist convictions to inform all stages of my involvement in research. This has articulated with the 'politics of identity' by drawing attention to the multiplicity and contingency of the researcher's identities and by acknowledging that no individual belongs to one, single, socially constructed category.

Acknowledgements

I am grateful to Maud Blair, Paul Connolly, Sarah Neal and Carol Vincent for their comments on an earlier version of this chapter.

8 | Struggles with the research self: reconciling feminist approaches to antiracist research

Sarah Neal

Introduction

Using autobiographic experiences gained from my qualitative doctoral research into the place of race in equality discourses and equal opportunities policies in higher education, this chapter focuses on the ways in which the researcher's gender impacts on the antiracist research project. While there has been commentary on the impact of the gender of the researcher on the research process (Oakely 1981; Smart 1984; Harding 1987; Padfield and Procter 1996), Finch notes that: 'systematic comparisons of men and women interviewers, in a range of research situations are not possible because we lack sufficient studies of accounts of the research process which consider the relationship of the gender of the interviewer to the research product' (Finch 1993: 170).

There has been a particular paucity in discussions of the relationship between the female/feminist researcher and her antiracist research. At the heart of this relationship is the tension between adopting both a traditional feminist (egalitarian, reciprocal) approach and an antiracist (challenging) approach. The difficulties in attempting to reconcile these approaches were made more acute in my own research situation given that the gaze of the research was upwards i.e. on institutions and the (often powerful) professionals that worked within them.

The first part of the chapter traces the rise of the antiracist and feminist critiques of social research, charting their points of connection and their points of difference. The chapter then moves on to reflexively analyse my own research, focusing on negotiating the complexities between *claiming* research as antiracist and feminist and that research actually *being* antiracist and feminist.

Connecting and disconnecting race and gender: mapping antiracist and feminist critiques of social research

While the antiracist and feminist critiques of the dominant strands of social research appear on the surface as well suited allies and have consequently often been placed together (as in my own research), it is nevertheless crucially important that this apparently natural alliance does not obscure the diversities in the critiques' perspectives or their different histories. Perhaps the main linking point between the antiracist and feminist critiques of social research, which both emerged predominantly in the early 1980s, is their shared notion that all research is political and involves issues of power, and in their shared rejection of the notion of objective, apolitical, scientific research. Given this, Rex and Tomlinson's (1979) attack on radical black sociology for fusing politics and sociological analysis, and thereby detracting from the latter, can also be read as an attack on feminist sociology. When Rex and Tomlinson argue that 'it is all too common today for sociologists to assert that their sociology is critical, non-value-free or reflexive and having done so to abandon any attempt to conform to the sorts of standards of reasoning and proof which are characteristic of scientific thought' (p. 314) they negate the reality of these standards having been constructed according to a white, male, canon (see also Blair, this volume).

The argument that all research is inherently political is not completely new. It can be traced to the critical theory tradition of the 1970s which had questioned what the role and focus of social research should be, what criteria should be used to measure its validity and the relationship between social research and political struggles (Mills 1959; Gouldner 1971; Lukacs 1971; Habermas 1972). In raising these questions, critical theorists, feminist and antiracist critiques have all highlighted the problematic direction of the social research gaze. In other words, much social research has tended to look downwards, leaning towards an interest in investigating those groups in society with marginal status – i.e. the poor or the 'deviant' (Liazos 1972; Gilroy 1980). As Punch notes: 'it is still painfully obvious that researchers have rarely penetrated to the territory of the powerful and many field studies still focus on lowly, marginal groups' (Punch 1986: 25). The downwards social research gaze tendency thus evades investigation into the activities of the powerful and thereby leaves patterns of oppression unchallenged. Goldberg highlights the political significance of a social research agenda dominated by a downwards gaze when he argues that:

> social science furnishes the State and its functionaries with information, and it is often employed in formulating and assessing State policies to satisfy social needs. Ideologically the State often invokes expedient analyses and the results of social science, whether by collaboration or appropriation, to legitimise State pursuits and to rationalise established relations of power and domination.
>
> (Goldberg 1992: 152)

Historically, research into the area of race has provided one of the primary examples of such a political and ideological role for social research. While this role may not simply be functional 'it is disingenuous for . . . researchers to expect that their racist and patriarchal conceptualisations of black people will not be of interest to the state institutions which oppress black people' (Lawrence 1981: 134). Within the context of research on race, or more specific-ally, race relations, the research gaze has been not on the 'state and its func-tionaries' but on black communities[1] themselves. Social research on race not only lost sight of the issues of power and provided distorted and damaging presentations of black peoples' experiences and realities, it also offered a veh-icle by which the collated data and information could be used to maintain and reinforce subordination and oppression (Bourne 1980; Gilroy 1980, 1987; Lawrence 1981, 1982; Parmar 1981; Gutzmore 1983).

The antiracist critique therefore arose from the damaging and distorting (re)presentations of black people and the feeding of these into social policy-making and common-sense discourses. The antiracist critique developed with the intention of conducting research that would aim to focus on how racism was reproduced and reinforced within different (white) social and state insti-tutions and (white) cultural discourses. In making these arguments the anti-racist critique can clearly be understood as a strategy for researching the powerful. Summarized (if crudely) the antiracist critique represents a call to social research to shift its gaze from black communities and to investigate instead the 'white speaking' position.

It is significant that historically, while black people have been constructed within social research agendas and via state-sponsored discourses as prob-lematic and a potential threat to social cohesion and control, women[2] as a whole have tended to have been rendered invisible by social research and excluded from its agendas (Harding 1987). In contrast to the antiracist cri-tique, the feminist critique arose therefore from the non-representation of women in social research. Du Bois (1983: 107) argues that this invisibilization within the (mainstream) research process not only rendered women unknown but, crucially, also unknowable. For Du Bois it is the 'actual experi-ence and language of women that is the central agenda for feminist social sci-ence and scholarship' (p. 108). Similarly, Duelli Klien states that it is only by having a 'methodology that allows for women studying women in an inter-active process . . . [that] will end the exploitation of women as research objects' (Klein 1983: 95). Feminist methodologies therefore developed around a commitment to doing non-hierarchical, reciprocal, emancipatory and subjective research which would be both about women, for women and conducted from within women's perspectives (Oakley 1981; Du Bois 1983; Duelli Klien 1983; Stanley and Wise 1983; Geiger 1986; Harding 1987). While I would endorse this project it is possible to question whether feminist methodologies, located within these parameters, have offered any more than 'better' ways to research the powerless – i.e. women. As Smart argues from her experiences of researching magistrates:

in both Oakley's discussion on doing feminist research and in Stanley and Wise's book on the problems of research for feminists there is an assump-tion that the power imbalance between the people 'being researched' and the researcher is basically in favour of the latter . . . But my experience of researching the 'locally powerful' does not fit with this model at all . . . I find this assertion remarkable and only explicable if we ignore all social class divisions and the structures of dominance in society outside the academic world of research.

(Smart 1984: 157)

In more recent developments, feminist methodologies have moved away from simply 'inserting' or visibilizing gender to a focus on issues of power in the context of gender as a social division and to a theorizing of women's experiences of gendered power relations (Currie and Kazi 1987; Gelsthorpe 1992; Opie 1992; Ramazanoglu 1992). However, because of the maintenance of this focus on women, these developments were not a call to research the 'male speaking' position in the same way that the antiracist critique clearly demanded that racism should be researched through the investigation of the 'white speaking' position. Given this space in terms of the comparability of the two critiques their compatibility becomes problematic for the researcher who is attempting to apply both critiques to her research process. Before exploring the tensions I experienced in reconciling antiracist and feminist approaches in the actual research field, I will first discuss the development and design of the research.

Developing and designing a research problem through antiracist and feminist perspectives

I intended my own research to be a project that would address the issues of equal opportunities and antiracism in higher education through inquiry into (predominantly) *white* institutions: four case study universities (two 'new' and two 'old'). The focus on universities as white institutions was directly linked to the antiracist demand that it is the ways in which racism is reproduced and reinforced within social and state institutions which requires research attention (Bourne 1980).[3] At its most basic level the validity of my claims for conducting antiracist and feminist research rested on my commitment to *problematizing* the issues of race (and gender) within the institutions being investigated. Building on this, I legitimized the antiracist/feminist identification of the research in terms of the ability of the research to make sense of the origins and nature of racist and sexist practices and discourses and the ability of the research to effectively critique countering practices (equal opportunities, antiracism) and discourses (Connolly 1993). This may appear a rather fragile foundation given that the wider context of what actually qualifies as antiracist and/or feminist research can be judged according to more tangible criteria: For example, the ability of the research to contribute towards specific antiracist and/or feminist struggles, most obviously through collaborative action research (Oakley 1981; Ben-Tovim *et al.* 1986; Lather 1986; Troyna and Carrington 1989; Ball 1991, 1992). While these writers have argued that it is collaborative action research which sits most comfortably with antiracist and/or feminist commitments, such a methodology only seems fully appropriate to those research sites which are concerned with powerless groups and in which the researcher inhabits a powerful position.

The research was qualitatively designed. This was because of the need for a more qualitative insight into the complex, micro politics of the everyday world of institutions (Farish *et al.* 1995) and because of the quantitative bias of the existing higher education and equal opportunities research (Williams *et al.* 1989; Jewson *et al.* 1991, 1993). The decision was not simply because of the association of qualitative research with antiracist and feminist methodologies. While quantitative and qualitative research are essentially neutral, it has been the way that each has been specifically employed that has rendered them objective/scientific/masculine/feminist/antiracist (Gelsthorpe 1992). As Morgan has noted, qualitative research has its 'own brand of machismo with its image of the male sociologist bringing back news from the fringes of society, the lower depths, the mean streets' (Morgan 1981: 86–7).

Within the four case studies I conducted 91 semi-structured interviews from a number of respondent groups. These respondent groups consisted of the powerful people within them – senior management, union officials, academics, personnel and equal opportunity officials. Although there were differential degrees of power amongst the individual respondents within the target group, I categorized them overall as powerful in terms of their being professionals. My research remit was to investigate the case studies' equal opportunities policies and structures: did they exist and if so how did they operate within the complex everyday world of each institution? In order to do this it was important for me to explore the discourses that surrounded equality policy formation and implementation. How did the respondent groups interpret notions of equal opportunities and antiracism? What aspects/issues of the equality agenda were contested/disputed, why, in what ways and by whom? Similarly, what aspects/issues were promoted/supported, why, in what ways and by whom? The findings of the research have been discussed elsewhere and do not need to be rehearsed here (see Neal 1995a, 1998). What I now want to explore are the political and ethical dilemmas I encountered as I tried to align my antiracist, feminist claims with the research process itself.

In the field: experiences of power and powerlessness

Doing antiracist research: the confrontational feminist researcher?

In the mid-1990s, antiracism as both a concept and an anti-oppressive strategy inhabits a complex and hazardous terrain as it negotiates and reshapes itself between the leftist rejection of its former essentialist black/white dichotomy (Gilroy 1990) and the successful New Right anti-antiracist attack (Lewis 1988). However, within these revisionist processes even an anti-essentialist version of antiracism retains the notions of dissent and challenge at its heart (see, for example, Macdonald *et al.* 1989: xxiii–iv). As I have argued elsewhere (Neal 1995a) the term (and concept of) antiracism continues to have oppositional and confrontational rather than harmonious and consensual connotations. Whilst having the former associations has contributed towards the populist perception of antiracism as extremism (Ben-Tovim *et al.* 1992) they have also imbued antiracism with a particular masculinity. The female/feminist, antiracist researcher then faces particular difficulties in adopting a masculinist (objecting/dissenting/challenging) approach in her research situation. Women do not tend to easily, comfortably or confidently inhabit this masculinist terrain. Despite the extent to which a female/feminist researcher is or may be committed to the antiracist project, being objecting/dissenting/challenging, and thereby antiracist can involve a complex internal struggle with (her)self. Similarly, research methodology itself does not always fit comfortably within a challenging framework and this can involve the feminist researcher in a complex external struggle with her research process. It is to my own negotiations of these struggles that I now turn.

I had not been long in the field before I recognized that the interview technique can become problematic when researching 'sensitive' issues like race, in that it provides very little space for dissent or objection on the part of the researcher to what a respondent may be saying. Although feminist standpoint research has been widely criticized for being essentialist, unrealistic and restricting (see Mirza, this volume) the flip side of symmetrical researching – white people interviewing white people about race and racism – carries as many complexities. Most obviously, such symmetry may entail the presumption that the researcher and the respondent, through their shared whiteness, will share the same (racist) views and ideas. While I did encounter this on occasions, more predominantly I experienced white respondents interpreting this research situation as a 'safe zone'. The most obvious indicators of this was a regularly professed 'fear' of 'saying the wrong thing' or not being sure of the 'right' language to use when discussing race issues in public. Such confessions were couched in terms of a well-meaning innocence or confusion. For example, this excerpt comes from an interview with the Women's Unit Coordinator in one of the 'new' university case studies:

> *WUC:*   With gender people are relatively happy about what the issues are and what needs to be done, but with race it's foggy, it's not often talked about and people feel unsure about what we should be doing, what language to use. They don't want to look like idiots and they don't want to offend anyone.
>
> *SN:*   Why do you think talking about race is so difficult?
>
> *WUC:*   Well for the reasons I've just said I suppose, not being certain of the issues and being scared of being called racist . . . race is a tricky area.

Echoing this sentiment, at the end of an interview with the Chair of the Race Advisory Committee in the same case study, he (a white man) asked me if I would comment, not on what I thought of the university's initiatives around racial equality or the work of the Committee, but on the language he had used to discuss race in the interview. Collapsing race into a language dilemma (for white people) serves to relegate race to a marginalized category which prevents race issues being discussed or addressed in any meaningful way.

Both these situations raised questions as to how a white researcher, researching race from a professed antiracist position, should respond to racist discourses and confessed language 'fear' encountered in the interview process. How does a researcher in this position offer objections or challenges to racism without jeopardizing the interview and perhaps, if the respondent is powerful, access to the whole case study? Even if the outcome is not so extreme, an objection could result in a significant alteration in the nature of what the respondent is prepared to tell the researcher. Similarly in what ways, if at all, should the researcher enter into a 'what is the right language' debate? Yet to remain silent implicitly signals either consent (Keith 1992; Back and Solomos 1992) or a shared uncertainty as to the 'right thing to say'.

My noncommittal probing of respondents meant that I encountered an uncomfortable gap between my self-definition as an antiracist political activist prioritizing the need to challenge racism in the variety of sites in which it emerged, and being an academic researcher. When I did remain silent when racism or problematic language use was encountered in the interview process my political dilemma was acute. That I had 'sold out', colluded and compromised were feelings that I continually dragged along with me through the fieldwork.

The nature of who I was researching and to some extent what I was researching meant that when I did encounter racism it was often couched in the terms of the new racism. In one particular incident I had been interviewing a pro-vice-chancellor. Throughout the interview he had been cooperative and friendly and had spoken repeatedly of his commitment to equal opportunities in the university. After the interview he showed me to his office door and commented on the complexity of the area I was researching. I was vaguely agreeing (as I was walking) when he started talking about 'difficulties between cultures': 'We have Asian students who are quiet and want to work hard and they get upset when the silence in the library gets disrupted by Afro-Caribbean [sic] students. They [Asian students] don't understand that its their [African Caribbean students] nature to be happy and exuberant'. At first I thought he was saying that these attitudes were common in the university and that they needed to be addressed, but then quickly realized he was giving me anecdotal evidence of his own (highly problematic) theory that it is cultural difference that leads to misunderstanding and racialized problems and conflicts. When I did realize this my first reaction was not to challenge this notion but memorize what he had said in order that I could go and record it accurately.

W. Ball (1990: 17) has argued that 'the fusing of the role of researcher and political activist are difficult to reconcile with the expectations of the academic world, with its emphasis on individual achievement, objectivity and academic publication'. Perhaps this is particularly so for a lone, low status, student researcher who is uniquely constrained by the standards and style required for a PhD and what counts as 'proper' or 'academic' research, and what counts as a 'contribution to knowledge' in the 'academic mode of production' (Morgan 1981; Stanley 1991).

Other commentators engaged in researching race have noted similar experiences. Back and Solomos (1992) write of being 'haunted' by the dilemmas surrounding these issues. In relation to his own research, Keith writes of 'sitting in an area car in one of the police divisions of the Metropolitan Police notorious for confrontation between police and the black community' and spending 'eight hours giving tacit approval to the policing judgements of the two officers in the car by my own failure to challenge several comments that I had found offensive' (Keith 1992: 554).

While not intending to detract from the experiences of these researchers, it is necessary to also understand the dilemma in the context of gendered power relations. I came to increasingly interpret this situation within a gendered framework. As I have argued earlier there is an inherent masculinity in the confrontational or oppositional associations of antiracism. When Lynn Barber ironically and incredibly argues that 'women are better at interviewing men, possibly because they are more experienced in listening and they don't feel obliged to correct or criticise or argue' (*The Guardian*, 14 February 1994) she is actually nearer to identifying a reality than the first reading of the quote indicates – i.e. if 'obliged' were to be replaced by 'expected'. This returns to my earlier point regarding the interview itself and the essentially passive and facilitating role of the interviewer. An antiracist researcher may feel the political need to counter racism in the research process whether they are male or female and equally face the dilemma of how to actually do this. However, given that women have traditionally been (structurally and culturally) associated with facilitating speech and with listening, then such a challenge becomes additionally difficult in that it is also a dissention from the conventionally perceived role and behaviour of women. A feminist researcher who remains silent on her encounter with racism implies her complicity with this racism *and* she conforms to the expectations of the 'typical model of male/female verbal exchange' (Smart 1984: 156). It is this specifically gendered experience of the research process that I now want to explore in more detail.

Doing antiracist research: struggling/colluding with the feminine self?

In perhaps his most legitimate criticism of feminist methodology and the issue of hierarchy Hammersley has noted that:

> where men are included as sources of data, hierarchy cannot or should not be eliminated from the research process. The men may impose a hierarchy and, whether they do or not, presumably feminist researchers must exploit whatever resources they have to exert control over the relationship, on the grounds that in present circumstances the only choice is between being dominant or being dominated.
>
> (Hammersley 1992b: 196)

Hammersley's argument has direct relevance to my research process for a number of reasons: that I was regularly interviewing men; that I was asking questions about difficult or contentious issues; and that I was a young, female researcher. The combination of these factors pushed me to a position in which my fieldwork constituted a specific site of domination and marginality with which I had to constantly struggle.

My awareness of my marginality was reinforced by the environment in which the interviews were conducted. Overwhelmingly, this would be in the respondents' own offices, a spatial symbol of professionalism. When interviewing senior management respondents I would have to announce my arrival for an arranged interview to a secretary or personal assistant. An interview would often be interrupted by seemingly urgent telephone calls or a secretary or personal assistant (PA) coming in and reminding the respondent that they had a meeting to go to directly after their interview with me. If I was offered coffee it was ordered for and bought in by the secretary or PA. This intimidating milieu intensified the experience of interviewing powerful people. Before such an interview I would be acutely anxious and would test my tape recorder many times to make sure it was set up correctly and check my interview schedule simply to make sure I had it to hand. The simple routines of doing these tasks became infused with the need to appear smoothly professional and capable, to fit into the environment. To discover that the tape was in the wrong way round or if I had to search all through my bag to find my interview schedule in front of the respondent were trivial situations that I dreaded happening. Nevertheless, being offered (the served) coffee, which I always felt I should accept, not only made me uncomfortably aware that it was made and brought to me by a (female) secretary, but it also presented particular ordeals simply in terms of drinking it at the right intervals and not spilling it. When interviewing one vice-chancellor in a midday slot he ordered that lunch should be bought up to his office for both of us. Negotiating eating the food, asking the interview questions and presenting myself as a professional was a particular ordeal. It is difficult to convey these anxieties – they appear almost comical now and can be explained in part by my inexperience. However, they can also be clearly interpreted in the gendered context of my marginality (Finch 1993; Wilkins 1993).

In responding to this marginality I increasingly reverted to an uneasy and ironic adoption of a traditional, 'malestream' academic persona, presenting myself as neutral, rational and objective in an attempt to claim an authority which I felt necessary to conduct interviews with respondents. Hammersley (1992b) argues that there is nothing intrinsically wrong with the researcher exercising control over the research process and that the researcher, simply by engaging in the research process, is unavoidably making a claim to intellectual authority of some form. However, trying to take on the guise of the objective academic engaged in neutral research was problematic not only because of the political and ethical compromises I was making, but also because women are not automatically perceived as being able to be neutral and objective or as having intellectual authority. This had repercussions in terms of how I began to think of my physical appearance. I not only had to (pretend to) be objective, I had to *look* as if I were objective. This requirement rendered bright-red lipstick, birds-nest hair, torn Levis and eight-hole Dr Martens boots unwearable. Measor (1985: 62) recommends that when interviewing (presumably only when you are a woman) 'it is very important to come over as very sweet and trustworthy, but ultimately rather bland'. Conforming to this gendered stereotype, I replaced what I would normally wear with an innocuous or neutral dress code. In a different context – that of lesbian fashion – Blackman and Perry (1990: 74) have made a relevant point when they refer to such a process as the presentation of the 'blank page': 'it is difficult to read into this fashion any indication of sexual politics or practice, and it will not always be clear whether the wearer is a lesbian'.

Although dress and appearance have been the subject of some feminist discussion (Wilson 1985; Blackman and Perry 1990), given the emphasis that traditional feminist methodologies have had on women interviewing women, it is not surprising that very little has been written from a feminist perspective about how women dress when they are in the field. Those feminist researchers who have written accounts as to how they dressed in their fieldwork have, significantly, been conducting research on men. Carol Smart indicates this dilemma about how to appear:

> one important element was how the researcher presented herself and a vital element of that was dress . . . in my research there were several pitfalls to avoid. One was dressing too casual as minor officials in particular would tend to disbelieve I was a bona fide researcher. It was difficult to gauge whether to try and look like a probation officer, a solicitor, or a stereotyped woman academic.
>
> (Smart 1984: 153)

Although in many ways dress and appearance may seem a minor or trivial aspect of the fieldwork process, it is actually an important part of all ethnographic research. In their research into street homelessness in Austin, Texas, Snow and Anderson (1993) write of how they 'dressed down' to fit more easily into the environment of frontline homelessness. Yet for women, dress and appearance are closely linked to a variety of sexual subtexts in ways that they are not for men.

My own dilemmas about what to wear were very much to the fore of my thinking when I was going to interview a man in an overtly powerful position. When I interviewed women who were in senior positions my anxieties over my physical appearance were much less intense. This would indicate the proximity of the context of (hetero)sexuality and interviewing men (see, for example, McKee and O'Brien 1983).

The account offered by Gewirtz and Ozga (1993) of their experiences of doing life story interviews with 'elites in educational policy making' raises connected issues of sexuality in the interviewing process, most significantly the notion of collusion with the (hetero)sexual subtexts. Gewirtz and Ozga note that as their research progressed: 'we were obliged to acknowledge . . . that the fact we were both women eased our access to our almost exclusively male interviewees. That in itself, of course, raises ethical issues, which are heightened when we acknowledged that our non-threatening and sympathetic self-presentation was also a useful research tactic' (Gewirtz and Ozga 1993: 1). Further into their paper Gewirtz and Ozga take up this theme again, stating: 'in effect we felt that we were viewed as women in very stereotypical ways . . . and we were obliged to collude, to a certain degree, with that version of ourselves because it was productive for the project. *We were given a great deal of help by our interviewees and they told us a great deal about themselves'* (p. 12, my emphasis). Clearly this successful collection of data was significantly en-hanced by the collusion of these women researchers and their manipulation of their marginality.

The collusion of women interviewers with the (hetero)sexual subtext which Gewirtz and Ozga highlight – and which my own adoption of a 'Miss Marks and Spencer look' also represented to a certain extent – has similarly arisen in a media context. For example, Anne Leslie of the *Daily Mail* advises that 'it is best to be neat but not gaudy; to be attractive but not so much that you have *Playboy* phoning up', and Nina Myskow of the *Sun* baldly asks 'isn't every inter-view a seduction?' (cited in *The Guardian*, 14 February 1994). Although such comments may be problematic they echo the same dilemmas as expressed by Smart (1984), McKee and O'Brien (1983), Gewirtz and Ozga (1993) and myself.

The interview then, can compound both the (hetero)sexual subtext and the traditional role of women as listeners. As Lynn Barber of the *Sunday Times* notes: 'listening with rapt attention is far more seductive than a mile of cleav-age' (*The Guardian*, 14 February 1994). Listening is essentially a feminized occupation and women are structurally located in and informally coerced into positions of encouraging and facilitating male speech (Spender 1980; Smart 1984). This process is being directly reproduced when women interview powerful men and this is irrespective of whether or not they are feminists or informed by feminism.

Doing antiracist research: experiencing hostility

My neutralized appearance and my attempts to present myself as objective were undermined to a large extent by what I was actually researching. As a young, woman researcher I represented very little threat to the powerful people I was interviewing (and I had gone some way to presenting myself as non-threatening), yet I still met with some hostility which can most accu-rately be understood in terms of the issues I was investigating. This hostility was not usually overt but tended to be expressed in a variety of ways that spilled over into my marginality and my gender. I would often be kept wait-ing for an interview, long after the arranged time. To be treated patronizingly, with seeming indifference or with the respondent continually looking at their watch was not unusual. I often felt I was being only barely tolerated and as if my questions were answered as if they were faintly ridiculous. Gilroy has noted that the battered concept of antiracism has meant it is a concept that is now 'almost impossible to utter in the still, serious places where . . . formal processes operate. Its use reflects badly on the credibility of those who invoke it' (Gilroy 1992: xi). This has become particularly so with the ascendancy of (anti) 'political correctness' discourses.

In one particular incident, a new vice-chancellor had taken over one of the university case studies near the end of my fieldwork. I wrote to him, explain-ing my research and asking if it would be possible to interview him, to which he agreed. As soon as I was in his office he demanded to know who had given me permission to use the university as a case study, who had I spoken to so far and what was the research for, although I had explained in my letter that it was doctoral research. Through this interviewing of me I felt it was clearly implied by the vice-chancellor that he wouldn't have allowed me access. When I explained which groups I was interested in talking to in the university, but reminded him that all my respondents were unnamed and anonymous, the situation became very confrontational. Although I thought (hoped) that the interview wouldn't go ahead, the vice-chancellor did allow me to ask him some questions. The following excerpt from the transcript is significant because it provides an illustration of the struggle for control of the interview process:

> SN: What is your own understanding or definition of the concept of equal opportunities?
> VC: You must know the literature on equal opportunities.
> SN: Yes, but what is your personal view?
> VC: Equal opportunities is what it says it is.
> SN: What would you say it was?
> VC: Equality of opportunity. You can't produce equality of outcome. You've got to distinguish between running an institution of higher education and improving the condition of mankind.

This excerpt is also significant in that it *simultaneously* demonstrates both the respondent's hostility towards me, to the nature of the questions I asked and, by implication, the concept of equal opportunities *per se*. Such experiences take an emotional toll and after this interview I had to go and sit in the safe space of the women's toilets to recover.

Conclusion

This chapter has sought to explore the issues surrounding the tensions that can arise in trying to simultaneously employ both antiracist and feminist approaches in the research field. There is a process of reconciliation that has to be negotiated between the reciprocal, subjective tenets of the feminist approach and the challenging, oppositional tenets of the antiracist approach. While the two are not exclusive of each other, the masculinity of the antiracist stance does not always sit easily with the femininity of the feminist stance. My own (unresolved) process of reconciliation was made more problematic because of the nature of my research site which involved an upwards gaze. In other words it was not always possible (or desirable) to be egalitarian, reciprocal and subjective when interviewing powerful, and overwhelmingly male, professionals. Conversely it was not always possible (if desirable) to be dissenting and confrontational when interviewing the same powerful, and overwhelmingly male, professionals. While there has been some feminist commentary on the difficulties of sustaining a feminist research approach (Smart 1984; Gewirtz and Ozga 1993) this does not address a race dimension. Similarly Back and Solomos (1992) and Keith (1992) have noted the difficulties of being confrontational antiracist researchers but have not incorporated a gender dimension into these discussions. What I have attempted to address are the (emotional) processes of compromise and distortion of both my anti-racist *and* feminist identities in my research practice. I have not sought to 'excuse' these compromises or distortions or give any 'right way' of conducting antiracist feminist research. Rather I have attempted to highlight the myriad of complexities that lie behind the intention to, or the assertion of, doing antiracist, feminist research and the impossibility of 'sustaining one ethical position in all contexts' (Back and Solomos 1992: 25).

Notes

1 While I use the term black inclusively to refer to peoples of African, Caribbean and South Asian descent it is not my intention to portray these groups as homogenous or deny difference and diversity.
2 Although I use the term 'women' generically, 'this is not to say that all women are oppressed in the same ways, but rather to recognise that while oppression is common the forms it takes are conditioned precisely by race/ethnicity, age sexuality and so forth' (Stanley 1991: 207).
3 I had not spent long in the field before I recognized that these institutions were not exclusively white and that it was necessary and valid for me to approach black members of university staff to request interviews. Facing a similar situation, Back and Solomos note that:

> for researchers to speak rhetorically about their mission to study white racism contains a subtle slight of hand. While superficially this seems more credible other important issues emerge. On one occasion Les offered an account of our 'studying the speaking position of the powerful' to a long established black activist. He reminded Les that to do so would be comparable to studying slavery by only speaking to slave masters. It was within this kind of context that the rhetoric of our position broke down.
>
> (Back and Solomos 1992: 13)

9 | 'Dancing to the wrong tune': ethnography, generalization and research on racism in schools

Paul Connolly

Introduction

The notion of generalizibility continues to haunt ethnographic researchers. In particular, ethnographers appear to be caught in a 'no win' situation where they are criticized when they fail to develop generalizations from their work and are equally criticized when they do. On the one hand there are writers such as Hammersley (1992a) who maintain that one of the principal means by which ethnographic research is often judged is in terms of its ability to generalize from the study of a particular social phenomena to a wider population. According to Hammersley (1992a) an in-depth study of a particular situation may be quite valid and methodologically sound but it is of limited use unless the conclusions drawn are of wider relevance. 'Relevance' in this sense is defined in terms of generalizability. As he argues: 'in planning, as well as assessing ethnographic research, we must consider . . . the question of how, as researchers and readers, we are able to generalise from findings about particular situations studied to conclusions that have such general relevance' (Hammersley 1992a: 85). On the other hand, there are those such as Keith (1993), writing from a post-structuralist perspective, who argue strongly against the very idea that ethnography can offer valid generalizations. In relation to his own ethnographic work on 'race' and policing, Keith argues that social phenomena can only be understood within the particular social, historical and spatial contexts within which they take place. Moreover, according to Keith, generalizations involve a process of 'forgetting' where the significance of particular social processes and practices are lost and researchers are inevitably left with little alternative than to focus on the shared experiences and characteristics of the minority ethnic population which invariably leads them to produce 'insidious stereotypes' (Keith 1993: 17).

The purpose of this chapter is to use these debates as a way into reassessing the role and purpose of ethnographic research in relation to studies of racism and schooling. The chapter will argue that the desire to judge ethnography in terms of its ability to generalize betrays a fundamental misunderstanding of its aims and underlying philosophy. Rather than producing generalizations, it will be argued that ethnographic research should be concerned with identifying and understanding particular social processes and practices and the specific sets of causal relations that exist within them. It will be from this perspective that the chapter will return to the theme of how 'relevance' can be judged in relation to ethnographic research. It will be argued that such research can be relevant to a much wider audience without succumbing to the misconceived need to generalize.

Quantitative vs. qualitative research?

It is useful to begin this reassessment of the role and purpose of ethnographic research with an important distinction made by Sayer (1992) between 'extensive' and 'intensive' research. While the distinction here is a little simplified and constructs a divide that is not so clear in reality (to be discussed later) it does serve as a good starting point for the arguments to follow. Extensive research, he argues, is concerned with identifying common patterns, regularities and distinguishing features of particular populations. Its methods are essentially quantitative and centre around large-scale surveys of representative samples of a population with the aim of producing generalizations about the population as a whole. However, while it may draw attention to correlations between particular variables (i.e. that there is a relationship between ethnic origin and educational performance, or gender and subject choice), Sayer contends that such methods can tell us very little about the precise nature of that relationship. In particular, he argues that extensive research does not have the ability to explain whether a causal relationship exists between two variables (i.e. does a child's ethnic origin *cause* educational performance?) or whether the correlation that exists between the two is simply a spurious one and the product of the methodological process. In relation to a correlation that may exist between ethnic origin and educational performance, for example, it has been argued that the correlation is not as direct or causal as the data suggests and that much of the relationship can actually be explained by social class, in that children from minority ethnic backgrounds who perform poorly in educational terms are actually far more likely to be from lower social class backgrounds (Reeves and Chevannes 1981; Burnhill et al. 1990). Similarly, just because a relationship exists between ethnic origin and educational performance, once all other variables such as social class are controlled for, this does not mean that it is a child's ethnic origin *per se* that is the cause of their poor educational performance. Thus it may well not be their cultural and/or religious background that is the root cause but racism. Yet, as Keith (1993) has argued, such broad surveys and statistical generalizations do involve a process of 'forgetting', where particular social processes and practices (in this case racism) are lost and all that is left is a generalization that educational performance is related to children's ethnic origin. As Troyna (1984) pointed out well over a decade ago, with such limited information it is not surprising to find that researchers are left to develop rather dubious and dangerous explanations in terms of the particular ethnic backgrounds of the children themselves (i.e. that the poor educational performance of black children is the result of what is assumed to be their greater likelihood of being raised in single parent families) rather than being able to seek explanations that may well be external to their ethnic background (i.e. racism).

It is because of the inability of extensive research to move beyond generalizations and offer insight into causal relations that Sayer (1992) contrasts it with what he terms intensive research. Intensive research, he explains, is concerned with identifying and analysing the particular social processes and practices that cause change. Its methods are therefore broadly qualitative and are interested in gaining an appreciation of *why* a particular individual or group behave in a certain way. This inevitably involves detailed observation of their behaviour and how they relate to other individuals, social groups and structures together with in-depth interviews with those involved to uncover the meaning they, and others they relate to, attach to their actions. Accordingly, such intensive research enables the researcher to begin to unravel the causes of an individual or a group's behaviour. In this respect causality can only be fully understood through an exploration of the understandings, meanings and intentions that individuals and groups associate with their actions.[1] Thus while extensive research may identify certain minority ethnic groups that perform less well in educational terms compared to their peers, intensive research can help to uncover some of the explanations as to why this is the case. In relation to ethnicity and schooling, a number of ethnographic studies have been invaluable in drawing attention to the role of racism in affecting minority ethnic children's educational performance and their experiences of schooling (see, for example, Wright 1986, 1992b; Mac an Ghaill 1988; Gillborn 1990; Mirza 1992). However, as Sayer is at pains to point out, intensive research may well be able to identify and explain particular causal relationships, but it can tell us very little about how representative these relationships are. In other words, intensive research, by its case study nature, is unable to develop generalizations.

This distinction between extensive and intensive research is one that I want to maintain in relation to this chapter. It offers an important insight into the respective roles and purposes of quantitative and qualitative research in that the former aims to produce generalizations but can tell us little about causal relations, while the latter can help to identify relations of causality but is unable to generalize from these. In reality, such a distinction is not as clear-cut. As Hammersley (1992a) rightly argues, there is a fair degree of overlap between the two methods. Qualitative researchers, for instance, often try to quantify their data and offer generalizations by use of descriptions such as 'sometimes', 'often', 'most of those studied' and so on. Similarly, with the advances in statistical techniques (see Drew and Demack, this volume), many quantitative researchers attempt to identify and account for as many social variables as possible in order to control for their influence and pinpoint the precise relationship between two particular variables. Moreover, no method can claim, with complete certainty, that its generalizations or the causal relations it has uncovered are beyond doubt. There will always be error and uncertainty associated with any claim. However, while neither quantitative nor qualitative methods can claim that their generalizations are without error, there is an important difference in relation to the degrees of certainty with which the two can make such claims, with the former being able to make generalizations with potentially less error than the latter. The same is true, vice versa, in relation to issues of causality.

Thus, while noting that some degree of overlap does occur, this should not detract us from the important differences which remain in relation to quantitative and qualitative research. Hammersley (1992a), for instance, while attempting to 'deconstruct' what he refers to as the 'qualitative-quantitative divide', does conclude that the choice of particular methods will inevitably involve a 'trade-off' in terms of the type of data required. As he explains, 'if we seek greater precision we are likely to sacrifice some breadth of description and vice versa'. Thus, as Hammersley goes on to argue, 'the costs and benefits of various trade-off positions will vary according to the particular goals and circumstances of the research being pursued' (Hammersley 1992a: 172).

This idea of a 'trade-off' taking place is an important one to stress in relation to notions of generalization and causality. Thus, while a qualitative, ethnographic researcher may choose a school that is broadly representative of other schools (in terms of the social class, gender and ethnic origin of its intake) she or he can never, with the degree of confidence associated with quantitative methods, claim that her or his findings can be applied to those other schools. In this case, quantitative methods would then be required to analyse these other schools and ascertain to what extent the particular relations that exist in the sample school are found to be more generally manifest in the others. Similarly, for as much as quantitative methods are able to control as many of the other variables as possible so as to try and isolate the effects of one variable on another, they can still never, in the last analysis, conclude with the degrees of certainty associated with qualitative methods that a particular correlation they are left with is a causal one. It remains the role of qualitative research to prove or disprove that by exploring and analysing the meanings and justificatory frameworks that those involved attached to their actions.

Generalizations and ethnography

It should be clear by now that attempts to judge the relevance of ethnography by its ability to generalize are tantamount to encouraging ethnographic researchers to 'dance to the wrong tune'. It is a 'tune' that has come to dominate the social sciences because of the desire of social researchers to claim their work as scientific. This form of 'scientism' as Sayer (1992) terms it, involves social researchers attempting to emulate the methods and procedures of the natural sciences. The production of universal laws of behaviour that can be rigorously and objectively tested obviously demands the use of quantitative methods and statistical analysis. According to positivist sociologists like

Merton (1967), social research should only focus on phenomena that can be observed and accurately measured. Such phenomena, once precisely identified and defined, can then be statistically analysed to ascertain what relationship, if any, exists between the phenomena and other social factors. Moreover, the use of precise mathematical techniques and of representative samples ensures that social research can meet one of the founding conditions of the natural sciences; that any particular study can be replicated and the findings corroborated or challenged.

It is not surprising that ethnography, in being encouraged to dance to this particular scientist tune, has been set up to fail. As argued above, ethnographic research cannot produce generalizations and thus engage in the production of universal laws of behaviour. Its underlying interpretivist philosophy, with its focus on the meaning that individuals and groups attach to their own and others' actions, requires that ethnographic research has to be intensive and small-scale. Moreover, the uniqueness and complex nature of social relations and the way in which they develop and change over time means that it is impossible to replicate any particular ethnographic study. It comes as little surprise therefore to find ethnography continually being dismissed for its perceived unscientific, subjective and merely anecdotal nature. Not only can existing ethnographic studies not be replicated, but it is also impossible precisely to define and measure the principal focus of ethnographic research – the 'meaning' that lies behind a person or group's behaviour.

It is for this reason that we need to reassess the role and purpose of ethnographic research. The first task involved in doing this is to exorcize the ghost of generalization once and for all. For as long as the requirement to generalize remains a central element of how ethnographic research is to be judged, so the findings of such work will continually be open to criticism and misinterpretation. The recent sustained critique of existing research on educational inequality by Foster *et al.* (1996) is a case in point. According to these writers, 'most, though not all, research makes claims, explicitly or implicitly, about cases beyond those which have actually been studied. In other words, it involves an element of generalizability' (Foster *et al.* 1996: 65). This statement allows them to critique much social research on educational inequalities in relation to 'race', gender and class (a fair proportion of which is ethnographic) in terms of its inability successfully to generalize from the data collected. Unfortunately, such a critique also helps to feed into their broader reassessment of qualitative studies on racism and schooling and allows them to reach the conclusions that no published study has, as yet, proven the existence of racism 'beyond reasonable doubt' (see Gillborn, this volume).

In attempts to challenge this applicability of generalization to ethnographic work, it is useful to begin with the two different forms of generalization that Foster and his colleagues identify, and address each in turn. For Foster *et al.* there are two basic forms of generalizability – 'empirical generalization' and 'theoretical inference' – which they then use as one particular yardstick to assess the research literature on educational inequalities. 'Empirical generalization', they argue, involves 'making claims about some larger, but finite, population of cases to which the case(s) studied belong' (Foster *et al.* 1996: 65).

In essence this involves claiming that, for example, the sample school under study is 'representative' of a range of other schools and therefore the findings in relation to that school can be applied to those other schools. Alternatively, it may simply involve making claims from the data about the experiences of a particular social group within the school such as *all* South Asian boys or *all* black girls for example. I want to argue, however, that whatever the level of generalization, such claims are incompatible with ethnographic research. Even if a school is chosen that is broadly representative in terms of its intake and surrounding demography, the importance of particular social and historical processes means that it can never claim fully to represent other schools. Each school will invariably differ along a number of axes including its ethos, the funding it receives, the influence of the particular headteacher and her or his senior management team, the role of the governing body and of the parents, the influence of specific events within the local community, the particular social and educational needs of the children involved and so on. It should already be apparent, therefore, that just because a school shares a similar intake and is located in an area that has a similar demography to another school this does not mean that the two schools are comparable. The specific character and influence of the variables outlined above will always act to differentiate one school from another. Moreover, all of these factors are not simply independent of one another so that they can be identified and isolated, but they feed into and, in turn, are influenced by, one another. There is thus an essential and unique history to each and every school where each specific factor contributes to the unfolding and developing sets of social relations in that particular school. To assume, for instance, that the forms that racism takes among children in one inner-city school is the same as another is to lose sight of the unique nature of that school and the ways in which specific events both within the school and beyond inevitably act to encourage a quite particular development of the sets of racialized relations found there.

Moreover, it would be equally wrong to make generalized claims about specific children within a particular school. Each child brings with them a unique biography and experiential history which then mediates the way they interpret and respond to particular incidents and events. Their response, in turn, can at times contribute to an elaborate self-fulfilling prophecy which will feed into how others decide to relate to them in the future. Gillborn's (1990) ethnographic study of a multi-ethnic secondary school demonstrates quite effectively the differing responses of black boys to the particular forms of racism found within the school. Similarly my own research shows that the experiences of young children from the same minority ethnic backgrounds differ widely in terms of their relations with teachers and their peers (Connolly 1998). It is not surprising, therefore, that ethnographic research on educational inequalities will always fare badly when judged in terms of its ability to generalize about the schooling experiences of particular groups of children and students. Not only are writers such as Foster *et al.* (1996) demonstrating a misconception of the nature and purpose of ethnographic research but they are also, by using the yardstick of generalizability, creating 'straw dolls' to knock down.

It may be argued that Foster and his colleagues are on safer ground when judging ethnographic research in relation to the second form of generalization, that of 'theoretical inference'. According to Foster *et al.* (1996: 65) 'theoretical inference . . . is employed by studies concerned with developing and testing theories. The claim here is that what is true of the case (or cases) studied is also true of all other members of the relevant theoretical category to which they belong'. It could be argued that while ethnography may not be able to develop empirical generalizations of the type discussed above, it is surely concerned with developing theoretical insights that may be used and/or adapted for understanding the schooling experiences and educational performance of particular social groups. This is true as far as it goes. However, we need to be careful in terms of how 'theory' is defined. Foster *et al.* define theory as that which: 'states a relationship between phenomena belonging to two or more categories; a relationship that it predicts will hold if certain conditions are met. The relationship is usually a causal one though it may be probabilistic – occurring in most (or a certain proportion) of cases relevant to the theory' (p. 43). The problem with this definition is that it is extremely limited and reflects the largely positivistic approach to theory proposed by Merton (1967), discussed earlier. It assumes that 'theories' can be developed which are applicable to all situations that meet certain prior requirements. The logic of this approach leads, inevitably, to the idea that one study can 'prove' or 'disprove' the findings of another. If this is not the case then what is the purpose developing such theories that claim to be applicable to all situations that meet particular criteria? To explain this point, consider an ethnographic study that, from its data and analysis, has developed a 'theory' that racist assumptions among teachers leads to the over-disciplining of black children in schools. Presumably, the theory will be dependent upon particular prior conditions being met (possibly that it relates to certain types of school; that it is more likely to occur in situations in large classes where the teacher is overworked and so on). Furthermore, it may not be claiming that this type of over-disciplining will occur in each and every situation that meets these criteria but that it is more *likely* to – that is, it is a probabilistic generalization.

Now, consider a second study conducted by another researcher who also focuses on a broadly similar school and also conducts their fieldwork for a significant period of time so that they are able to develop a good 'feel' for the ethos of the school and the nature of relations between teachers and students. The difference this time, however, is that this second study finds no tendency for black students to be adversely disciplined compared to their fellow pupils and thus develops a 'theory' from the data that racism does not significantly impinge upon relationships between teachers and students. Presumably, by definition, this second theory is also supposed to apply to all types of school that meet certain conditions. It may, as with the earlier 'theory', be based upon a probabilistic generalization – that is, that its findings should be true in more cases than not. The problem inevitably arises, however, that, because of their desire to generalize and claim much wider applicability, both theories cannot be true. The logic of generalization therefore leads both researchers into what Keith (1993) terms the process of 'forgetting' where, in their desire to generalize, they both attempt to underplay the many aspects of their particular school that are specific to it and, rather, overemphasize its 'representative' nature.

This is not to say that, should ten or even twenty ethnographic studies all show a tendency for black students to be unfairly and disproportionately disciplined, a reviewer of the literature cannot claim, with due precaution, that a more generalized pattern does appear to be emerging. Such claims would be inevitable and quite reasonable. But they do involve a quite different type of generalization in that it is a generalization *about a number of different ethnographic studies*. The problem I have attempted to highlight above emerges when ethnographers attempt to develop a theory from just the data gathered in relation to their own study, and claim that it has much wider and general applicability. It is within such a context that a theory developed from one study cannot easily sit alongside a contradictory one developed from another study. In such circumstances researchers are inevitably drawn into the logic of 'proving' and 'disproving' the work of others.

The problem with this approach to theory therefore is that it fails to recognize the importance of particular social contexts and the complexities of the relations found there. As already argued, no two schools are the same. The notion of theory testing underpinning the work of Foster *et al.* (1996) is therefore simply inappropriate as researchers are not comparing like with like. If, as discussed in the above scenario, the second ethnographic study found that the teachers in one specific school did not discriminate against the minority ethnic children in their class, does that 'disprove' the findings of an earlier study that did find discrimination in a different school? Even if we assume that the two studies were conducted by the same researcher making use of the same research techniques and employing similar definitions of racism and discrimination, the only real conclusion we can reach is that there is something different about the two schools and their respective teachers and/or children that lead to discrimination in one school and not the other. The same is true in relation to the effects of time. The salience of racism in students' and teachers' lives will inevitably change from one period to another. Local events, such as a vicious racist attack or the escalation of tensions between young people and the police can all act to increase the salience of 'race' among students and teachers within a particular school. Similarly, the moral panics over black mugging within the national press (see Hall *et al.* 1978) or events such as the Rushdie affair or the Gulf war can also have a profound effect on the nature of racialized relations at a local level and within the school. The point is that the incidence and degree of racism in any particular context is not pre-given and fixed but changes over time. Even if the same researcher was able to return to the same school where they had previously conducted some research and focus on the same student cohort, there is no guarantee that they will come to similar findings in relation to the nature and incidence of racism as they did previously. To find, on the second visit, that the incidence of racism is significantly less than that found during the first study, is therefore not to 'disprove' the findings of that study. Rather it could simply be to draw attention to the differing social relations that have developed *at that particular time*.

It is because of the complexity of racism and the way that its nature and form changes over time and from one context to the next, that ethnography just cannot emulate the natural sciences in terms of theory generation and testing. Ethnographers cannot control their environments to such an extent that they can create the same 'laboratory conditions' that existed in a previous study. Similarly, the focus of the study – teachers, children, parents, school governors – are not inanimate objects that respond to a particular event in the same way time after time but are thinking, reflexive beings who can interpret events in very different ways and respond to them in an equally diverse manner. Thus, even if a researcher can find a school that is exactly the same as one used in a previous piece of research, they can never control for the individuals within it. To assume a definition of theory that relies on the ability to control for particular schools and individuals is thus, again, to fundamentally misunderstand the nature and role of ethnographic research. Because of the divergence and complexity of social relations, ethnography cannot, by its nature, be used to generate and test universal laws of behaviour, which appears to be, in essence, how Foster and his colleagues (1996) define 'theory'. It is not surprising that, again, with such a definition, it is relatively easy to criticize and undermine the findings of ethnographic research on educational inequalities.

The call so far for ethnographers to resist the urge to generalize, rather than restricting and severely limiting the role of ethnographic research, actually helps to broaden its application and relevance. To forego the logic of generalization does not, in any sense, mean a spiral into a simplistic form of relativism where researchers are either restricted to making statements about individuals and/or are prevented from considering and discussing the wider relevance of their own work. On the contrary, ethnographers can still make claims about the school 'as a whole', or a particular social group of children within the school and, similarly, it is important that they do fully consider the wider application of their work. However, the problems in relation to generalization discussed above mean that these two needs have to be approached and addressed more cautiously. This chapter will now consider each in turn.

The purpose of ethnographic research

It is clear that, in order fully to understand the schooling experiences of particular social groups of children, it is important for ethnographic research to incorporate an understanding of the wider influence of the school 'as a whole' and of the broader context of the local community. However, the problem arises as to how such claims can be made without recourse, at some level, to generalization. The way to address this concern is to begin by looking again at what we mean by the term 'generalization'. The definition of empirical generalization offered by Foster *et al.* (1996) and quoted above, is nearest to how many of us probably understand the notion of generalization. To repeat, generalizing in this sense involves 'making claims about some larger, but finite, population of cases to which the case(s) studied belong' (Foster *et al.* 1996: 65). Now I want to argue that an ethnographic study can involve an analysis of the

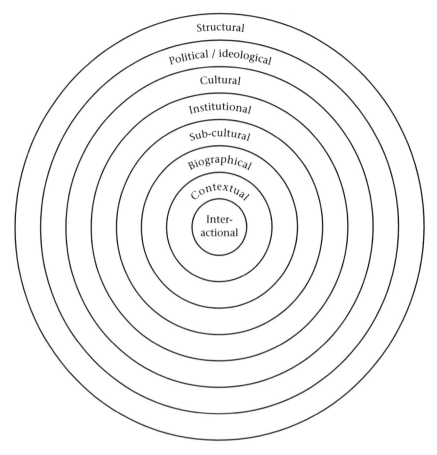

Figure 9.1. A model for analysing racist incidents in schools
Source: Troyna and Hatcher 1992: 40

interplay of various levels of the social formation without the need to gener-alize in this sense. To understand this it is useful to consider Troyna and Hatcher's (1992) ethnographic study of racist incidents among 10- and 11-year-old children as an example. In essence they argue that in order fully to understand why a specific racist incident occurred at a particular time between a group of children, we need to be aware of a number of events taking place at various levels of the social formation and how these come to impact upon each other. To this end they offer a diagrammatical model consisting of a number of concentric circles, shown in Figure 9.1, each representing a differ-ent social level. They define each of the particular layers as follows:

Structural: The differential relations of power and structurally induced conflict between groups perceived as racially different in society.

Political/ideological: Prevailing systems in play at the time of the incident. On the one hand, racism: justified in terms of the current *zeitgeist*. On the other, anti-racism: defended in terms of egalitarian ideals.
Cultural: The level of lived experience and common-sense understanding within the locality and community, especially as these are refracted through the family and its networks.
Institutional: The ideologies, procedural norms and practices which are promoted, sanctioned and diffused by the school.
Sub-cultural: The children's sub-cultural worlds.
Biographical: Those factors and characteristics which are specific to the individuals involved in the incident.
Contextual: The immediate history of a racist incident.
Interactional: The actual event/incident; what was done, what was said.

(Troyna and Hatcher 1992: 41)

It is not necessary to outline and assess the specific way in which Troyna and Hatcher make use of this particular model. Rather, the important point for the moment is simply to highlight the existence of these differing levels and the importance of each. In particular, I want to argue that while it is essential to understand how the events manifest at these different levels influence each other and contribute to the emergence of racist incidents, it is important to not extend unilaterally the claims made from one layer to another. Thus, while an ethnographic study may draw attention to particular features of a specific school (i.e. the institutional level) such as its strong disciplinary code, we cannot simply assume that this will be represented in the behaviour of the children in any direct way (i.e. the sub-cultural level). Similarly, while a high degree of racism may be found among the children's peer-group relations (i.e. the sub-cultural level), this does not mean that we can simply claim that those children are endemically racist (i.e. the biographical level) or that what they do will necessarily be informed by racism (i.e. the contextual and interactional levels). And vice versa, the fact that a researcher has observed a number of racist incidents in the playground cannot be used to then assume that the children's peer-group relations are inherently structured by racism.

In other words, the claims made at a particular level of analysis cannot be applied to, or be used to generalize to, other levels. Each level of the social formation, as identified by Troyna and Hatcher (1992) has to be studied in its own right as a complex set of social processes and practices with a focus on the sets of relations that have been developed among key agents at that level (whether these be individuals at the micro levels of analysis or groups at the more meso and macro levels). Thus it may well be found that, as in my own research (see Connolly 1998), the particular school under study has developed a specific disciplinary ethos that does tend to disproportionately affect black children or that there is a significant level of competition over status within the children's peer-group relations that results in a tendency for South Asian children to be victimized and verbally and/or physically abused. However, while these are valid claims to make at this level with the appropriate evidence, it would be wrong to then assume from this that *all* black children experience the same degree of over-disciplining or that *all* South Asian children are equally likely to experience racial abuse from their peers. To do so would involve an attempt to apply data gained from one level (i.e. the school or the peer group) where the unit of analysis is the group to another level (interactional) where the unit of analysis is the individual or vice versa. This would involve, in effect, an attempt to generalize from one level to another (i.e. individual to the group or vice versa).

Rather, what we need to do in the examples listed above is to assess, through empirical investigation, what the range of experiences of black and/or South Asian children is to these broader processes and then identify the diversity of the children's responses to them. As I found in my own research, while the school's disciplinary processes did tend to over-focus on black children, there was a diverse range of experiences among the children of these processes ranging from those that were able to evade the disciplinary processes altogether to those that were being constantly drawn into them (see also Connolly 1995a, 1995b). Similarly, my research found that not all South Asian children were the focus of racial abuse. Some were successfully able to evade it while others were relatively frequently picked upon. Attempts to generalize from these different experiences would be severely to restrict and simplify the analysis to the point where it would be of little use. Rather, the focus for the analysis should be to develop an understanding of the different social processes and practices involved and how and why some children are affected by them while others are able to evade them. This is precisely what I attempted to do in my own research (see Connolly 1998). In this sense, rather than severely restricting the analysis by refusing to develop generalizations, this refusal actually opens up and extends it.

To summarize, the purpose of ethnographic research is to identify and explain causal social processes; to understand why certain individuals and groups experience what they do and behave in a particular way. A more comprehensive understanding will inevitably involve the identification of layers of analysis within the social formation such as those identified by Troyna and Hatcher (1992). In my own study these involved the national political level, the local estate, the school and the children's male and female peer-group relations. This in turn requires an analysis, at each level, of the way in which racism has influenced the specific relationships between the individuals/ groups found at each particular level. The final task is then to understand how the specific forms of racism manifest at one particular level of the social formation come to influence and be taken up at the other levels. In my own research, for example, I found that the local estate, and especially the racism manifest there and the reputation the estate had gained, was a significant factor in influencing the ways in which the school staff and the children thought about issues of 'race' and therefore how they took these racial understandings with them into the level of the school (in relation to the teachers) and into their peer-group relations (for the children).

One final point that needs to be addressed is that it could be argued that, by definition, attempts to make claims about racism on the local estate or the disciplinary ethos of the school involve a form of generalization. In relation to my own work, for instance, the claim that the school's disciplinary processes did tend to over-focus on black children cannot be seen as anything but a generalization. Similarly, how could I write about the nature of racism on the estate without making generalizations? In response it is important to make clear that the 'tendencies' that I highlight at any particular level of analysis are not claimed to either be the most prominent or the most important. Rather, I am purposely being highly selective about the particular social processes and practices I wish to focus on at these broader levels, with the sole intent of trying to identify those that have a direct bearing on the interaction between the children who constitute the principal focus of my study. Because I found, for example, that there existed a number of popular derogatory and negative stereotypes held by many of the black and white children about their South Asian peers, I was therefore interested in trying to identify and understand some of the sources of these stereotypes in relation to the broader levels of the school, the local community and national politics. In examining how particular racist stereotypes were generated and produced at each of these levels and then, consequently, how they came to shape and inform each other, I was not making generalized claims about the precise incidence or magnitude of these stereotypes at each level. To claim, for instance, that South Asian people tend to be constructed as 'alien' and the 'other' in national political discourses about immigration and 'race' relations, is not to claim that this is the most important or significant way in which they are depicted (although it may well be). It is simply to identify that such a process exists and has an influence, in turn, on the relations that develop within a particular local community. The point is that, because my primary focus is on the young children themselves, I only ever intend selectively to draw out and highlight particular elements that exist at these broader levels. In other words, I am primarily interested in identifying and understanding causal relations (that is, what particular social processes and practices at varying levels of the social formation *cause* children to behave and think in a certain way?). As such, my study of the local estate and/or the national political level has not been designed to develop and make generalizations about these levels. To do so would involve a quite different research focus and, possibly, the use of very different methods.

The relevance of ethnographic research

So far I have argued for the need to resist generalization in ethnographic research and have briefly looked at how ethnography can be used to identify and understand a number of causal processes without succumbing to the pressure to generalize. For some commentators, however, while such work may be very laudable it would not be judged too favourably in relation to its relevance. As we have seen, for Hammersley (1992a), among others, ethnographic research is only relevant if it can be used to generalize to other cases. This would typically involve, as Foster *et al.* (1996) have outlined, either generalizing from the case study to a wider, but finite, population (empirical generalization) or generating and testing hypotheses (theoretical inference). As it has been argued that these two forms of generalization are not appropriate to ethnography, it remains the task of this chapter to outline how ethnographic research can be judged as relevant. It is useful to do this by addressing, in turn, the two forms of generalization listed above and the alternative ways in which ethnography may be judged as relevant in each case.

Empirical relevance

Once we have rejected the notion of empirical generalization, it does seem at first glance to leave ethnographic research quite bare. How can a particular study be relevant if its findings have no wider application? Such a question, however, defines relevance strictly in terms of generalizability. As we discussed earlier, the problem with this is that it places ethnography in an impossible situation. Because of the uniqueness of every school or social locality, the findings of one ethnographic study can never claim to be directly applicable (and thus 'relevant') to another. Thus each time an ethnographer makes such claims about their own case study they will always be vulnerable to criticism that their study was not representative, that it was merely anecdotal and that the situation in other schools to which she or he is trying to generalize is different enough that the findings from his or her case study are just not applicable. Again, the desire to generalize actually tends to restrict the debate rather than extend it.

Rather, we should begin to see the findings of ethnographic research for what they are – insights into particular social processes and practices that exist within a specific social location – in our case the school. The findings can therefore be directly applicable to that school at that time but not to any other. However, this does not mean that the findings are not relevant to other schools. It may well be that some of the processes found in one school are also to be found in another. Rather than assuming this to be the case, however, such applicability needs to be empirically tested (Sayer 1992; Layder 1994). Thus, in relation to the schooling experiences of black students, Wright (1986) found that they were adversely effected, in her school, by excessive disciplinary control from teaching staff. This finding has since provided a 'resource', or sensitizing device which has been used by a number of other studies to help them ascertain and empirically test whether similar processes were occurring in their schools and, if so, what the precise nature of those were (see, for example, Mac an Ghaill 1988; Gillborn 1990; Connolly 1995b).

In this sense the relevance of successive ethnographic studies is found in the way that they cumulatively provide an ever-increasing catalogue of particular social processes and practices which researchers can draw upon to help sensitize them to and consequently identify the complex range of processes that could be occurring in their school. It is important to note that there are no claims to generalizability here. Rather, those findings can only help to orientate the researcher in relation to a range of possible processes that may be occurring in their school. In this sense, ethnographic studies can be highly relevant to other social localities without the need to generalize.

The same is true for the relevance of ethnographic studies for teachers and educationalists. Such work provides a growing resource from which teachers are able to assess their own practice. In my own research, for instance (Connolly 1995b), I found that because some black boys were more likely to be publicly disciplined within the school, these boys were more likely to gain a reputation for being 'bad' among their fellow peers. This in turn created a tendency for some of their male peers to view them as quintessentially masculine which, as a consequence, would at times act to threaten their own sense of masculinity. As a result, some of the white boys would pick fights with these black boys as a way of publicly reaffirming their own masculine credentials. This meant that a self-fulfilling prophecy existed where some black boys were more likely to be drawn into fights and therefore publicly disciplined by the teachers, thus reinforcing their reputation for being 'bad'. In my research I made no claims that these processes were the most prominent within the school. nor that they were equally likely to be experienced by all black boys in the same way or to the same degree. It stood to reason, therefore, that such findings were not to be directly and uncritically applied to other similar schools. As a result, teachers could not simply assume that if they find a black boy involved in a playground fight it was a result of the complex processes discussed above. However, my findings could be used by those teachers to sensitize themselves to the fact that those processes *may* be occurring. Thus, rather than simply disciplining the child in question, the teacher should, partly as a consequence of my study, be aware of the possibility that the child's involvement in a fight could be a result of more complicated processes. It would still be the responsibility of the teacher to investigate this and prove it one way or the other.

In summary, the role of my own research and, moreover, that of many others, is therefore to help sustain and support a critical reflexivity among teachers; to help them to be aware of the complex range of processes and practices occurring within the school that may be adversely affecting their children's social and educational development. While ethnographic research is unable to make definite claims to generalizability in the sense that their findings are directly applicable to other similar schools, they do provide a growing resource for researchers, teachers and educational practitioners to enable them to think critically and question their taken for granted assumptions and/or current practice.

Theoretical relevance

This discussion of empirical relevance leads, finally, on to a reconsideration of the role of ethnographic research in relation to the development of theory. Rather than seeing theory as something that can be tested and proven or disproven by further ethnographic investigation, we need to rethink the role of theory in a more eclectic manner. In particular we need to move away from the idea that there can ever be grand theories (which the tendency towards generalization inevitably encourages) that can be used to state universal laws of human behaviour and social organization. Rather we need to see theory as being grounded in empirical investigation and representing a developing resource that can draw attention to and help understand the range and diversity of social processes, practices and relations.

There is therefore a central role for ethnographic research in addressing existing theories and developing and/or challenging them, but not in such a crude and absolutist way as to then 'prove' or 'disprove' them. As argued earlier, just because the particular social processes identified in one study were not consequently found in another does not mean that the former study was wrong. If a discrepancy exists in this way between the findings of one study and another the task of the researcher should be twofold. First they need to examine what particular processes and practices, specific to their sample school, were in play that could possibly differentiate it from the school in the other study and thus help to explain the different findings. Second, the researcher can also re-examine their own methodology and that of the other study to see whether their findings or those of the other were actually an arte-fact of the research process. In other words, did the particular methodologies employed differ with the result that different data were collected and analysed in a different way? This latter concern would involve not just a consideration of the particular methods of data collection used but also of the theoretical framework employed in the analysis and interpretation of the data together with the politics and ethics of the research. This, of course, is precisely the form of debate currently occurring in relation to 'race' and education (see Gill-born, this volume; Hammersley, this volume).

In general, however, there has been little conflict over the findings of suc-cessive ethnographies of 'race' and education. Rather, the area provides a good example of how theory can be developed and refined through ethnographic research. For example, in relation to the schooling experiences of minority ethnic students, Wright's (1986) seminal work helped to confirm and develop the findings of researchers such as Driver (1980) and Furlong (1984) that a labelling process existed in relation to black students where some teachers car-ried with them stereotypes of what they saw as their 'aggressive' and 'con-frontational' style. It was a process which then tended to manifest itself through the greater likelihood that some black students would be disciplined and chastised in comparison to their peers. Mac an Ghaill (1988) developed this theory to include the differential experiences of South Asian male students, demonstrating how the different racial stereotypes that some teachers held about black and South Asian students meant that their treat-ment of the students differed in important respects. In particular he showed how the behaviour of South Asian male students was often overlooked or rein-terpreted by the teacher through their perception that South Asian students were 'hard working' and 'obedient'. Mac an Ghaill also drew attention to the differing responses to teacher racism that the minority ethnic students devel-oped. In particular he showed that while the black male students were more likely to reject the formal education of the school and resist the authority of the teachers directly, the black and South Asian female students were more likely to still value education but not the teachers or the school. They would therefore strive to do well in educational terms while resisting the authority of the teachers in more subtle and less confrontational ways – a strategy that Mac an Ghaill described as 'resistance within accommodation' (1988: 11; see also Fuller 1984).

Since then, Gillborn (1990) has further added to this perspective by drawing attention to the diversity of responses to teacher racism developed by the black and South Asian students and Mirza (1992) has helped to further develop our understanding of some of the particular experiences and social processes that help to explain black female student's approach to education. The later work of Wright (1992b), Troyna and Hatcher (1992) and myself (Connolly 1998) has extended the analysis to primary schools to show how similar processes are present in the earlier years of education. Moreover, my own work and that of Troyna and Hatcher has also extended our understanding of the role of peer group relations in effecting the schooling experiences of minority ethnic children.

As can be seen from this brief (and inevitably incomplete) account of the ethnographic research literature on racism and schooling, the development of theory has been a cumulative process where the findings of each study have been taken on board, empirically tested and refined by other studies. The development of theory, in this sense, has been a growing and vibrant enterprise and has not reflected the very restricted approach to generalization and theory-testing described above. Each successive study has not set out to 'prove' or 'disprove' earlier studies but has rather used the earlier work to sensitize itself to the potential processes and practices that could be occurring in its own sample school. As stated earlier, this avoidance of generalization within particular ethnographic studies does not preclude a person reviewing the cumulative weight of the number of ethnographies that now exist and concluding that a more general tendency does, indeed, appear to be emerging in relation to the experiences and treatment of minority students.[2] It is important to stress that this is a separate procedure and involves its own tests of credibility and validity for the claims generated. In relation to ethnographic research, this is the only valid arena for the production of generalizations. However, as outlined at the start of this chapter, it will still involve a number of potentially serious errors relative to the proper employment of quantitative methods of analysis.

Conclusions

This chapter represents a modest attempt to reassess the role and purpose of ethnography in relation to research on racism and schooling. It has argued for the need to resist, once and for all, the scientist agenda set for ethnography around the need to generalize. The chapter has contended that such an agenda betrays a fundamental misunderstanding of the aims and functions of ethnography. Rather than attempting to develop generalizations, ethnography should be concerned primarily with the identification and understanding of causal processes and practices, developing an appreciation of why certain individuals and groups behave in the way that they do. It has been argued that, because of the historical and social specificity of each case study, such work cannot then be used to develop generalizations.

It was from this basis that the chapter has attempted to look again at how the relevance of ethnographic research can be understood. In assessing both its empirical and theoretical relevance the chapter has shown that ethnography can be relevant without succumbing to the need to generalize. Moreover, in resisting the blunt instrument of generalization, the role and purpose of ethnography can be freed up and expanded to contribute to the growing and rich understanding of the complexity of causal relations and the diverse range of social processes and practices that underpin them.

Acknowledgements

I would like to thank the following for their useful comments on an earlier draft of this chapter: David Gillborn, Martyn Hammersley, Brendan Murtagh and Karen Winter.

Notes

1 It could be argued that the search for causality cannot but involve the use of generalizations. In this sense, it has been suggested that claims about causality are in effect claims about regularities; change in phenomena of type x causes change in phenomena of type y (providing other phenomena are controlled for). The problem with this is that, as is argued later in the chapter, the particular social settings which ethnographers study do not just involve phenomena x and y but also a, b, c, d, e and so on.. Moreover, these phenomena articulate with each other and their basic nature and form develops through these articulations and therefore changes over time. For example, a person's racist beliefs and the particular racial stereotypes they may subscribe to will change over time as they are influenced by other factors such as gender, class, sexuality and age and as they also interact with others and learn from them and adapt the way they behave with them. It therefore makes little sense to develop a causal relation that, for instance, x (teacher racism) causes change in y (the educational performance of minority ethnic students). This is because the properties of variable x are not constant. Similarly, the students' responses will never be constant but, because of each student's particular life history and biography, will be diverse and varied. It therefore makes little sense to attempt to identify two discrete variables from within complex social settings and claim that their nature and form are constant and that, consequently, it can be predicted with sufficient accuracy that change in one variable produces a particular change in another. It is because of this that it is argued in this chapter that 'causality' can only be understood in relation to interaction within particular social settings and through the method of attempting to unravel the many constituent elements that have combined in unique ways to influence that behaviour. This in turn requires an interpretivist focus on the meanings and understandings that those concerned attribute to their actions so that we can begin to ascertain *why* they actually behaved in the way that they have done.

2 For a good, recent example of this type of review see Gillborn and Gipps (1996).

10 | A league apart: statistics in the study of 'race' and education

David Drew and Sean Demack

Introduction

The subject area of this chapter should be seen in the context of a number of different worlds. The first of these, and probably the most important, is the world in which black and Asian young people live out their schooling and prepare for the world of work. It is their hopes, fears and aspirations which are the subject of this chapter and also their experiences of disadvantage and racism at school or at work. The second world is the world of those who affect their lives: the teachers; the schools; those who make educational policy; and the employers who will be offering these young people work. Much rests in their hands. The third world is that of research, be it qualitative or statistical, carried out for government or as independent research. The task of statistical research is to study the way the first two worlds interact, and to generalize about these through systematic study. A successful piece of research would be one which realistically reflects the experiences of students and assesses the impact of educational and labour market policies upon them. A criticism occasionally made of statistical analysis is that statistics are sometimes a poor reflection of reality and one of the purposes of this chapter is to examine this. One of the individuals who was acutely aware of this was Barry Troyna, and his paper about the deficiencies of the statistical analyses of ethnic differences in the early 1980s (Troyna 1984) was a spur to those who felt that improved analyses were urgently required.

The last decade has seen many changes both in the factors affecting young people and in the way these have been systematically researched. For example, educational policies of government have led to increasing constraints on what is taught in schools because of the National Curriculum, and market-led policies have meant that parents have more choice about where their children should go to school; a level of choice which almost certainly benefits children of middle-class parents rather than children of working-class parents. How were black and Asian children affected by this?

The research world has fought to keep up with a decade of change in education and to monitor and measure the effects of the changes on different groups. This task is difficult because, in order to test the effect of change, a large number of factors need to be taken into account. Technological improvement (the availability of software and hardware to cope with large and complex data sets and speed up the calculation process) is beginning to make this possible but it is no easy task. Whilst the analysis of data is probably less costly than it ever was, the collection of data is still very expensive.

The aim of this chapter is to show the contribution that statistical analysis can make to an understanding of 'race' and education differences. The chapter will attempt to place recent research findings in a methodological perspective so that both the findings and the models which produced them can be seen together. This builds on previous critiques (see Plewis 1988; Drew and Gray 1991; Gillborn and Drew 1992). In these critiques the findings of studies carried out in the 1980s were reviewed. They were criticized as being limited in a number of respects: the size of the samples was often small; the ethnic categories used were very broad; and the studies focused on certain geographical areas – particularly London – so the results could not necessarily be generalized to other parts of the country. Also, the measures of educational attainment were sometimes crude, other factors (for example gender and social background) had not been controlled for in the analysis, and the statistical models used were sometimes simple and did not take account of the multivariate nature of the data. It is interesting to see that many of the proposals made by Plewis in 1988 to put the analysis of ethnic differences in education on a sound footing have been taken up and considerable progress has been made.

It is not the purpose of this chapter to fully review the findings of statistical studies in the area of 'race' and education not least because such a review would take up a lot of space. Reviews of the area can be found elsewhere (see Drew 1995 for a review of research on ethnicity, education and the youth labour market, and Gillborn and Gipps 1996 for a review of research on ethnicity and achievement, produced for the Office for Standards in Education (OFSTED). Rather, the purpose of the chapter is to review a number of areas in which statistical analyses have been used and discuss the usefulness and pitfalls of such analyses.

Using the metaphor of the tool box we can view statistical techniques as a particular set of tools to do a particular job. (We have provided a glossary of the statistical terms referred to here at the end of the chapter.) In certain circumstances the statistical tool box will be entirely inappropriate and other research tools – for example qualitative or ethnographic methods – will be appropriate to get the job done. In this sense we do not see the use of statistical analysis and model building as in conflict with qualitative research but rather as a complementary set of methods. Some researchers see a tension between methodologies and problems of validity with certain types of study. We prefer to see qualitative approaches (see, for example, Mac an Ghaill 1988; Gillborn 1995) as studies of the processes affecting young people's lives which complement statistical studies of their educational experiences. It is the purpose of this chapter to spell out the role of statistical analysis and how it complements qualitative research. Other parts of this book point to the role of qualitative methods and ethnography in particular in uncovering social processes and focusing on causal relations (see Connolly, this volume). Statistical approaches also have this ideal in mind. Statistical approaches have particular strengths that ethnographic approaches do not have, in particular the ability to generalize from results by using carefully designed random samples. The probable difference between the sample estimate and the true value in the population can be estimated using standard errors and confidence intervals produced from survey results.

Statistical analysis draws attention to the associations between various factors and thus the likely relationship between particular variables. This can then form the basis of more detailed qualitative analysis of social processes to determine if and why the relationship exists. The relationship could be a spurious one or it could be that change in one variable is a cause of change in the other.

The approach that has been adopted in the chapter is to single out three particular areas of recent research and to use these to discuss the methods utilized and their strengths and weaknesses. This is offered up in a spirit of positive criticism. It is rather uncommon for researchers to provide a 'warts and all' description of research (including their own) in a journal article or a book. There is considerable pressure on researchers, supported by funders and acutely aware of critics, to focus on what their findings show, rather than on the confusions, uncertainties and mistakes which led up to them and the caveats which should be put around the results. The examples chosen are not meant to be representative of all the research in the area though they do relate to important areas of current debate. The three areas are: educational attainment; the educational and labour market transitions from the ages of 16–19; and studies of school effectiveness.

Statistical procedures

Before we are able to understand and offer a critique of the problems of particular models we need to begin by outlining the general procedures. There are four distinct stages in this: model formulation; creating the data; model fitting; and making empirical generalizations. These are detailed in Table 10.1.

These are the well established steps of social science research (see Rose and Sullivan 1993) and some of them have particular relevance for studies of 'race' and education. During the first stage, the model formulation stage, the process involves a comprehensive review of the literature. Researchers are expected to draw on previous work in an area and models which have previously been used and are found to fit the data well. If new research represents a radical departure from previous work a justification for the new approach should be provided. Any research which draws only on literature which gives support to the author's standpoint is suspect.

At this juncture we need to briefly discuss the nature of modelling in statistics and the meaning of cause and effect. The central idea of a causal relationship is that one event, or state, or variable, produces another outcome in the

Table 10.1   Stages in model building

Model formulation
Hypotheses; concept formation; use of previous work; comprehensive review of literature
Creating data
Operationalization of key concepts; research design and sampling; questionnaire design; collection of data via interviews or questionnaires
Model fitting
Choice of model; analysis; testing model adequacy; consideration of alternative models and explanations
Making empirical generalizations
Making inferences; generalizations from the model; suggested reformulations

---

course of time. Much has been written about the difficulties of establishing such a relationship by philosophers of science and many volumes have been produced on the subject. At one level a causal relationship may appear to be a deceptively simple one to appreciate. For example, if a metal is heated then, within certain temperature boundaries, it expands. This is why mercury rises up a tube when the weather is hot – the principle of the thermometer. But is the same true in the social sciences where outcomes appear to be affected by a multiplicity of factors and the measurement of cause and effect is far less simple? Marsh puts this succinctly:

> How can patterns in a survey produce proof of a causal process operating through time, starting with a cause and ending with an effect? The simple answer is that they cannot. But just because there is nothing in the cross-sectional evidence to clinch a causal argument does not mean that such evidence cannot help corroborate a hypothesis. Finding a correlation between smoking and lung cancer in no way proves that smoking causes lung cancer, but it does mean that the hypothesis cannot be ruled out. If we have reason to believe that it is a plausible connection, and if we can demonstrate to critics of the theory that the correlation holds up even after we have controlled for the factors that they believe to be responsible, the argument gets stronger and stronger.
>
> (Marsh 1982: 71)

This is the philosophy of statistical methodology in educational research.

It is this idea of controlling for other factors in an analysis that is at the heart of statistical modelling and will be illustrated in later examples in this chapter. The core notion in the pursuit of an explanation of how these things work is the concept of variability. In a situation in which a causal relationship exists then the strength of this relationship can be assessed by focusing on the variability between and within subgroups. Take the causal relationship between educational attainment and income, for example. If the population is split into groups according to their educational background then those with high qualifications would have, on average, higher incomes than those with no qualifications. Furthermore the variation in income would be smaller within each qualification group than the variation overall. Such an analysis, which focuses on the variability between groups and within groups (the analysis of variance) has become the standard approach in many types of statistical model building. This has been the case since the classical agricultural experiments concerned with the way in which fertilizers affect crop yield, analysed by R. A. Fisher at Rothampstead Research Station in England in the 1920s and 1930s (see Fisher 1925). Visitors from around the world still visit this sleepy Hertfordshire village where one of the most important techniques of statistical methodology of this century was developed.

This analysis of variability in the data can be extended. For example, if the causal relationship between, say, educational attainment and income is to be tested then there are two questions. First, does analysis of separate attainment groups show that these groups are relatively homogeneous with respect to income? Second, are these two factors still correlated even after other factors are taken into account? An 'other factor' could be, for example, gender. The question then becomes: 'Are qualifications and income associated for each gender group?' This method, the examination of relationships between variables whilst keeping others constant, has become the standard approach in this type of statistical model building.

At the second stage, creating data, the operationalization of concepts is a key aspect. Operationalization means defining variables so that concepts can be statistically measured. Take, for example, the measurement of educational attainment. This could be operationalized by measuring attainment at 16 or at 18 or at some other time point. If attainment at 16 is measured then this could be operationalized in a number of different ways by counting the number of passes at GCSE, for example, or by calculating a score based on the grades as well as the number of passes. There are a number of choices to be made here. A further aspect is sampling design. Choice of an appropriate sampling scheme can produce an efficient design for a fixed cost, the adequacy of the scheme being measured by sampling errors. Of equal importance for the researcher is the size of survey non-response and the bias that is created by this. It is commonly felt that a response rate of 80 per cent in a survey is good. Yet considerable bias can be introduced by the missing 20 per cent, because the non-respondents are likely to differ from the respondents in key ways, by being over-represented, for example, in particular attainment groups. In classic sampling texts (Cochran 1977) the serious nature of such bias is given emphasis and yet much higher non-response rates than 20 per cent are frequently reported.

At the third stage, model fitting, there are always a number of options available and the model choice is likely to be influenced by the models that have previously been used to research the topic. Much statistical work uses time-honoured techniques, the main difference between now and say a decade ago being that model fitting is relatively painless given the rapid improvements in computer technology. There are occasionally real innovations when models are introduced which are of a different type to those used before. Multilevel modelling comes into this category. These are models which came into use in educational research in the mid-1980s (Aitkin and Longford 1986; Goldstein 1987). They explicitly take into account the hierarchical nature of much of this data, for example that children are grouped into classes which are in turn grouped into schools. The issue of interest might be at the individual level – that is, the progress of individual pupils – or it might be at school level – that is, the differences between schools in examination results. These models enable the variability between individuals and the variability between schools to be studied within the same model. This has a number of advantages, one being that the variability between schools can be measured once account has been taken of the variability between individuals, i.e. the differences between school intakes. This variability between schools is commonly described as 'school effectiveness'.

At this stage it is also important to test for model adequacy. For example, whether the model enables us to make predictions, using the available data, which are close to outcomes observed. Ways in which this can be done will be discussed in the next section. Researchers are almost bound to include measures of goodness of fit (i.e. how well their model matches the actual data) when publishing their results but the subject is sometimes dealt with rather briefly and this is sometimes because the fit is rather poor. This is often not a reflection on the researcher but reflects the fact that in much educational and social research there is a considerable amount of variation that cannot be explained by a statistical model.

At the fourth stage, making empirical generalizations, the crucial aspect for the researcher is the extent to which the results of the study can be generalized. This depends on the way the sampling was carried out and the definition of the original survey population. For example, if a sample was taken from schools in metropolitan authorities then, strictly speaking, the results of the study can only be generalized to similar such schools and may not be generalizable to the whole of, say, England and Wales, because the original population excluded rural areas. National studies are expensive and relatively rare and therefore studies may focus on a small number of areas or even one area for reasons of cost. It is important to generalize from such studies with care.

Model building

Although there appears to be a large number of statistical models applied to research data in education, they do in fact fall into a small number of groups. The main group is the group of general linear models, so called because they are based on the premise that the relationship between the explanatory variables and the outcome variable is a linear and additive one. The adequacy of the models is usually tested in two ways. The first method is to examine the extent to which the variation in the outcome variable is explained by the explanatory variables and what residual, unexplained variation remains. The second way is to test the relative importance of each of the individual explanatory variables using tests of statistical significance.

The general procedures of model building in practice can be illustrated by an example of linear regression in which one outcome variable of educational attainment (y), is predicted by some measure of prior attainment (x). The data illustrated in Figure 10.1 is for a random sample of students at the University of Sierra Leone giving their final year examination results (y) expressed as a grade point average, as predicted by the second year results (x). This illustrates a strong association between the second year score and the final year score. The regression line passes through the scatter of points so that the sum of the squared distances from the points to the line is as small as possible.

It would appear that the fit of this regression line is quite good, which means that knowledge of year two results enables a reasonably good prediction to be made of attainment in the final year. (Students who obtained a grade point average of 4.2 or above in their final year were awarded a first class honours degree). The prediction for a student with a year 2 score of 4.27 is a score of 4.13 in their final year, illustrating that, in general, students were doing less well in their final year than previously. This prompted questions about whether the work had become much more difficult in the final year or whether the marking had become harder.

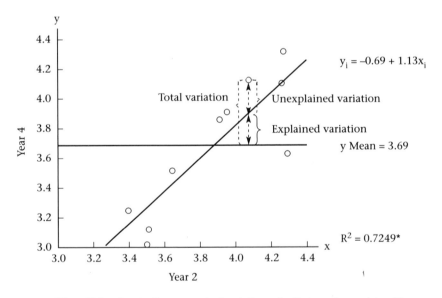

Figure 10.1 Prediction of Year 4 examination results from Year 2 examination results for BA education students in Sierra Leone

How can we assess the adequacy of the model? One way to do this is to imagine that no information was available about year 2 scores at all. In this case the best prediction that could be made of an individual's final year results would be the final year mean (3.69), hardly a prediction at all really. When we add information about second year scores then of course the predictions become much better. This improvement can be illustrated by the variance. If no prior information is available then the variability in predictions is given by the deviations about the overall mean, whereas if the regression line is fitted, as in Figure 10.1, then the variability in predictions is given by the deviations about the regression line. The difference between the prediction and the mean is the 'explained' difference, and the difference between the line value and the actual y value is the residual, 'unexplained' difference. An overall measure of how much of the variability in the final year score can be accounted for by the year 2 score can be calculated by adding up these differences which leads to the expression:

Total variance = explained variance + unexplained variance

This rather simple equation is the key to the analysis of many complex models and the explained variance (expressed in percentage terms) is the most often used measure of model adequacy or goodness of fit. If it is 100 per cent this means that the outcome measure can be perfectly estimated given the value of the predictor variable. For the data from Sierra Leone, the explained variance was 72 per cent, indicating a reasonable but not perfect fit. Some first class degrees, for example, could be predicted but some students did not come up to expectation in their final year. There are a number of variants of the regression model, dealing with slightly different situations, but the principles of model fitting and testing model adequacy are the same.

Case one: Educational attainment at 16

When the Swann report was published in 1985 there was great concern about the lamentable lack of statistical evidence within the report. The Committee was charged with establishing the educational needs and attainments of children from ethnic minority groups and yet within the 806 page report the main evidence for underachievement is contained in only seven tables from the Department of Education's School Leavers Survey and only the briefest statistical analysis (DES 1985: 110). This led James Cornford, one of the Committee members, to comment on the 'inadequacy of official statistics to provide anything but the crudest indications of the extent of differences between ethnic groups in academic achievement' (DES 1985: 171). He also commented on the 'failure of the Department to keep itself adequately informed on what has for many years been acknowledged to be an urgent problem' and called for the Department to establish a research programme to examine these problems in a regular and systematic way. It is interesting to look back on this to see what progress has been made in the last decade.

How large are ethnic differences in attainment? This is shown in Figure 10.2, taken from the 1991 Population Census (Drew and Fosam 1994). It shows the

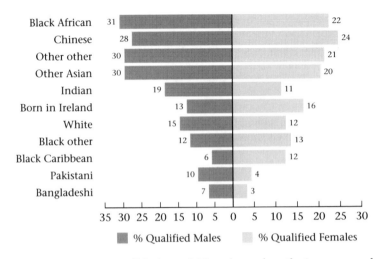

Figure 10.2 Percentage qualified, aged 18 and over by ethnic group and gender
Source: Drew and Fosam 1994: 25

percentage in each group with diploma or degree level qualifications in the adult population. The reason this graph has been chosen is that it provides a convenient benchmark for the population as a whole against which we can begin to discuss the attainment of children. The ethnic categories that were used for the first time in the Census in 1991 are utilized here.

The graph appears to reinforce some well known findings. There are apparently large differences between ethnic groups and the Black Caribbean, Pakistani and Bangladeshi groups do less well than others. There are sizeable gender differences here also with Black Caribbean females having higher attainment levels than their male counterparts but the reverse being true for Pakistanis and Bangladeshis. The graph shows some characteristics which were not so well known before this data became available. A number of groups appear to have higher attainment levels than whites; the Chinese and the Black Africans in particular.

However, this data is not all that it first appears and we need to ask a number of questions. The process described previously alerts us to a number of issues and we will use this apparently straightforward graph taken from the Population Census to discuss the kind of questions that other researchers will be asking when they see a graph like this.

The first question is about the research design that has been used. The Census is a cross-sectional survey, albeit a very large one, and attempts to measure an individual and family's circumstances at one moment in time. Most research studies are cross-sectional in nature, that is they are based on measurement at one point in time with one sample of respondents. Within such a study some data might be collected retrospectively (for example about examination results one or two years ago) but recall error is likely to be a problem when this is done. Cross-sectional studies therefore have limited value in measuring change over time. In longitudinal studies the same individuals are followed over a period by interviewing them at a number of time points and this enables changes over time to be studied more effectively. Longitudinal studies are, by their nature, very expensive and for this reason they are relatively rare. There is one major national longitudinal study of education from 16–19, the Youth Cohort Study of England and Wales (Courtenay and McAleese 1994), and a major national study of 5000 households to measure social and economic change, the British Household Panel Survey (Scott 1995).

Survey design has a major effect on the questions that can be studied and, not surprisingly, the most interesting questions can sometimes only be answered using the most complex and expensive surveys. The case in point here is educational attainment (see Figure 10.2). The question that a cross-sectional study will help us answer is: how do ethnic differences in educational attainment in 2001 compare with those in 1991? A very interesting question that only a longitudinal survey can address is: how did people in different ethnic groups and different age groups improve their qualifications by part-time study between 1991 and 2001? The Census does, in fact, have a longitudinal sample survey associated with it which will, in all probability, enable such questions to be answered from the next Census.

The second question is about sampling and the representativeness of the results. This would appear to be trivial here because this is the Population Census and so no sampling has been involved. Yet even here there is need for caution, due to bias introduced by non-response. There was a 2 per cent under-count in the Census (the so called 'missing million') and this differentially affected ethnic minorities. The undercount for the Black African group is estimated to be 5 per cent (Simpson 1996).

The third question is about the operationalization of the ethnic categories here. (Operationalization is about specifying specific variables in a way which can be quantitatively measured.) There has been a large volume of debate about this, particularly in the context of the 1991 Population Census (Bulmer 1996). There have been long and detailed discussions over two decades about the most effective way to ask questions on ethnicity in the Population Census (Drew 1980) and there are current moves to revise the ethnic question for the 2001 Population Census (Aspinall 1996). There is a difficult compromise between what is practical, what is reliable and what is valid. The practicalities are that government wants a question appropriate for its use in policy analysis and needs to collect data with samples large enough to identify these groups. The reliability issue is illustrated by the fact that, in the USA, it has been found that people may self-classify themselves in two different ways within a short space of time; for example, as Hispanic on one occasion and white on another (Farley and Levin 1982), and this was likely to have been a problem in the Population Census here. The validity issue is about what ethnicity means and how ethnic, cultural, religious and nationality groupings can be adequately described. To give a very small but important example, the term 'Asian' has often been used to describe people from a number of countries

(India, Pakistan and Bangladesh) and a number of religions (Moslems and Hindus, for example). It is generally agreed that such a description has limited utility now because so many groups are included together. It is unusual now, relative to a decade ago, to see Asians discussed as though they are a homogeneous group, even though limitations in the data sometimes force us still to group together data in this way.

The fourth question is about the outcome measures used in the analysis. What measure of outcome has been used and has the analysis been carried out in the most appropriate way? There are many ways in which educational attainment could be measured. This depends on the stage of education. At 23, for example, this could include A-level passes, vocational qualifications and degree and diploma results. At 16 the focus is usually on General Certificate of Secondary Education (GCSE) results. There is a second issue though and this is how success at GCSE is operationalized. Should the number of passes be used? Should a score be created which combines the grades obtained for each subject, giving for example a score of seven for grade A, a score six for grade B, a score of five for grade C and so on? For a group of individuals, should the percentage that reach a certain threshold be calculated? For example, the percentage obtaining five or more GCSE passes at grades A–C? Should the number of such passes be expressed as a percentage of all pupils in the group or only of all those entered for the examination? All these choices have ramifications for the way the results can be analysed and interpreted.

One answer is to use the measure that gives the most information about results, so in this case the GCSE score appears to be a useful one combining as it does a measure of the grades of passes as well as the number of them. (For example, six grade Bs and one grade C gives a score of 41). Another answer is to highlight high attainment, a measure which may have a direct appeal when emphasizing achievement. However, the latter may be a rather deceptive indicator because using a threshold value of attainment may exaggerate group differences. Take for example the data on diploma and degree results (see Figure 10.2). A relatively small number of people in general have degree or diploma level qualifications (about one in seven overall). This means that, in statistical terms, the focus of such measures is on the tail of the attainment distribution. Put another way, it may be the case that 19 per cent of Indian males have diplomas and degrees compared with 10 per cent of Pakistani males, a nearly twofold difference, but this gives us no information about the large majority of either group who have no such qualifications. We found this to be an important consideration when analysing GCSE results using the Youth Cohort Study of England and Wales (YCS) (Drew 1995). In analyses we carried out in the late 1980s, the measure of high attainment used was obtaining five passes at grades A–C, a commonly utilized measure because such students usually stay on at school or college beyond the age of 16. It was found that only 7 per cent of African Caribbeans reached this threshold compared with 21 per cent of whites, a three-fold difference. If, on the other hand, a measure of overall group performance is obtained using a score then a very different picture emerges. The overall exam score was 17 for African Caribbeans and 22 for whites, which shows a much smaller difference. Clearly the threshold measure suggests a poor performance for the African Caribbean group whilst the overall score suggests a rather more optimistic picture. It actually took us quite a long time in our own research on this subject to realize the very simple statistical point that a focus on extremes could be somewhat misleading. Poor high attainment for a group is not the same as poor average attainment.

The fifth question is about contextualizing the analysis. The model used in this example is a very simple one in which ethnicity and gender differences are analysed. What other factors have been used to place the ethnic differences in context? One of the failings of research on ethnic differences in educational attainment in the decade since the Swann report has been the lack of attention to social class differences (see Burnhill *et al.* 1990) and how this particularly affects Black and Asian young people. At an individual level it seems natural to feel the need to distinguish between, for example, the experiences of a Pakistani girl from a comfortably middle-class background with professional parents from that of a Pakistani girl whose parents are unemployed and who lives in a poor inner city area. Although studies have focused over many decades on the social class differences in education such research has not previously also included an ethnic dimension. Also, many of the studies on ethnic differences in the 1980s were either carried out in London or in Local Education Authorities (LEAs) with relatively large numbers of ethnic minority students and this, therefore, did not give a representative view of outcomes at a national level until data became available in the Youth Cohort Study of England and Wales, a nationally representative study funded by what is now the Department for Education and Employment (Drew 1995). The reason for this is that results for, say, London schools cannot be generalized beyond London. For one thing the GCSE results for London are, for a variety of reasons, considerably lower than for other parts of the country and furthermore the social class composition of the inner part of London is very different from that of other areas. This relates very directly to the question of population definition. If the focus is on inner London schools then pupils in such schools are defined to be the survey population and, if the sampling is appropriately carried out, the results will be representative of that population. It is not necessarily the case that the results can be generalized to other areas. If such generalizations had been made in 1985, for example, we would have concluded that nearly twice as many Asians as whites obtain five or more GCSE passes at the higher grades (Kysel 1988). An analysis on the other hand of the YCS data shows that the results for Asians and whites were very similar at this particular time.

The interaction between gender, social class and ethnic differences in GCSE attainment in the YCS are shown in Figure 10.3. This uses the scoring system mentioned earlier – i.e. a score of seven for a grade A, a score of six for a grade B and so on. The analysis shows that whilst ethnic differences are quite large, social class differences are even greater. Whilst African Caribbean young people perform less well than their white and Asian counterparts we find that black middle-class pupils perform well at GCSE and white working-class males perform poorly. The stereotyped view of high Asian achievement and low African Caribbean achievement is therefore seen to be an oversimplification and it is to be hoped that such analyses will become more common to

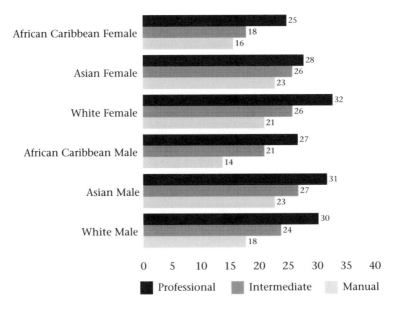

Figure 10.3 Average exam score by ethnic origin, sex and socio-economic group
Source: Drew and Gray 1990: 114

break down the stereotypes that a focus on group differences helps to maintain.

These questions about research designs, sampling and data reliability, ethnic classification, choice of outcome variables and choice of appropriate contextual variables recur with regularity. Comparisons between this and related studies is shown in Table 10.2. This table shows the way in which studies in this area have increased in size and complexity since the early 1980s. The earliest studies were based on a small number of schools in particular areas with a very limited number of control variables and so the studies lacked reliability, validity, and generalizability.

The YCS is a longitudinal survey in which individuals are questioned three times over a 30 month period, commencing at age 16. This enables quite detailed analysis to be carried out of the first three years of post-compulsory education. The response rate is high, nearly 80 per cent for each sweep of the cohort – very high for a postal survey. Since the analysis of the GCSE results was for data from the first sweep, non-response is not so great a problem. Nevertheless this does create problems for the later sweeps of the survey, for example when studying A-level results, because the attrition is cumulative. If the response rate for each sweep is approximately 80 per cent (and in fact it was only slightly lower than this in practice) by the end of the third sweep the response rate overall will be:

0.8 x 0.8 x 0.8 = 0.512

Table 10.2 Features of British studies comparing examination performance at age 16 for ethnic minority groups

Study and authors	Year of exam results	Sample size (total) Afro-Caribbean Asian	Nature of sample	Controls for social background and intake
Maughan and Rutter (1986)	1972	2866 250 Not stated	12 non-selective secondary schools in 6 Inner London boroughs	Gender, 7 point teacher ratings of verbal reasoning at 11, reading test score at 14
Driver (1980)	1974–7	2310 590 580	5 comprehensives in 5 LEAs in the north, the Midlands and the Home Counties	Gender
Mabey (1986)	1976	21,662 2382 389	All pupils in single cohort of Inner London Education Authority (ILEA) schools	Gender, reading attainment at 15, verbal reasoning at secondary school transfer
Craft and Craft (1983)	1979	2237 207 524	16 schools in one Outer London borough	Gender, social class
Eggleston et al. (1986)	1981	562 110 157	23 comprehensives in 6 LEAs	Gender
DES (1985)	1979	6196 718 466	A 10 per cent sample of pupils in 6/5* LEAs with high numbers of ethnic minority pupils	None
	1982	5942 653 571		
Kysel (1988)	1985	17,058 5981 1124	All pupils in a single cohort of ILEA schools	Gender, verbal reasoning band (3 groups)
Drew and Gray (1990)	1985	14,429 244 435	Random sample of 2362 maintained schools in England and Wales	Gender, socio-economic group
Smith and Tomlinson (1989)	1986	1154 146 664	18 schools in 4 LEAs	Gender, socio-economic group, second year reading score
Nuttall et al. (1989)	1985–7	31,623 Not stated Not stated	Pupils in 3 cohorts of ILEA schools	Gender, verbal reasoning band, school type and proportion with free school meals

Source: Drew and Gray 1991: 161
* Note: 6 LEAs in relation to 1979 study and 5 LEAs in relation to 1982 study.

That is, about 50 per cent. This gives quite serious cause for concern about response bias, because those respondents that continue to reply in different sweeps of a survey will have rather different characteristics to those who have left the sample for whatever reason. The size of the non-response bias is itself a subject of study in surveys of this size. Comparisons are made between the survey results and those of another available data set. In this case the population distributions were compared with those from the Labour Force Survey and the examination results with those provided by the Department for Education and Employment (see Drew 1995). Some biases were evident. The way this is conventionally dealt with in surveys is to reweight data at the analysis stage using known characteristics. In the case of YCS these characteristics were gender, region, school type, attainment and whether the respondent was a stayer or leaver at 16. The data is reweighted so that, for example, the regional distribution is the same as that of the external data source. In addition considerable efforts have now been made to reduce the survey attrition by recontacting young people who had not returned survey questionnaires at an early sweep (Courtenay *et al.* 1994).

Although there are limitations to all studies, even large surveys, and the problem of survey attrition is particularly acute for longitudinal studies, it remains the case that the more general availability of large government-funded data sets represents a major advance for research in this area and the greater availability of data is to be warmly welcomed.

Case two: Transitions from 16–19

The process of taking GCSEs at the age of 16 is, for many young people, the beginning of a period of post-compulsory education which leads to A levels or vocational qualifications and possibly university. Levels of attainment at 16 and 18 are crucial to a successful transition to the next stage. Important decision points within the system in England and Wales are first the decision to stay on at 16 and second the decision at 18 about whether or not to go to university. (For students of vocational courses there are other slightly different possibilities.) The purpose of modelling here is to unravel the factors which affect the decision to stay on. There are a variety of 'push' and 'pull' factors which contribute to the decision to stay on at 16. The 'push' factors relate to young people's attainments, aspirations, experiences and expectations of post-compulsory education. The 'pull' factors are about the attractions of work and income (Raffe and Willms 1989; Micklewright *et al.* 1990). Local labour markets and unemployment have a number of effects. If youth unemployment is high, this may tend to discourage early leaving (the 'discouraged worker' effect) but, on the other hand, parental unemployment works in the opposite direction, encouraging early leaving because the family needs a wage earner. Whether or not these various factors operate in a similar way for ethnic minority young people relative to white young people is an interesting question.

Before considering the decision to stay on at 16 using a logit model, it is worth examining the general pattern of participation from 16–19. This is

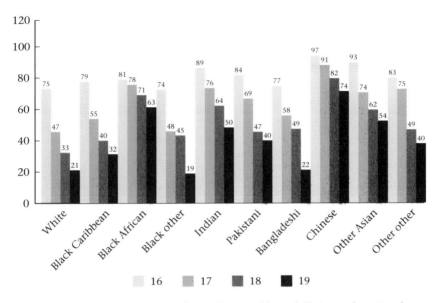

Figure 10.4 Participation rates of 16–19-year-olds in full-time education by age and ethnic group
Source: Drew *et al.* 1997: 19

illustrated in Figure 10.4, using data from the 1991 Population Census (Drew *et al.* 1997). The participation rates of all ethnic minority groups in 1991 was higher than that for whites, suggesting a high commitment of ethnic minority young people in general to education post 16. Some groups have particularly high staying-on rates – for example, black Africans, Indians, other Asians and the Chinese. This participation remains at over 50 per cent of the cohort at the age of 19. Gender differences are also of importance with more females than males in general staying on, but this *not* being the case for some ethnic minority groups – for example, Pakistanis and Bangladeshis. Variations in course participation are also complex.

For the logit model, the focus is on the decision about whether or not to stay on at 16 and the factors that affect this. For this model, data from the Youth Cohort Study of England and Wales is used, based on a postal survey of 28,000 young people (Drew 1995). For this model, the variables used are attainment, ethnic origin, social class, gender, parental education and whether or not the family is a single parent family (see Table 10.3). As discussed before there are two ways to approach this. One is to obtain a measure of how useful the model is by measuring how much variability is explained by the model, and the second is to measure the relative importance of particular variables. The deviance shown in the table reflects the variability accounted for as each of the variables enter the model. For example, the attainment in GCSE is the single most important factor in determining staying on, and has the highest explained deviance. The overall adequacy of the model is measured by a single

Table 10.3   Staying on in full-time education at 16: a logit model*

	Deviance explained	Degrees of freedom	Estimate	Standard error	Odds ratio
Grand mean			1.94	0.07	–
Attainment	4540	2	–	–	–
4+ higher grades	–	–	–	–	1.0
1–3 higher grades	–	–	−1.59	0.05	0.2
0 higher grades	–	–	−2.82	0.05	0.1
Ethnic origin	299	3	–	–	–
White	–	–	–	–	1.0
Afro-Caribbean	–	–	1.17	0.16	3.2
Asian	–	–	2.35	0.16	10.5
Other	–	–	0.18	0.11	1.2
Social class	248	3	–	–	–
Professional	–	–	–	–	1.0
Intermediate	–	–	−0.18	0.05	0.8
Manual	–	–	−0.67	0.05	0.5
Gender	132	1	–	–	–
Male	–	–	–	–	1.0
Female	–	–	0.46	0.04	1.6
Parental education	66	1	–	–	–
Graduate	–	–	–	–	1.0
Non-graduate	–	–	−0.51	0.06	0.6
No. of parents	7	1	–	–	–
Two parents	–	–	–	–	1.0
Single parent	–	–	−0.16	0.06	0.9

Pseudo R-square	0.95
Deviance for grand mean	5571 with 226 degrees of freedom
Deviance for model	279 with 216 degrees of freedom

Notes:
* Base groups are those with 4+ higher grade passes, white, parents in professional occupations, male, graduate parents, two-parent families.

Source: Drew 1995: 102

measure of goodness of fit, here called a pseudo R-square, of 0.95 in this case. This means that 95 per cent of the variation in the data is explained by the model, with 5 per cent left unexplained. Such a small unexplained variation is uncommon, and means the model is fitting well.

The parameter estimates reflect the difference each variable makes. These are reflected in logit models by odds ratios which reflect the increased probability of staying on, relative to a comparison group. For example, the odds ratio for females is 1.6 (the comparison group being males) which means that the odds of staying on for females is 60 per cent higher relative to males, other factors having been taken into account.

The substantive point to be made about this particular model is that compared with all other factors it is ethnicity that has the highest odds ratios, particularly for Asians and African Caribbeans. It has already been seen in Figure 10.4 that the participation rates for ethnic minority young people are very high and this result shows that when attainment and other character-istics are taken into account the staying-on rates are still high for ethnic minorities relative to the white group.

The addition of particular variables in this model throws ethnic differences into sharp relief. In the original model (see Table 10.3) there are a number of factors which are correlated with ethnic origin which would lead us to expect a low staying-on rate for black and Asian young people. For example, social class, parental education and, for African Caribbeans, lone parents. Coming from a single parent family, having a working-class background and having non-graduate parents are all characteristics which are associated with a reduced probability of staying on, even after educational background is taken into account. These are family characteristics which some members of some ethnic minority groups are more likely than white young people to have. The high staying-on rates of these groups, despite such disadvantages, is thus quite striking. (See Cheng 1994 and Drew *et al.* 1997 for later analyses.)

A very similar model was fitted to YCS data for transitions into the labour market at 19. One of these was for the probability of being unemployed at 19 (Drew 1995). This model also showed high odds ratios for the probability of being unemployed, showing that African Caribbean and Asian young people with a similar educational background to white young people had a much higher chance of being unemployed (by a factor between 1.5 and 2.2). This corroborates evidence from other studies using tester applicants for jobs indi-cating levels of discrimination by employers as bad as those in the early 1970s (Brown and Gay 1985). It also shows the need for triangulation where a number of research methods are used to approach a research problem from different directions.

Case three: Ethnicity and school effectiveness

As part of their commitment to parental choice the Department of Education and Science (DES) published in 1992 the first set of secondary school league tables. The tables consisted of statistics at school level – for example, the per-centage of pupils with five or more GCSE passes at grade C and above. The main problem with these statistics was their inability to provide a valid basis for comparison between schools because prior attainment and other factors of importance had not been taken into account. This meant that it was impossible to determine whether a high league table position was an indi-cation of a particularly academically effective school or that the students were particularly academically able. Critics of such tables argued that by including measurements of student attainment on *entry* to a school into the analysis (and other factors), then the academic progress of a pupil through secondary school could be measured. This approach, which uses multilevel modelling, is sometimes described as 'value added' as it is trying to measure the academic value the school experience adds to an individual student. (For an introduction to the use of multilevel modelling in educational research see Gray and Wilcox 1995.)

Mutilevel models are designed to analyse hierarchically structured data which is particularly relevant to studies of schools. Pupils are clustered together in classes which are clustered together in schools which are themselves clustered into LEAs, and the analysis can then be considered on all these levels. Prior to multilevel techniques the hierarchical structure of such data system was largely ignored.

Multilevel modelling builds upon regression techniques which have been described earlier in this chapter. Initially a regression line is fitted that shows a linear relationship between a pupil's academic performance on entry to a school, and their performance at GCSE, for each school separately (see Figure 10.5a). Each school is represented by a line and each line is the best fitting line for the pupils within a particular school. Other characteristics of the pupil, which might also affect a pupil's attainment (for example, ethnicity, gender and social class) are also included into the model. There is an overall relationship for all schools taken together – an overall line reflecting the average for all schools (not shown in Figure 10.5). This stage is called the 'fixed effects' part of the model.

From this regression line significant differences between all pupils in the study can be calculated in terms of GCSE points. For example, pupils who displayed high academic performance on entry to the school could be found to have a higher GCSE score on average than pupils who displayed a low academic performance on entry. As well as analysing the differences between pupils, the differences between schools can also be analysed at this stage. Schools whose regression line falls above the overall line are seen as being more effective, on average, than expected (taking prior attainment and background characteristics of pupils into account) and those below the line less effective than expected. (Only schools for which the line is more than two standard deviations above the expected line would be regarded as significantly more effective on average than expected.) The spread of all the lines represents the difference in effectiveness between all schools, and it is from this that the measure of the school effect is calculated. In many applications the lines are assumed to be parallel and the differences between the schools is assumed to be the same whether pupils are at the lower or higher end of ability range. If the lines are not assumed to be parallel and they vary in slope (as illustrated in Figure 10.5b) then this allows us to focus on differential school effectiveness. For example, if the lines representing two schools cross, then the school with the steepest slope is comparatively more effective with its high ability pupils and less effective with its low ability pupils.

As with all statistical studies, the adequacy of the model depends heavily on the operationalization of the key variables and on the appropriateness of the sampling methodology. In terms of ethnicity, some interesting questions that multilevel modelling techniques allow us to investigate are:

- What are the differences in academic progress, on average, between ethnic groups once prior attainment, gender, social class and other factors have been taken into account ?

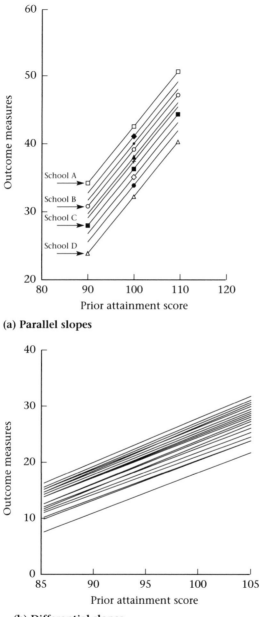

(a) Parallel slopes

(b) Differential slopes

Figure 10.5 Multilevel models with parallel or differential slopes
Source: Gray and Wilcox 1995: 220

- Which schools are particularly effective (or ineffective) on average for ethnic minority groups?
- Is there any evidence to suggest that schools are differentially effective in respect of specific ethnic minority groups – that is, are some schools significantly more effective on average for one ethnic group while simultaneously being significantly less effective on average for another?
- What are the characteristics of schools that are particularly effective for ethnic minority young people, and are these different from the characteristics that make schools effective for white pupils?

In order to discuss the strengths and weaknesses of this multilevel approach we will focus on two school effectiveness studies both carried out at London University Institute of Education. The first was carried out in Inner London for the Association of Metropolitan Authorities (AMA) over the three year period 1990–2 (Thomas *et al.* 1994; Thomas *et al.* 1996). The second was carried out in 1993 and analysed GCSE examination results in Lancashire (Thomas and Mortimore 1994, 1996). Both focused on GCSE results and the results of both these studies can be seen in Table 10.4. In both studies the outcome variable was the GCSE points score. The scoring system is the same as that used in the YCS study: seven points to a grade A, six points to a grade B, five points to a grade C and so on. Thus, a student with four subjects at grade C scores 20 points.

A number of the issues raised in the first case study (for example, on sampling methodology or the operationalization of the variables) also apply here, but for this case study discussion of these problems will be kept to a minimum except to mention non-response bias. This was a feature of both studies; a sizeable proportion of both the Lancashire and London samples had to be excluded because of lack of information concerning their prior attainment scores. Students with no prior attainment score obtained much lower GCSE scores on average (20 points) than students with a prior attainment score (27 points). Thus the estimates of attainment for individuals and means for schools will be biased upwards. Whilst the effect of this bias on the absolute level of scores is clear, the effect of the bias on the measurement of the size of school effects is less obvious.

The variables considered for inclusion in the fixed part of the models are shown in Table 10.4. The most important of these is prior attainment, as would be expected. In the London study this is measured using one indicator, the verbal reasoning band, and in the Lancashire study, using the three NFER (National Foundation for Educational Research) cognitive ability tests. As the London study uses an indicator with only three bands this controls in rather a crude way for prior attainment. That is to say, within one of the prior attainment bands we would expect to find quite a wide range of ability at secondary school entry and this means that as a predictor the ability band will be poor. In comparison, the use of three tests at 11 in the Lancashire study represents a rather more sophisticated attempt to control for prior knowledge and skills.

It is not surprising to find that prior attainment accounts for more of the variation in GCSE outcomes than any other factor. But other factors are also of importance. Gender is one of these because it is consistently found that girls

Table 10.4 Details of two quantitative studies of school effectiveness using multilevel modelling techniques

Study and authors	Location	Year of exam results	Sample sizes	Nature of sample	Non-response	Student level variables	School level variables
Thomas et al. 1994 Thomas et al. 1996	Inner London	1990 1991 1992	4633 (42 schools) 11,334 (116 schools) 11,875 (87 schools)	1992 sample: 11,875 15+ pupils in 87 secondary schools across 7 LEAs	18 per cent lost due to incomplete prior attainment scores; 3 per cent lost due to other incomplete data	Prior attainment (verbal reasoning band 1–3); gender; entitlement to free school meals (FSM); ethnicity (DfE defined)	School status (county/voluntary); coeducational or not; percentage absence on given day; percentage FSM; percentage of pupils for whom English is second language
Thomas and Mortimore 1994, 1996	Lancashire	1993	8566 (79 schools)	11,881 15+ pupils in 87 secondary schools	28 per cent lost due to incomplete prior attainment scores	Prior attainment (NFER cognitive abilities tests: verbal (VQ); quantitative (QQ); non-verbal (NQ)); gender; FSM; ethnicity; pupil mobility (no. of years in UK secondary schools and no. of previous secondary schools attended); special needs; child statemented or not; 30 pupil level census measures	30 school level census variables matched to pupil level census measures Aggregated pupil level data: size of school (as above); status (as above); coeducational? (as above); FSM (as above); percentage of Asian students; percentage of low attainers on entry (band 3); percentage high attainers on entry (band 1)

obtain better results than boys. Social class is also of importance because of the advantages that accrue to those whose parents are in professional and managerial occupations. In these studies social background is reflected in a measure based on whether or not a pupil has free school meals, but this is a crude dichotomy and of limited value as a measure of social class background, although it does give a limited indication of the relative disadvantage of being in a very low income group.

The results for the London data show the importance of prior attainment. The difference in attainment between a pupil in verbal reasoning (VR) band 3 and VR band 1 is equivalent to more than five subjects at grade C in GCSE. The effects of the other factors are that girls, on average, have higher attainment than boys and that pupils from socially disadvantaged backgrounds do less well. In the Lancashire study, census variables were included as proxy measures of socio-economic status and whilst some of these were statistically significant they also depended on simple dichotomies and are unlikely to adequately reflect the full effect of social background on GCSE attainment.

From the results in Table 10.5 it can be seen that ethnic minority young people make better progress on average than their white counterparts (with one small exception, the 'other' group). Comparing the progress of ethnic groups with studies into levels of examination attainment, an interesting difference is found. In terms of the raw results the white group obtained higher GCSE scores than other ethnic groups except the Chinese (not shown in Table 10.5) but in terms of progress through secondary school, this picture is reversed. All ethnic minority groups obtained higher GCSE scores once background factors are taken into account (except for the black Caribbean and black other groups, where the differences were not statistically significant). This suggests that the academic progress of ethnic minority young people (particularly the Chinese) through secondary school is greater on average than the white group. One explanation put forward by both studies for this finding is that students for whom English is a second language (and are from particular ethnic groups) begin secondary school as low attainers but make substantial progress as they become fluent (Thomas *et al.* 1994 and Thomas and Mortimore 1994). This effect is particularly evident in language subjects. Another interpretation is that this progress reflects the high commitment of many ethnic minority young people to education both at the secondary school level and beyond into further and higher education (Modood and Shiner 1994; Drew *et al.* 1997).

The purpose of modelling is to measure the separate influences of different factors but it is important not to lose sight of the complex interconnecting process that may deny some pupils equal opportunities to succeed. We know that ethnicity, social class and gender are interrelated but the models used are all additive ones, so the effects are simply added together. For example, for the London data (see Table 10.5) black African pupils apparently have an advantage over white pupils (by +4.6 points) but those having free school meals do less well (by −4.5 points). These two factors offset each other so that we estimate that black Africans from low income households are making progress that is relatively poor. In school effectiveness modelling, the progress of ethnic minority

Table 10.5 Fixed part of multilevel models used in the analyses of total GCSE scores in London (1992) and Lancashire (1993)

Fixed part	Association of Metropolitan Authorities	Lancashire
Prior attainment		
Verbal reasoning band 1 (verbal reasoning band 3)	+27.9	–
VR1 v. VR2	+13.0	–
Verbal CAT subtest[1]	–	+0.52
Quantitative CAT subtest[1]	–	+0.41
Non-verbal CAT subtest[1]	–	+0.19
Gender		
Girls v. Boys	+3.2	+4.1
Ethnicity		
Black (African) v. white	+4.6	+6.9
Black (Caribbean) v. white	(−0.6)	(+2.5)
Black (other) v. white	(+0.3)	(−5.3)
Indian v. white	+8.2	+9.5
Pakistani v. white	+7.2	+9.0
Bangladeshi v. white	+6.3	+10.6
Chinese v. white	+10.7	+17.3
Other v. white	+5.7	−2.5
Social economic status		
Free school meals v. no free school meals	−4.5	−4.8
Percentage head of household in registrars generals social class five[2]	–	−0.3
Percentage persons 18+ with higher education qualification[2]	–	+0.1
Pupil mobility		
Previous school v. no previous school	–	−3.1
Less than 5 years UK education v. 5 years UK education	–	−11.04
Other factors		
Age[3]	–	+0.2

Source: Table constructed from those found in the following two papers: Thomas *et al.* 1994; Thomas and Mortimore 1994

Notes:
[1] per point on subtest
[2] per percentage point
[3] per month
(Figures in brackets = not significant)

CAT = Cognitive Ability Tests

pupils will be judged after taking account of social class and other factors. This means that the disadvantage that ethnic minority children from low income families experience will be measured in, for example, the social class variable as well as the ethnic variable. Such disadvantage should not be overlooked.

The misunderstanding that may arise when attainment and progress are confused was illustrated by the publicity given to a similar earlier study by

Smith and Tomlinson (1989). Some right-wing commentators in the press gleefully pointed to the good progress of ethnic minority children in secondary schools. For example, Ray Honeyford commented that

> a damning reversal of everything the race relations industry has pumped out about ethnic children's educational prospects in this country . . . West Indian and Asian children, the study found, are doing as well in our schools as white children – and in some cases better – I would advise our schools to learn several lessons from this report. Forget about skin colour. Forget about race.
>
> *(Daily Mail*, 9 June 1989)

This is a misinterpretation of the research in this area. At the time we pointed out that many teachers now cite 'the school effect' as evidence that there is no longer a problem of underachievement (of ethnic groups) in English schools and, hence, that 'race' is no longer an educational issue. However, in terms of achievement there still is a gap between white and other ethnic groups. Progress through secondary school is greater on average for minority ethnic groups but not large enough to close the gap in achievement completely (Gillborn and Drew 1992).

Earlier in this chapter the data from Sierra Leone was used to show how a model's adequacy could be discussed using the idea of explained variation. As a model is improved by the addition of new factors the variance explained is increased. With multilevel models this concept has to be widened because there is variability both at the level of the individual and the level of the school, so these need to be discussed separately.

Most of the variation in GCSE scores can be explained by the prior attainment of pupils and their socio-economic characteristics. For London, 64 per cent of the school level variation in GCSE scores was explained by such factors and for Lancashire it was 72 per cent. This shows that once account has been taken of prior attainment and other characteristics of the students in each school there is much less variation between schools than it at first appears. A school effect was identified in both of the studies; 12 per cent of the variation in GCSE scores for London and 10 per cent of the variation in the case of Lancashire was found to be attributable to schools, once background factors had been controlled for. These findings are consistent with those of previous studies and highlight that the effect of a school is but a small proportion of the combined effects of background factors such as academic ability and social position in determining the GCSE scores of a student. Nevertheless, school effects are significant.

The analysis up to now assumes that the differences between the schools is the same whether the pupils are at the lower or higher end of the ability range. This is reflected in the parallel slopes in Figure 10.5. If the slopes are assumed to be different then the analysis can tackle the question: are some schools more effective than others for pupils of high prior attainment and other schools more effective with pupils of relatively low prior attainment? The question can also be asked: are some schools more effective with ethnic minority students than others? Whilst there is some evidence of differential effectiveness for ethnic minority groups from the London study, this issue has not yet been fully explored. We concluded in 1991 that none of the studies to date provided convincing evidence about the school's contribution to the gap in the attainment of white and ethnic minority young people and this conclusion still holds (Drew and Gray 1991).

How then have the London and Lancashire studies helped in addressing the questions regarding ethnicity and GCSE attainment posed earlier in this section?

- It has been shown that when ethnicity is studied (while controlling for factors such as prior attainment, gender and social class) there are still significant differences between certain ethnic groups. When compared with the white group, most other ethnic groups are shown to perform significantly better on average and none performed significantly worse. This partially obscures the fact that in terms of actual raw performance there remains a 'black–white gap'.
- Schools which were particularly effective (or ineffective) in teaching certain ethnic groups when background factors have been controlled for were not identified in either study but the quantitative methods could be used to identify such schools for further investigation using qualitative case study methods.
- Some schools perform better than expected for some ethnic groups while performing worse than expected for other groups. The extent of this has yet to be satisfactorily explored in a large-scale study. To date we lack a study with a sufficient number of pupils and schools covering a sufficient range of variables, with a nationally representative sample, combining both qualitative and quantitative forms of data gathering to answer these questions.

In terms of the original questions posed earlier in this section (see p. 158) only the first of these is satisfactorily answered by these multilevel studies but the relative importance of teaching methods, individual teachers, discipline, departmental differences, class size, school ethos, the headteacher and other factors are difficult to assess. The significance of such factors for ethnic minority pupils has also yet to be assessed in studies of this kind.

Conclusion

The aim of this chapter has been to set out the methodology for carrying out a piece of statistical research and then to give three case studies: the study of ethnic differences in educational attainment at 16; the study of educational differences in transitions from 16–19; and the study of ethnicity and school effectiveness. The case studies have shown that much has changed in the last decade and there have been improvements in the way the subject has been researched and the data analysed.

First of all there are the changes in the last decade in children's educational progress. Despite the pressures on schools and teachers, the educational achievements of the large number of black and Asian young people who have moved successfully through secondary school and post-compulsory education into higher education have been considerable (see Modood and Shiner 1994 for data on university entrance). Although this gives some cause for optimism there is also cause for concern, particularly about the achievements of some African Caribbean, Pakistani and Bangladeshi pupils. Furthermore, the under-achievement of working-class children in schools is a serious issue and this affects black and Asian children coming from working-class backgrounds just as it affects white children. When these young people seek work, the prospects for employment are not good and the qualifications of black and Asian young people appear not to have the same value in the labour market as those of their white counterparts.

Second, there have been changes in research methodology in the last decade. Although the cost of data collection is still high, advances in computing have meant that the cost of data transfer and data analysis have become much lower. Does this mean that data will become more freely available? There has been a welcome shift in this direction so that data producers (for example government departments) can and will make their data available to users in universities, local authorities and in other public sector research bodies. But there is still a long way to go.

As for research on ethnicity, we now have much more *statistical* research. The picture that has emerged in recent years is very different from the crude picture of underachievement painted in the Swann report in 1985 – a picture which could easily lead to a caricature of all Asian young people as docile and diligent and all black young people as failures. The progress of pupils can now be compared with those of like academic and social backgrounds rather than the previous simplistic analyses which looked at differences without taking other factors into account.

In some ways, multilevel models have failed to answer some of the most important questions about ethnic minority young people and educational attainment. The effect of home background tends to be understated in these models and when it comes to the school effects themselves the question of differential school effectiveness – i.e. whether or not African Caribbean and Asian young people make better progress in some schools rather than others – has not been adequately addressed. Modelling school effects tends to lead, by definition, to a focus on school differences. If this leads to increased funding to schools in inner city areas this could bring benefit to ethnic minority young people living in those areas. But to suggest that ethnic differences are relatively unimportant and that the main need is for general school improvement is a mistake. An overall view needs to be taken of the educational progress of children through secondary school as well as the social disadvantage some African Caribbean and Asian young people experience, and of the gap between ethnic minority and white young people that develops at the primary and junior school level.

This leads inexorably to the conclusion that what is really needed is an overall view of what happens to young people from birth to the end of their schooling, using longitudinal research. Only then could the effects of the home environment, the junior school and the secondary school be unravelled. Such a study would be very expensive and there would be a time factor – the results would take two decades to produce! It is more realistic to propose that we continue to bring together the results of large government funded surveys, together with LEA-produced research, smaller studies, and qualitative research to produce a triangulated picture. There is an urgent need that such a project continues.

Writing in 1984, Barry Troyna warned that 'the greatest danger lies in the possibility that ill-conceived and poorly formulated studies will perpetuate the notion of black underachievement as a given rather than a problematic that requires sensitive interrogation' (Troyna 1984: 64). More than a decade later it is safe to conclude that the notion of black underachievement is not assumed as given. However, there is always a need for vigilance about bad research and carefully conceived and well formulated studies are as crucial as ever. The need for sensitive interrogation continues.

Glossary

Advances in statistical techniques are, as in all academic disciplines, accompanied by the development of language. Many of the following terms are explained in the main part of the text but we thought it would be useful to provide a glossary of some of the statistical terms that have been used. The glossary has been adapted from O'Muircheartaigh and Francis (1981) and Vogt (1993).

analysis of variance   a test of statistical significance which is commonly used to test the effect of a number of different categorical variables on one interval scale outcome variable.

bias   a systematic and non-random (but not necessarily intentional) distortion in a result or sample. There are many possible sources of bias – for example biased questions, defective sampling frames and non-response.

causal inference   a conclusion drawn from a study designed in such a way that it is legitimate to infer cause. Most people who use this term mean that an experiment in which subjects are randomly assigned to control and experimental groups is the only design from which researchers can properly infer cause.

census   a complete enumeration of the survey population.

coefficient   in a regression equation, the number by which a predictor variable is multiplied. This is the gradient (or slope) in a straight line equation.

contextual factors   a possible explanatory variable relating to the context in which individuals are placed. Students may be advantaged by going to a school in which there are many high-achieving pupils. The percentage of pupils in the school with high levels of prior attainment could be a predictor of an individual's GCSE success. This is a contextual factor.

correlation   the extent to which two or more things are related (co-related) to one another. Usually measured by a correlation coefficient (ranges from –1, indicating perfect negative correlation, to +1, indicating perfect positive correlation).

cross-sectional study   a study using data referring to a particular point in time. Thus the analysis cannot take into account changes over time in the variables analysed. Much social survey data are of this type.

explanatory variable or independent variable   one of a number of predictor variables from which an outcome is said to have resulted. For example, in school effectiveness studies the academic attainment of a student on entry to a school is used to predict the students' performance in GCSE examinations.

goodness of fit   a measure of how well a model matches actual data. A measure of the agreement between observed and expected values.

heterogeneous   mixed or diverse; used to describe samples (and populations) with high variability.

homogeneous   the same or similar; used to refer to samples (and populations) that have low variability.

hypothesis   a supposition or conjective which acts as a starting point in an investigation, irrespective of its probable truth or falsity. In the most usual case the hypothesis is a null hypothesis – for example, that there is no difference between GCSE scores of boys and girls. Methods of testing are employed to decide whether or not to reject the null hypothesis.

intercept   the point at which a regression line crosses the vertical y axis, i.e. when the value on the x (horizontal) axis is zero. Also known as the regression constant.

logit model   a regression model where the outcome variable is binary. A binary variable has only two values, for example whether a student has passed or failed an examination.

longitudinal study   a study in which information is sought from the same sample of respondents on more than one occasion. Longitudinal studies provide a good opportunity for studying change over time, for example in circumstances or attitudes.

mean   (arithmetic mean) the total of a set of values divided by the number of them.

model   an attempt to summarize the complexity of the real world in the form of simplified statements or relationships. One of the most common forms of statistical model is a mathematical equation which presents a set of statistical relationships in a formal, mathematical language (for example, a regression equation).

multilevel model   a model that takes into account the natural hierarchy in the data and allows simultaneous analysis of these levels. For example, students are clustered in schools and schools are clustered within LEAs. This suggests a 3-level model of the data.

multiple regression model   a regression technique where a number of predictor variables (for example, prior attainment and background characteristics) are used to predict an outcome variable (for example, a GCSE score).

multivariate analysis   methods for examining a number of outcome variables at the same time.

operationalization   to define a variable or concept in such a way that it can be measured. For example, in the London and Lancashire school effectiveness studies, the socio-economic status of a student was operationalized on the basis of whether the student was in receipt of free school meals or not.

outcome or dependent variable   a variable which can be predicted by reference to other (predictor) variables.

population   a collection of units for analysis – for example, objects, people and organizations. The units could **be** children in schools or, at another level, the schools themselves.

random sampling   a sampling method that ensures that each member of a population has a known, non-zero probability of being included in the sample.

regression analysis   a method used to explain the variability of an outcome variable using information about one or more predictor variables. Regression analysis attempts to answer questions like: 'How well can I predict the GCSE score of a student (outcome variable – y) with knowledge of the student's academic attainment on entry to secondary school (independent variable – x)?'

residual   a model uses actual data from one source (say the x value) to predict an outcome variable (the y value). This prediction rarely corresponds exactly to the actual outcome, although hopefully the two will frequently be close. The difference between what is predicted for a particular case and what the actual outcome is, is known as a residual. If the actual outcome is higher than expected the residual is positive; if the actual outcome is lower than expected, the residual is negative.

sample   a group of units selected from the population. It may be too expensive to study the population as a whole but results may be generated from a carefully selected sample.

standard deviation   a statistical measure of the spread (or dispersion) of scores around the mean. The square root of the average sum of squared deviations from the mean.

standard error   a measure of sampling error; it refers to error in our estimates due to random fluctuations in our samples. The smaller the standard error the better the sample statistic is as an estimate of the population parameter.

statistically significant   a test of statistical significance is one where a sample set of data is tested against a null hypothesis for the population as a whole. Working with particular probability levels, rules are applied in order to either accept or reject the null hypothesis. An example of this would be a null hypothesis that the mean difference between male and female examination results in the population was zero. The significant test based on a sample of examination results would enable us to conclude whether or not this test hypothesis should be rejected.

survey   a research design in which a sample of subjects is drawn from a defined population and studied (usually using a questionnaire or interview) to make inferences or generalizations about the population.

triangulation   the use of a number of research methods to study a particular problem from a number of different perspectives. A study could, for example, include secondary analysis of data, a statistical sample survey and a qualitative study.

variance   a statistical measure of the spread (or dispersion) of scores around the mean. The square of the standard deviation. The average sum of squared deviations from the mean.

References

Aboud, F. (1988) *Children and Prejudice*. Oxford: Basil Blackwell.

Adelman, C. (1985) Who are you? Some problems of ethnographer culture shock, in R. G. Burgess (ed.) *Field Methods in the Study of Education*. London: Falmer Press.

Aitkin, M. and Longford, N. (1986) Statistical modelling in school effectiveness studies. *Journal of the Royal Statistical Society*, 149: 1–43.

Ali, Y. (1992) Muslim women and the politics of ethnicity and culture in Northern England, in G. Shagal and N. Yuval-Davis (eds) *Refusing Holy Orders*. London: Virago Press.

Apple, M.W. (1996) *Cultural Politics and Education*. Buckingham: Open University Press.

Aronowitz, S. and Giroux, H.A. (1991) *Postmodern Education: Politics, Culture and Social Criticism*. Oxford: University of Minnesota Press.

Asian Women Writer's Collective (1990) Acknowledgements, in R. Ahmad and R. Gupta (eds) *Flaming Spirits*. London: Virago Press.

Aspinall, P. (1996) *The Development of an Ethnic Group Question for the 2001 Census*. London: London Office for National Statistics.

Back, L. and Solomos, J. (1992) Doing research, writing politics: the dilemmas of political intervention in research on racism. Conference paper, Birkbeck College, University of London, 23 April.

Ball, S. J. (1985) Participant observation with students, in R. Burgess (ed.) *Qualitative Methods*. London: Falmer Press.

Ball, S. J. (1987) *The Micro-Politics of the School: Towards a Theory of School Organization*. London: Methuen.

Ball, S. J. (1990) Self-doubt and soft data: social and technical trajectories in ethnographic fieldwork. *International Journal of Qualitative Studies in Education*, 32 (2): 151–71.

Ball, S. J. (1994) Some reflections on policy theory: a brief response to Hatcher and Troyna. *Journal of Education Policy*, 9 (2): 171–82.

Ball, S. J. and Goodson, I. (eds) (1985a) *Teachers' Lives and Careers*. Lewes: Falmer Press.

Ball, S. J. and Goodson, I. (1985b) Understanding teachers: concepts and contexts, in S. J. Ball and I. Goodson (eds) *Teachers' Lives and Careers*. Lewes: Falmer Press.

Ball, W. (1990) A critique of methods and ideologies in research on race and education. Conference paper presented to XIIth World Congress of Sociology, 28 July–1 August.

Ball, W. (1991) The ethics and politics of doing anti-racist research in education: key debates and dilemmas. *European Journal of Intercultural Studies*, 2: 35–49.

Ball, W. (1992) Critical social research, adult education and anti-racist feminist praxis. *Studies in the Education of Adults*, 24: 1–25.

Banks, J. A. (1993) The canon debate, knowledge construction, and multicultural education. *Educational Researcher*, 22 (5): 4–14.

Banks, J. A. and Lynch, J. (eds) (1986) *Multicultural Education in Western Societies*. London: Holt.

Baudrillard, J. (1983) *Simulations*. New York: Semiotext(e).

Becker, H. S. (1964) Introduction, in H. S. Becker (ed.) *The Other Side*. New York: Free Press.

Becker, H. S. (1967) 'Whose side are we on?' *Social Problems*, 14: 239–47.

Becker, H. S. (1970) *Sociological Work: Method and Substance*. New Brunswick, NJ: Transaction Books.

Becker, H. S. (1971) Reply to Riley's 'Partisanship and objectivity'. *American Sociologist*, 6: 13.

Becker, H. S. and Horowitz, I. L. (1972) Radical politics and sociological research: observations on methodology and ideology. *American Journal of Sociology*, 78: 48–66.

Ben-Tovim, G., Gabriel, J., Law, I. and Stredder, K. (1986) *The Local Politics of Race*. London: Macmillan.

Ben-Tovim, G., Gabriel, J., Law, I. and Stredder, K. (1992) A political analysis of struggles for racial equality, in P. Braham, A. Rattansi and S. Skellington (eds) *Racism and Anti-Racism: Inequalities, Opportunities and Policies*. London: Sage.

Bertaux, D. (ed.) (1981) *Biography and Society: The Life History Approach in the Social Sciences*. Beverley Hills, CA: Sage.

Beynon, J. (1985) Institutional change and career histories in a comprehensive school, in S. Ball and I. Goodson (eds) *Teachers' Lives and Careers*. Lewes: Falmer.

Bhachu, P. (1991) Culture, ethnicity and class among Punjabi Sikh women in 1990s Britain. *New Community*, 17: 401–12.

Bhavnani, K. K. (1990) What's power got to do with it? empowerment and social research, in I. Porter and J. Shotter (eds) *Deconstructing Social Psychology*. London: Routledge.

Bhopal, K. (1994) Asian women within the family: patriarchy or patriarchies? Conference paper, University of Central Lancashire, British Sociological Association Annual Conference 'Sexualities in Context', 28–31 March.

Billingsley, A. (1970) Black families and white social science. *Journal of Social Issues*, 26: 127–42.

Blackman, I. and Perry, K. (1990) Skirting the issue: lesbian fashion in the 1990s. *Feminist Review*, 34: 67–78.

Blauner, B. (1994) Talking past each other: black and white languages, in F. L. Pincus and H. J. Ehrlich (eds) *Race and Ethnic Conflict*. Boulder, CO: Westview Press.

Bloor, D. (1976) *Knowledge and Social Imagery*. London: Routledge.

Blumer, H. (1979) *Critiques of Research in the Social Sciences: An Appraisal of Thomas and Znaniecki's 'The Polish Peasant in Europe and America' with a New Introduction*. New York: Social Science Research Council.

Bonnett, A. (1991) Forever white? Challenges and alternatives to a 'racial' monolith. *New Community*, 20 (1): 173–80.

Bourne, J. (1980) Cheerleaders and ombudsmen: the sociology of race relations in Britain. *Race and Class*, 21: 331–5.

Bradbury, M. (1975) *The History Man*. London: Secker and Warburg.

Brah, A. (1992) Difference, diversity and differentiation, in J. Donald and A. Rattansi (eds) *'Race', Culture and Difference*. London: Sage.

Brah, A. and Minhas, R. (1985) Structural racism or cultural difference: schooling for Asian girls, in G. Weiner (ed.) *Just a Bunch of Girls*. Milton Keynes: Open University Press.

Brah, A. and Shaw, S. (1992) *Working choices: South Asian young Muslim women and the labour market*. Research paper no. 91, Sheffield: Department of Employment.

Brannen, J. (1988) Research note: the study of sensitive subjects. *Sociological Review*, 36: 552–63.

Brar, H. S. (1991) Unequal opportunities: the recruitment selection and promotion prospects for black teachers. *Evaluation and Research in Education*, 5 (1 and 2): 35–47.

Brar, H. S. (1992) Unasked questions, impossible answers, the ethical problems of researching race and education, in M. Leicester and M. Taylor (eds) *Ethics, Ethnicity and Education*. London: Kogan Page.

Brewer, J. (1994) The ethnographic critique of ethnography: sectarianism in the RUC. *Sociology*, 28 (1): 231–44.

British Council of Churches Report (1976) *The New Black Presence in Britain*. London: British Council of Churches.

Britzman, D., Santiago-Valles, K., Jimenez-Munoz, G. and Lamash, M. (1993) Slips that show and tell: fashioning multiculture as a problem of representation, in C. McCarthy and W. Crichlow (eds) *Race, Identity and Representation in Education*. London: Routledge.

Broad, B. (1994) Anti-discriminatory practitioner social work research: some basic problems and possible remedies, in B. Humphries and C. Truman (eds) *Re-Thinking Social Research*. Aldershot: Avebury.

Brown, C. and Gay, P. (1985) *Racial Discrimination: 17 Years after the Act*. London: Policy Studies Institute.

Bulmer, M. (1986) Race and ethnicity, in R.G. Burgess (ed.) *Key Variables in Social Investigation*. London: Routledge.

Bulmer, M. (1996) The ethnic group question in the 1991 Census, in D. Coleman and J. Salt (eds) *Ethnicity in the 1991 Census, volume 1: Demographic Characteristics of the Ethnic Minority Populations*. London: HMSO.

Burgess, R. G. (ed.) (1984a) *The Research Process in Educational Settings: Ten Case Studies*. Lewes: Falmer Press.

Burgess, R. G. (1984b) *In the Field: An Introduction to Field Research*. London: Unwin Hyman.

Burgess, R.G. (1986) *Sociology, Education and Schools*. London: Batsford.

Burnhill, P., Garner, C. and McPherson, A. (1990) Parental education, social class and entry to higher education, 1976–86. *Journal of Royal Statistical Society: A*, 153: 233–48.

Cameron, D., Frazer, E., Harvey, P., Rampton, M. B. H. and Richardson, K. (1992) *Researching Language: Issues of Power and Method*. London: Routledge.

Carby, H. (1982) White women listen! Black feminism and the boundaries of sisterhood, in Centre for Contemporary Cultural Studies *The Empire Strikes Back: Race and Racism in 70s Britain*. London: Hutchinson.

Carlen, P., Gleeson, D. and Wardhaugh, J. (1992) *Truancy: The Politics of Compulsory Schooling*. Buckingham: Open University Press.

Carrington, B. and Wood, E. (1983) Body talk. *Multiracial Education*, 11 (2): 29–38.

Casey, K. (1993) *I Answer With My Life: Life Histories of Women Teachers Working for Social Change*. New York: Routledge.

Cashmore, E. (1979) *Rastaman*. London: Allen and Unwin.

Cashmore, E. and Troyna, B. (eds) (1982) *Black Youth in Crisis*. London: Allen and Unwin.

Centre for Contemporary Cultural Studies (CCCS) (1982) *The Empire Strikes Back: Race and Racism in 70s Britain*. London: Hutchinson.

Cheng, Y. (1994) *Education and Class: Chinese in Britain and the US*. Aldershot: Avebury.

Christian, B. (1989) But who do you really belong to – black studies or women's studies? *Women's Studies*, 17: 17–23.

Clarricoates, K. (1980) The importance of being Ernest . . ., Emma . . ., Tom . . ., Jane: the perception and categorisation of gender conformity and gender deviation in primary schools, in R. Deem (ed.) *Schooling for Women's Work*. London: Routledge.

Clifford, J. and Marcus, G.E. (eds) (1986) *Writing Culture: The Poetics and Politics of Ethnography*. Berkeley, CA: University of California Press.

Cochran, W.G. (1977) *Sampling Techniques*. New York: John Wiley.

Cohen, P. (1992) 'It's racism what dunnit': hidden narratives in theories of racism, in J. Donald and A. Rattansi (eds) *'Race', Culture and Difference*. London: Sage.

Coleman, J. (1958) Relational analysis: the study of social organizations with survey methods. *Human Organization*, 16 (4): 28–36.

Collins, P. H. (1990) *Black Feminist Thought*. London: Unwin Hyman.

Collins, P. H. (1991) Learning from the outsider within: the sociological significance of black feminist thought, in M. Fonow and J. Cook (eds) *Beyond methodology*. Bloomington, IN: Indiana University Press.

Commission for Racial Equality (CRE) (1988) *Ethnic Minority Schoolteachers: A Survey in Eight Local Education Authorities*. London: CRE.

Connell, R. J. (1987) *Gender and Power*. Oxford: Polity Press.

Connolly, P. (1992) Playing it by the rules: the politics of research in 'race' and education. *British Educational Research Journal*, 18 (2): 133–48.

Connolly, P. (1993) Doing feminist and anti-racist research as a white male – a contradiction in terms? Conference paper, University of Essex, British Sociological Association Annual Conference, 5–8 April.

Connolly, P. (1994) All lads together? Racism, masculinity and multicultural/anti-racist strategies in a primary school. *International Studies in Sociology of Education*, 4 (2): 191–211.

Connolly, P. (1995a) Boys will be boys? racism, sexuality and the construction of masculine identities amongst infant boys, in J. Holland, M. Blair and S. Sheldon (eds) *Debates and Issues in Feminist Research and Pedagogy*. Clevedon: Multilingual Matters.

Connolly, P. (1995b) Racism, masculine peer-group relations and the schooling of African/Caribbean infant boys. *British Journal of Sociology of Education*, 16 (1): 75–92.

Connolly, P. (1996a) Seen but never heard: rethinking approaches to researching racism and young children. *Discourse: Studies in the Cultural Politics of Education*, 17 (2): 171–85.

Connolly, P. (1996b) Doing what comes naturally? Standpoint epistemology, critical social research and the politics of identity, in E. Stina Lyon and J. Busfield (eds) *Methodological Imaginations*. Basingstoke: Macmillan.

Connolly, P. (1997) Racism, postmodernism and Bourdieu: towards a theory of practice, in D. Owen (ed.) *Sociology After Postmodernism*. London: Sage.

Connolly, P. (1998) *Racism, Gender Identities and Young Children*. London: Routledge.

Cotterill, P. (1992) Interviewing women: issues of friendship, vulnerability and power. *Women's Studies International Forum*, 15: 593–606.

Courtenay, G. and McAleese, I. (1994) *Cohort 4: Young people 17–18 years old in 1990*. Report on Sweep 2, ED Research Series, Youth Cohort Report No. 27. Department of Employment.

Courtenay, G., Hedges, B. and Lynn, P. (1994) Monitoring transitions to the labour market. *Survey Methods Centre Newsletter*, 14 (1).

Craft, M. and Craft, A. (1983) The participation of ethnic minority pupils in further and higher education. *Educational Research*, 25 (1): 10–19.

Cross, M. (1989) Soapbox. *Network: Newsletter of the British Sociological Association*, 43: 20.

Currie, D. and Kazi, H. (1987) Academic feminism and the process of de-radicalisation: re-examining the issues. *Feminist Review*, 25: 74–98.

Davey, A. (1983) *Learning to be Prejudiced*. London: Edward Arnold.

Davies, L. (1985) Ethnography and status: focusing on gender in educational research, in R. G. Burgess (ed.) *Field Methods in the Study of Education*. Lewes: Falmer Press.

Denscombe, M. and Aubrook, L. (1992) 'It's just another piece of schoolwork': the ethics of questionnaire research on pupils in schools. *British Educational Research Journal*, 18 (2): 113–31.

Denzin, N.K. (1992) *Symbolic Interactionism and Cultural Studies: The Politics of Interpretation*. Oxford: Blackwell.

Department for Education and Employment (1992) *Exclusions: A Discussion Document*. London: DFE.

Department of Education and Science (DES) (1985) *Education for All: The Report of the Committee of Enquiry into the Education of Children from Ethnic Minority Groups*. London: HMSO.

Dhondy, F. (1974) The black explosion in British schools. *Race Today*, February: 44–7.

Drew, D. (1980) The politics of statistics, in Runnymede Trust and Radical Statistics Race Group (eds) *Britain's Black Population*. London: Heinemann Educational Books.

Drew, D. (1995) *Race, Education and Work: The Statistics of Inequality*. Aldershot: Avebury.

Drew, D. and Fosam, B. (1994) Gender and ethnic differences in education and the youth labour market. *Radical Statistics*, 58: 16–35.

Drew D. and Gray, J. (1990) The fifth year examination achievements of black young people in England and Wales. *Educational Research*, 32 (2): 107–17.

Drew, D. and Gray, J. (1991) The Black-white gap in exam achievement: a statistical critique of a decade's research. *New Community*, 17 (2): 159–72.

Drew, D., Fosam, B. and Gillborn, D. (1995) Statistics and the pseudo-science of 'race' and IQ: interrogating 'The Bell Curve'. Conference paper presented at the Royal Statistical Society Annual Conference, Telford, 13 July.

Drew, D., Gray, J. and Sporton, D. (1997) Ethnic differences in the educational participation of 16–19 Year Olds, in V. Karn (ed.) *Ethnicity in the 1991 Census* (vol. 4). London: HMSO.

Driver, G. (1977) Cultural competence, social power and school achievement: West Indian secondary school students in the West Midlands. *New Community*, 5 (4): 353–9.

Driver, G. (1980) *Beyond Underachievement*. London: Commission for Racial Equality.

Du Bois, B. (1983) Passionate scholarship: notes on values, knowing and method in feminist social science, in G. Bowles and R. Duelli Klein (eds) *Theories of Women's Studies*. London: Routledge and Kegan Paul.

Duelli Klein, R. (1983) How to do what we want to do: thoughts about feminist methodology, in G. Bowles and R. Duelli Klein (eds) *Theories of Women's Studies*. London: Routledge and Kegan Paul.

Dyer, R. (1988) White. *Screen*, 29 (4): 44–65.

Edwards, R. (1990) Connecting method and epistemology: a white woman interviewing black women. *Women's Studies International Forum*, 13: 477–90.

Edwards, R. (1993) An education in interviewing: placing the researcher and the research, in C. Renzetti and R. Lee (eds) *Researching Sensitive Topics*. London: Sage.

Eggleston, J. (1991) Facing the realities of a no win situation, *Times Educational Supplement*, 25 January: 29.

Eggleston, J., Dunn, D.K. and Anjali, M. (1986) *Education for Some: The Educational and Vocational Experiences of 15–18 year-old Members of Minority Ethnic Groups*. Stoke-on-Trent: Trentham.

Epstein, D. (1993) *Changing Classroom Cultures: Anti-Racism, Politics and Schools*. Stoke-on-Trent: Trentham.

Essed, P. (1991) *Understanding Everyday Racism.* London: Sage.

Farish, M., McPake, J., Powney, J. and Weiner, G. (1995) *Equal Opportunities in Colleges and Universities.* Buckingham: Open University Press.

Farley, R. and Levin, M. (1982) Historical comparability of ethnic designations in the United States. Conference paper presented to the annual meeting of the American Statistical Association, Cincinnati, Ohio, August.

Finch, J. (1984) It's great having someone to talk to: the ethics and politics of interviewing women, in C. Bell and H. Roberts (eds) *Social Researching: Politics, Problems, Practice.* London: Routledge.

Finch, J. (1993) It's great having someone to talk to: the ethics and politics of interviewing women, in M. Hammersley (ed.) *Social Research: Philosophy, Politics and Practice.* London: Routledge.

Fisher, R. A. (1925) *Statistical Methods for Research Workers,* first edition. Edinburgh: Oliver and Boyd.

Foster, L. and Seitz, A. (1985) Applications of oral history in the sociology of ethnic relations. *Journal of Intercultural Studies,* 6 (3): 5–15.

Foster, M. (1994) The power to know one thing is never the power to know all things: methodological notes on two studies of black American teachers, in A. Gitlin (ed.) *Power and Method.* London: Routledge.

Foster, P. (1990a) *Policy and Practice in Multicultural and Anti-Racist Education.* London: Routledge.

Foster, P. (1990b) Cases not proven: an evaluation of two studies of teacher racism. *British Educational Research Journal,* 16 (4): 335–49.

Foster, P. (1991) Case still not proven: a reply to Cecile Wright. *British Educational Research Journal,* 17 (2): 165–70.

Foster, P. (1992) Equal treatment and cultural difference in multi-ethnic schools: a critique of the teacher ethnocentrism theory. *International Studies in Sociology of Education,* 2 (1): 89–103.

Foster, P. (1993) 'Methodological purism' or 'a defence against hype'? Critical readership in research in 'race' and education. *New Community,* 19 (3): 547–52.

Foster, P., Gomm, R. and Hammersley, M. (1996) *Constructing Educational Inequality: An Assessment of Research on School Processes.* London: Falmer.

Foster, P. and Hammersley, M. (1996) Researching educational inequality: a critique. *Research Intelligence: British Educational Research Association Newsletter,* 56: 18–20.

Frankenberg, R. (1993) *White Women, Race Matters: The Social Construction of Whiteness.* London: Routledge.

Freilich, M. (1977) *Marginal Natives At Work: Anthropologists in the Field.* Cambridge, MA: Schenkman.

Fuller, M. (1984) Black girls in a London comprehensive school, in M. Hammersley and P. Woods (eds) *Life in School: The Sociology of Pupil Culture.* Milton Keynes: Open University Press.

Furlong, J. (1984) Black resistance in the liberal comprehensive, in S. Delamont (ed.) *Readings on Interaction in the Classroom.* London: Methuen.

Gabriel, J. (1994) *Racism, Culture, Markets.* London: Routledge.

Geiger, S. (1986) Women's Life Histories: method and content. *Signs,* 11 (6): 334–51.

Gelsthorpe, L. (1992) Response to Martyn Hammersley's paper 'On feminist methodology'. *Sociology,* 26 (2): 213–18.

Gewirtz, S. and Ozga, J. (1993) Sex, lies and audiotape: interviewing the education policy elite. Conference paper, University of Warwick, 1988 Education Reform Act research seminar, 4 February.

Gewirtz, S., Ball, S. J. and Bowe, R. (1995) *Markets, Choice and Equity in Education.* Buckingham: Open University Press.

Ghuman, P. A. S. (1995) *Asian Teachers in British Schools*. Clevedon: Multilingual Matters Ltd.

Giddens, A. (1984) *The Constitution of Society*. Cambridge: Polity.

Gillborn, D. (1990) *'Race', Ethnicity and Education: Teaching and Learning in Multi-Ethnic Schools*. London: Unwin-Hyman.

Gillborn, D. (1995) *Racism and Antiracism in Real Schools: Theory, Policy, Practice*. Buckingham: Open University Press.

Gillborn, D. (1996) Student roles and perspectives in antiracist education: a crisis of white ethnicity? *British Educational Research Journal*, 22 (2): 165–79.

Gillborn, D. and Drew, D. (1992) 'Race', class and school effects. *New Community*, 18 (4): 551–65.

Gillborn, D. and Gipps, C. (1996) *Recent Research on the Achievements of Ethnic Minority Pupils*. London: HMSO.

Gilroy, P. (1980) Managing the underclass: a further note on the sociology of race relations in Britain. *Race and Class*, 22: 47–62.

Gilroy, P. (1987) *There Ain't No Black in the Union Jack*. London: Hutchinson.

Gilroy, P. (1990) The end of anti-racism, in W. Ball and J. Solomos (eds) *Race and Local Politics*. London: Macmillan.

Gilroy, P. (1992) Foreword, in B. Hesse, R. Dhanwant, C. Bennet and P. McGilchrist (eds) *Beneath the Surface, Racial Harassment*. Aldershot: Avebury.

Giroux, H. A. (1991) Democracy and the discourse of cultural difference: towards a politics of border pedagogy. *British Journal of Sociology of Education*, 12 (4): 501–19.

Gitlin, A. (ed.) (1994) *Power and Method*. New York: Routledge.

Gleeson, D. (1992) School attendance and truancy: a socio-historical account. *Sociological Review*, 40 (3): 437–90.

Glucksmann, M. (1994) The work of knowledge and knowledge of women's work, in M. Maynard and J. Purvis (eds) *Researching Women's Lives From a Feminist Perspective*. London: Taylor & Francis.

Goldberg, D. T. (1992) *Racist Culture: The Politics and Philosophy of Meaning*. Oxford: Basil Blackwell.

Goldberg, D. T. and Zegeye, A. (1995) Editorial Note. *Social Identities*, 1 (1): 3–4.

Goldstein, H. (1987) *Multilevel Models in Educational and Social Research*. London: Charles Griffin and Company.

Gomm, R. (1993) Figuring out ethnic equity. *British Educational Research Journal*, 19 (2): 149–65.

Goodson, I. (1980) Life Histories and the Study of Schooling. *Interchange*, 11 (4): 62–76.

Goodson, I. (1981) Becoming an academic subject: patterns of explanation and evolution. *British Journal of Sociology of Education*, 2 (2): 163–80.

Goodson, I. (ed.) (1992) *Studying Teachers' Lives*. London: Routledge.

Gore, J. (1993) *The Struggle for Pedagogies*. London: Routledge.

Gouldner, A. (1971) *The Coming Crisis in Western Sociology*. London: Heinemann.

Gouldner, A. (1975) *For Sociology: Renewal and Critique in Sociology Today*. Harmondsworth: Penguin.

Graham, H. (1991) The concept of caring in feminist research: the case of domestic service. *Sociology*, 25: 61–78.

Gray, J. and Wilcox, B. (1995) *Good School, Bad School: Evaluating Performance and Encouraging Improvement*. Buckingham: Open University Press.

Greed, C. (1990) The professional and the personal: a study of women quantity surveyors, in L. Stanley (ed.) *Feminist Praxis: Research, Theory and Epistemology in Feminist Sociology*. London: Routledge.

Green, G., Barbour, R., Barnard, M. and Kitinger, J. (1993) Who wears the trousers? Sexual harassment in research settings. *Women's Studies International Forum*, 16: 627–37.

Griffiths, M. (1995) Making a difference: feminism, post-modernism and the methodology of educational research. *British Educational Research Journal*, 21: 219–36.

Gutzmore, C. (1983) Capital, 'black youth' and crime. *Race and Class*, 25 (2): 13–31.

Habermas, J. (1972) *Knowledge and Human Interests*. London: Heinemann.

Hall, S. (1992a) New ethnicities, in J. Donald and A. Rattansi (eds) *'Race', Culture and Difference*. London: Sage.

Hall, S. (1992b) The West and the Rest: discourse and power, in S. Hall and B. Gieben (eds) *Formations of Modernity*. Cambridge: Polity.

Hall, S., Critcher, C., Jefferson, T., Clarke, J. and Roberts, B. (1978) *Policing the Crisis*. London: Macmillan.

Hamilton, P. (1992) The Enlightenment and the birth of social science, in S. Hall and B. Gieben (eds) *Formations of Modernity*. Cambridge: Polity.

Hammersley, M. (1980), 'A peculiar world? Teaching and learning in an Inner City school', unpublished PhD thesis, University of Manchester.

Hammersley, M. (1990) *Classroom Ethnography: Empirical and Methodological Essays*. Buckingham: Open University Press.

Hammersley, M. (1990) *Reading Ethnographic Research*. London: Longman.

Hammersley, M. (1992a) *What's Wrong with Ethnography?* London: Routledge.

Hammersley, M. (1992b) On feminist methodology. *Sociology*, 26 (2): 187–206.

Hammersley, M. (1992c) A response to Barry Troyna's 'children, "race" and racism: the limits of research and policy', *British Journal of Educational Studies*, 40(2): 174–7.

Hammersley, M. (1993a) On methodological purism: a response to Barry Troyna. *British Educational Research Journal*, 19 (4): 339–41.

Hammersley, M. (1993b) Research and 'anti-racism': the case of Peter Foster and his critics. *British Journal of Sociology*, 44 (3): 429–48.

Hammersley, M. (1994) On feminist methodology: a response. *Sociology*, 28 (1): 293–300.

Hammersley, M. (1995) *The Politics of Social Research*. London: Sage.

Hammersley, M. (1997) Taking sides against research: an assessment of the rationales for partisanship, in D. Scott (ed.) *Values and Educational Research*. Bedford Way Papers, Institute of Education, University of London.

Hammersley, M. and Atkinson, P. (1995) *Ethnography: Principles in Practice*, 2nd edn. London: Routledge.

Hammersley, M. and Gomm, R. (1993) A response to Gillborn and Drew on 'race', class and school effects. *New Community*, 19 (2): 348–53.

Hammersley, M. and Gomm, R. (1996) Exploiting sociology for equality? *Network: Newsletter of the British Sociological Association*, 65: 19–20.

Harding, S. (1986) *The Science Question in Feminism*. Milton Keynes: Open University Press.

Harding, S. (ed.) (1987) *Feminism and Methodology: Social Science Issues*. Milton Keynes: Open University Press.

Harding, S. (1991) *Whose Science? Whose Knowledge? Thinking from Women's Lives*. Buckingham: Open University Press.

Hargreaves, D. (1967) *Social Relations in a Secondary School*. London: Routledge.

Hargreaves, D., Hestor, S. and Mellor, F. (1975) *Deviance in Classroom*. London: Routledge.

Harris, C. and James, W. (1993) Introduction, in W. James and C. Harris (eds) *Inside Babylon*. London: Verso.

Harvey, L. (1990) *Critical Social Research*. London: Unwin Hyman.

Herbert, C. (1993) Researching adolescent girls' perceptions of unwanted sexual attention, in M. Kennedy, C. Lubelska and V. Walsh (eds) *Making connections*. London: Taylor & Francis.

Holmwood, J. (1995) Feminism and epistemology: what kind of successor science? *Sociology*, 29: 411–28.

hooks, b. (1984) *Feminist Theory: From Margin to Center*. Boston, MA: South End Press.

Hurrell, P. (1995) Do teachers discriminate? Reactions to pupil behaviour in four comprehensive schools. *Sociology*, 29 (1): 59–72.

Jayaratne, J. and Stewart, A. (1995) Quantitative and qualitative methods in the social sciences: feminist issues and practical strategies, in J. Holland, M. Blair and S. Sheldon (eds) *Debates and Issues in Feminist Research and Pedagogy*. Clevedon: Multilingual Matters.

Jewson, N., Mason, D., Bowen, R., Mulvaney, K. and Parmar, S. (1991) Universities and ethnic minorities: the public face. *New Community*, 17: 183–99.

Jewson, N., Mason, D., Broadbent, J., Jenkins, S. and Thandi, H. (1993) *Polytechnics and Ethnic Minorities: The Public Face*. Department of Sociology Discussion Paper. Leicester: University of Leicester.

Kamin, L. J. (1974) *The Science and Politics of IQ*. Harmondsworth: Penguin.

Kamin, L. J. (1981) in H.J. Eysenck versus L. Kamin *Intelligence: The Battle for the Mind*. London: Pan.

Kamin, L. J. (1995) Behind the curve. *Scientific American*, February: 82–6.

Keith, M. (1992) Angry writing, (re)presenting the unethical world of the ethnographer. *Space and Society*, 10: 551–68.

Keith, M. (1993) *Race, Riots and Policing: Lore and Disorder in a Multi-Racist Society*. London: UCL Press.

Kelly, E. and Cohn, T. (1988) *Racism in Schools – New Research Evidence*. Stoke-on-Trent: Trentham Books.

Kishwar, M. (1994) A horror of isms, in M. Evans (ed.) *The Woman Question*, 2nd edn. London: Sage.

Klein, G. (1993) *Education Towards Race Equality*. London: Cassell.

Kovel, J. (1988) *White Racism, a Psychohistory*. London: Free Association Books.

Kysel, F. (1988) Ethnic background and examination results. *Educational Research*, 30 (2).

Lacey, C. (1970) *Hightown Grammar: The School as a Social System*. Manchester: Manchester University Press.

Ladner, J. A. (1975) Introduction, in J. A. Ladner (ed.) *The Death of White Sociology*. New York: Vintage Books.

Lather, P. (1986) Research as praxis. *Harvard Educational Review*, 56 (3): 257–77.

Lawrence, E. (1981) White sociology, black struggle. *Multiracial Education*, 9 (3): 3–17.

Lawrence, E. (1982) In the abundance of water the fool is thirsty: sociology and black 'pathology', in CCCS, *The Empire Strikes Back: Race and Racism in 70s Britain*. London: Hutchinson.

Layder, D. (1994) *New Strategies in Social Research*. London: Sage.

Lee, R. (1993) *Doing Research on Sensitive Topics*. London: Sage.

Lewis, R. (1988) *Anti-Racism: A Mania Exposed*. London: Quartet Books.

Liazos, A. (1972) The poverty of sociology of deviance: nuts, sluts and perverts. *Social Problems*, 20: 103–20.

London Borough of Ealing (1988) *Ealings Dilemma: Implementing Race Equality in Education*. Ealing: Race Equality Unit.

Lukacs, G. (1971) *History and Class Consciousness: Studies in Marxist Dialectics*. London: Heinemann.

Mabey, C. (1986) Black pupils' achievement in Inner London. *Educational Research*, 28 (3): 163–73.

Mac an Ghaill, M. (1988) *Young, Gifted and Black: Student-Teacher Relations in the Schooling of Black Youth*. Milton Keynes: Open University Press.

Mac an Ghaill, M. (1989) Beyond the white norm: the use of qualitative methods in the study of black youths' schooling in England. *International Journal of Qualitative Studies in Education*, 2 (3): 175–89.

Mac an Ghaill, M. (1991) 'Young, Gifted and Black': methodological reflections of a teacher/researcher, in G. Walford (ed.) *Doing Educational Research*. London: Routledge.

McCall, G. and Simmons, J. L. (eds) (1969) *Issues in Participant Observation*. Reading, MS: Addison-Wesley.

McCarthy, C. and Crichlow, W. (1993) *Race, Identity and Representation in Education*. London: Routledge.

Macdonald, I., Bhavnani, R., Khan, L. and John, G. (1989) *Murder In The Playground: The Report of the Macdonald Inquiry into Racism and Racial Violence in Manchester Schools*. London: Longsight Press.

McKee, L. and O'Brien, M. (1983) Interviewing men: taking gender seriously, in E. Gamarnikow, D. Morgan, L. Purvis and D. Taylorson (eds) *The Public and the Private*. London: Heinemann.

McLennan, G. (1995) Feminism, epistemology and postmodernism: reflections on current ambivalence. *Sociology*, 29: 391–410.

Mama, A. (1989) *The Hidden Struggle*. London: London Race and Housing Research Unit.

Mama, A. (1995) *Beyond the Masks: Race, Gender and Subjectivity*. London: Routledge.

Marland, M. (1990) A mirror to our work, *Guardian*, 27 November: 20.

Marsh, C. (1982) *The Survey Method*. London: George Allen and Unwin.

Marshall, A. (1994) Sensuous sapphires: a study of the social construction of black female sexuality, in M. Maynard and J. Purvis (eds) *Researching Women's Lives from a Feminist Perspective*. London: Taylor & Francis.

Mason, D. (1995) *Race and Ethnicity in Modern Britain*. Oxford: Oxford University Press.

Maughan, B. and Rutter, M. (1986) Black pupils' progress in secondary schools II: examination achievements. *British Journal of Developmental Psychology*, 4: 19–29.

Maynard, M. (1993) Feminism and the possibilities of a postmodern research practice. *British Journal of Sociology of Education*, 14 (3): 327–31.

Maynard, M. (1994) 'Race', gender and the concept of 'difference' in feminist thought, in H. Afshar and M. Maynard (eds) *The Dynamics of 'Race' and Gender: Some Feminist Interventions*. London: Taylor & Francis.

Measor, L. (1985) Interviewing – a strategy in qualitative research, in R. Burgess (ed.) *Strategies in Educational Research: Qualitative Methods*. London: Falmer.

Measor, L. and Sikes, P. (1992) Visiting lives ethics and methodology in life history, in I. Goodson (ed.) *Studying Teachers' Lives*. London: Routledge.

Merton, R. K. (1963) *Social Theory and Social Structure*. Glencoe: Free Press.

Merton, R. K. (1967) *On Theoretical Sociology*. New York: Free Press.

Micklewright, J., Pearson, M. and Smith, S. (1990) Unemployment and early school leaving. *The Economic Journal*, 100: 163–9.

Mills, C.W. (1959) *The Sociological Imagination*. Harmondsworth: Penguin.

Milner, D. (1983) *Children and Race: Ten Years On*. London: Ward Lock.

Minh-ha, T. (1989) *Woman, Native, Other*. Bloomington, IN: Indiana University Press.

Mirza, H. S. (1992) *Young, Female and Black*. London: Routledge.

Mirza, K. (1989) *The Silent Cry: Second Generation Bradford Muslim Young Women Speak*. Birmingham: Centre for the study of Islam and Christian-Muslim Relations.

Mirza, M. (1994) Feminist and anti-racist methodologies: ethical dilemmas in fieldwork. Unpublished paper presented to the British Educational Research Association Annual Conference, St Anne's College, Oxford, 9 September.

Mirza, M. (1995) Some ethical dilemmas in fieldwork: feminist and anti-racist methodologies, in M. Griffiths and B. Troyna (eds) *Antiracism, Culture and Social Justice in Education*. Stoke-on-Trent: Trentham Books.

Modood, T. (1988) 'Black', racial equality and Asian identity. *New Community*, 14 (3): 397–404.

Modood, T. (1990) Catching up with Jesse Jackson: being oppressed and being some-body. *New Community*, 17 (1): 85–96.

Modood, T. (1992) *Not Easy Being British: Colour, Culture and Citizenship*. Stoke-on-Trent: Runnymede Trust and Trentham Books.

Modood, T. and Shiner, M. (1994) *Ethnic Minorities and Higher Education: Why are there Differential Rates of Entry?* London: Policy Studies Institute.

Morgan, D. (1981) Men, masculinity and the process of sociological inquiry, in H. Roberts (ed.) *Doing Feminist Research*. London: Routledge.

Morrison, T. (1992) *Playing in the Dark: Whiteness and the Literary Imagination*. Cambridge, MA: Harvard University Press.

Mortimore, P., Sammons, P., Stoll, L., Lewis, D. and Ecob, R. (1988) *School Matters: The Junior Years*. Wells: Open Books.

Mullard, C. (1985) *Race, Power and Resistance*. London: Routledge.

Mullard, C. (1986) *Pluralism, Ethnicism and Ideology: Implications for a Transformative Pedagogy*. Working paper no. 2, CRES, University of Amsterdam.

Murdock, G. and McCron, R. (1973) Scoobies, skins and contemporary pop. *New Society*, 29 March: 690–2.

Murdock, G. and Phelps, G. (1973) *Mass Media and the Secondary School*. London: Macmillan.

Neal, S. (1995a) A question of silence? Antiracist discourses and initiatives in higher education: two case studies, in M. Griffiths and B. Troyna (eds) *Antiracism, Culture and Social Justice in Education*. Stoke-on-Trent: Trentham Books.

Neal, S. (1995b) Researching powerful people from a feminist and anti-racist perspective: a note on gender, collusion and marginality. *British Educational Research Journal*, 21: 517–32.

Neal, S. (1998) *The Making of Equal Opportunities Policies in Universities*. Buckingham: Open University Press.

Nehaul, K. (1996) *The Schooling of Children of Caribbean Heritage*. Stoke-on-Trent: Trentham Books.

Nixon, J. (1985) *A Teacher's Guide to Multicultural Education*. Oxford: Blackwell.

Nuttall, D., Goldstein, H., Prosser, R. and Rashbash, J. (1989) Differential school effectiveness. *International Journal of Educational Research*, 13: 769–76.

O'Muircheartaigh, C. and Francis, D. (1981) *Statistics: A Dictionary of Terms and Ideas*. London: Arrow Books.

Oakley, A. (1981) Interviewing women: a contradiction in terms? in H. Roberts (ed.) *Doing Feminist Research*. London: Routledge.

Opie, A. (1992) Qualitative research, appropriation of the 'other' and empowerment. *Feminist Review*, 40: 52–69.

Padfield, M. and Proctor, I. (1996) The effect of interviewer's gender on the interviewing process: a comparative enquiry. *Sociology*, 30 (2): 355–66.

Parmar, P. (1981) Young Asian Women: a critique of the pathological approach. *Multi-racial Education*, 9 (3): 19–29.

Parmar, P. (1982) Gender, race and class: Asian women in resistance, in CCCS, *The Empire Strikes Back: Race and Racism in 70s Britain*. London: Hutchinson.

Parmar, P. (1990) Black feminism: the politics of articulation, in J. Rutherford (ed.) *Identity: Community, Culture, Difference*. London: Lawrence and Wishart.

Patai, D. (1994) When method becomes power, in A. Gitlin (ed.) *Power and Method*. London: Routledge.

Perez, L. E. (1993) Opposition and the education of Chicana/os, in C. McCarthy and W. Crichlow (eds) *Race, Identity and Representation in Education*. London: Routledge.

Phoenix, A. (1987) Theories of gender and black families, in G. Weiner and M. Arnot (eds) *Gender Under Scrutiny: New Inquiries in Education*. London: Unwin Hyman.

Phoenix, A. (1994a) Practising feminist research: the intersection of gender and 'race' in the research process, in M. Maynard and J. Purvis (eds) *Researching Women's Lives From a Feminist Perspective*. London: Taylor & Francis.

Phoenix, A. (1994b) Narrow definitions of culture: the case of early motherhood, in M. Evans (ed.) *The Woman Question*, 2nd edn. London: Sage.

Plewis, I. (1988) Assessing and understanding the educational progress of children from different ethnic groups. *J.R. Statistical Society*, 151: pt 2.

Popular Memory Group (1982) Popular memory: theory, politics and method, in R. Johnson, G. McLennan, B. Schwarz and D. Sutton (eds) *Making Histories*. London: Hutchinson.

Pryce, K. (1979) *Endless Pressure*. London: Penguin.

Punch, M. (1986) *The Politics and Ethics of Fieldwork*. Thousand Oaks, CA: Sage.

Quicke, J. (1988) Using structured life histories to teach the sociology and social psychology of education, in P. Woods and A. Pollard (eds) *Sociology and Teaching*. London: Croom Helm.

Raffe, D. and Willms, J. D. (1989) Schooling the discouraged worker: local labour market effects on educational participation. *Sociology*, 23 (4): 559–81.

Ramazanoglu, C. (1992) On feminist methodology: male reason verses female empowerment. *Sociology*, 26 (2): 207–12.

Rattansi, A. (1992) Changing the subject? Racism, culture and education, in J. Donald and A. Rattansi (eds) *'Race', Culture and Difference*. London: Sage.

Rattansi, A. (1994) 'Western' racisms, ethnicities and identities in a 'postmodern' frame, in A. Rattansi and S. Westwood (eds) *Racism, Modernity and Identity on the Western Front*. Cambridge: Polity Press.

Reeves, F. and Chevannes, M. (1981) The underachievement of Rampton. *Multiracial Education*, 10 (1): 35–42.

Reinharz, S. (1992) *Feminist Methods in Social Research*. Oxford: Oxford University Press.

Reissman, C. (1987) When gender isn't enough: women interviewing women. *Gender & Society*, 1: 172–207.

Rex, J. and Tomlinson, S. (1979) *Colonial Immigrants and the British City: A Class Analysis*. London: Routledge.

Rhodes, P. J. (1994) Race of interviewer effects in qualitative research: a brief comment. *Sociology*, 28 (2): 547–58.

Ricoeur, P. (1970) *Freud and Philosophy*. New Haven, CT: Yale University Press.

Riemer, J. (1977) Varities of opportunistic research. *Urban Life*, 5 (4): 467–77.

Roman, L. G. (1993) White is a color! White defensiveness, postmodernism and anti-racist pedagogy, in C. McCarthy and W. Critchlow (eds) *Race, Identity and Representation in Education*. New York: Routledge.

Rose, D. and Sullivan, O. (1993) *Introducing Data Analysis for Social Scientists*. Buckingham: Open University Press.

Said, E.W. (1978) *Orientalism: Western Conceptions of the Orient*. London: Penguin.

Sayer, A. (1992) *Method in Social Science*, 2nd edn. London: Routledge.

Scanlon, J. (1993) Challenging the imbalances of power in feminist oral history. *Women's Studies International Forum*, 16: 639–45.

Scarman, Lord (1981) *The Brixton Disorders, 10–12 April 1981*, Cmnd 8427. London: HMSO.

Schaeffer, N. (1980) Evaluating race-of-interviewer effects in a national survey. *Sociological Methods and Research*, 8 (4): 400–19.

Scheurich, J. J. (1993) Towards a white discourse on white racism. *Educational Researcher*, 22 (8): 5–10.

Scott, J. (1995) Using household panels to study micro-social change. *Innovation*, 8 (1).

Seiber, J. E. (1993) The ethics and politics of sensitive research, in C. Renzetti and R. Lee (eds) *Researching Sensitive Topics*. London: Sage.

Sewell, T. (1995) A phallic response to schooling: black masculinity and race in an inner-city comprehensive, in M. Griffiths and B. Troyna (eds) *Antiracism, Culture and Social Justice in Education*. Stoke-on-Trent: Trentham.

Sharp, R. and Green, A. (1975) *Education and Social Control*. London: Routledge.

Sikes, P., Measor, L. and Woods, P. (1985) *Teacher Careers: Crises and Continuities*. Lewes: Falmer.

Sikes, P., Troyna, B. and Goodson, I. (1996) Talking about teachers: a conversation about life history. *Taboo: The Journal of Culture and Education*, 1: 35–54.

Simpson, S. (1996) Non-response to the 1991 census: the effect on ethnic group enumeration, in D. Coleman and J. Salt (eds) *Ethnicity in the 1991 Census, vol. 1, Demographic Characteristics of the Ethnic Minority Populations*. London: HMSO.

Singh, R., Brown, T. and Darr, A. (1988) *Ethnic Minority Young People and Entry to Teacher Education*. Bradford: Bradford and Ilkley Community College.

Siraj-Blatchford, I. (1994) *Praxis Makes Perfect: Critical Educational Research for Social Justice*. Derbyshire: Education Now Books.

Sivanandan, A. (1988) Left, right and Burnage. *New Statesman*, 27 May. Reprinted in A. Sivanandan (1990) *Communities of Resistance: Writings on Black Struggles for Socialism*. London: Verso.

Sleeter, C. (1993) How white teachers construct race, in C. McCarthy and W. Crichlow (eds) *Race, Identity and Representation in Education*. London: Routledge.

Smart, C. (1984) *The Ties That Bind: Law, Marriage and the Reproduction of Patriarchal Relations*. London: Routledge.

Smith, D. (1979) A sociology for women, in J. Sherman and E. Torton Beck (eds) *The Prism of Sex: Essays in the Sociology of Knowledge*. University of Wisconsin Press.

Smith, D. J. and Tomlinson, S. (1989) *The School Effect: A Study of Multi-Racial Comprehensives*. London: Policy Studies Institute.

Smith, R. (1993) Potentials for empowerment in critical educational research. *The Australian Educational Researcher*, 20 (2): 75–94.

Snow, D. and Anderson, L. (1993) *Down On Their Luck: A Study of Homeless People*. Los Angeles, CA: University of California Press.

Socialist Review Collective (1994) Arranging identities, framing the issue/s. *Socialist Review*, 1 and 2: 1–19.

Solomos, J. and Back, L. (1995) *Race and Social Change*. London: Routledge.

Song, M. (1995) Between 'the front' and 'the back': Chinese women's work in the family business. *Women's Studies International Forum*, 18: 285–98.

Song, M. and Parker, D. (1995) Cultural identity: disclosing commonality and difference in in-depth interviewing. *Sociology*, 29: 241–56.

Spender, D. (1980) *Man Made Language*. London: Routledge.

Stacey, J. (1988) Can there be a feminist ethnography? *Women's Studies International Forum*, 11: 21–7.

Stanfield, J. H. (ed.) (1993a) *A History of Race Relations Research: First Generation Recollections*. London: Sage.

Stanfield, J. H. (1993b) Epistemological considerations, in J. H. Stanfield and R. M. Dennis (eds) *Race and Ethnicity in Research Methods*. London: Sage.

Stanfield, J. H. (1994) Empowering the culturally diversified sociological voice, in A. Gitlin (ed.) *Power and Method*. London: Routledge.

Stanley, L. (1991) Feminist auto/biography and feminist epistemology, in J. Aaron and S. Walby (eds) *Out of the Margins: Women's Studies in the Nineties*. London: Falmer.

Stanley, L. and Wise, S. (1983) *Breaking Out*. London: Routledge.

Stanley, L. and Wise, S. (1990) *Feminist Praxis*. London: Routledge.

Stanley, L. and Wise, S. (1993) *Breaking Out Again*, 2nd edn. London: Routledge.

Stanworth, M. (1983) *Gender and Schooling: A Study of Sexual Divisions in the Classroom*. London: Hutchinson.

Thomas, D. (ed.) (1995) *Teachers' Stories*. Buckingham: Open University Press.

Thomas, S. and Mortimore, P. (1994) *Report on Value Added Analysis of 1993 GCSE Examination Results in Lancashire*. London: Institute of Education, University of London.

Thomas, S. and Mortimore, P. (1996) Comparison of value added models for secondary school effectiveness. *Research Papers in Education*, 11 (1): 5–33.

Thomas, S., Pan, H. and Goldstein, H. (1994) *Report on Analysis of 1992 Examination Results*. London: Association of Metropolitan Authorities.

Thomas, S., Sammons, P., Mortimore, P. and Smees, R. (1996) Differential School Effectiveness. *British Educational Research Journal*, 23 (4): 451–69.

Thompson, P. (1988) *The Voice of the Past: Oral History*. Oxford: Oxford University Press.

Tizard, B., Blatchford, P., Burke, J., Sarquhan, C. and Plewis, I. (1988) *Young Children in the Inner City*. Hove: Lawrence Earlbaum Associates.

Tomlinson, S. (1984) *Home and School in Multicultural Britain*. London: Batsford.

Tomlinson, S. (1992) Review of David Gillborn 'Race', Ethnicity and Education: Teaching and Learning in Multi-Ethnic Schools'. *New Community*, 18 (2): 343.

Troyna, B. (1978) 'Reggae and black youths in Britain: an exploratory study', unpublished MPhil thesis, University of Leicester.

Troyna, B. (1979) Differential commitment to ethnic identity by black youths in Britain. *New Community*, 7 (3): 406–14.

Troyna, B. (1984) Fact or artefact? The 'educational under-achievement' of black pupils. *British Journal of Sociology of Education*, 5 (2): 153–66.

Troyna, B. (1991a) Children, 'race' and racism. *British Journal of Educational Studies*, 39 (4): 425–36.

Troyna, B. (1991b) Underachievers or underrated? The experiences of students of South Asian origin in a secondary school. *British Educational Research Journal*, 17 (4): 361–76.

Troyna, B. (1992) Ethnicity and the organisation of learning groups: a case study. *Educational Research*, 34 (1): 45–55.

Troyna, B. (1993) Underachiever or misunderstood? A reply to Roger Gomm. *British Educational Research Journal*, 19 (2): 167–74.

Troyna, B. (1994a) The 'Everyday World' of teachers? Deracialised discourses in the sociology of teachers and the teaching profession. *British Journal of Sociology of Education*, 15 (3): 325–39.

Troyna, B. (1994b) Reforms, research and being reflexive about being reflective, in D. Halpin and B. Troyna (eds) *Researching Education Policy: Ethical and Methodological Issues*. London: Falmer Press.

Troyna, B. (1994c) Blind faith? Empowerment and educational research. *International Studies in Sociology of Education*, 4 (1): 3–24.

Troyna, B. (1995) Beyond reasonable doubt? Researching 'race' in educational settings. *Oxford Review of Education*, 21(4): 395–408.

Troyna, B. (forthcoming) Reflexivity, in R. G. Burgess (ed.) *Encyclopedia of Social Research*. London: Routledge.

Troyna, B. and Carrington, B. (1989) Whose side are we on? Ethical dilemmas in research on 'race' and education, in R. Burgess (ed.) *The Ethics of Educational Research*. Lewes: Falmer Press.

Troyna, B. and Hatcher, R. (1992) *Racism in Children's Lives: A Study of Mainly White Primary Schools*. London: Routledge.

Turner, G. (1979) Review of 'Learning to Labour'. *Sociology*, 13 (2): 336–8.

Verhoeven, J. C. (1989) *Methodological and Metascientific Problems in Symbolic Interactionism*. Leuven: Departement Sociologie, Katholieke Universiteit Leuven.

Vogt (1993) *Dictionary of Statistics and Methodology: A Nontechnical Guide for the Social Sciences*. London: Sage Publications.

Walker, J. C. (1985) Rebels without applause? *Journal of Education*, 167 (2): 63–83.

Walker, R. (1986) The conduct of educational case studies: ethics, theory and procedures, in M. Hammersley (ed.) *Controversies in Classroom Research*. Milton Keynes: Open University Press.

Warren, C. A. B. (1988) *Gender Issues in Field Research*. London: Sage.

Weis, L. (1992) Reflections on the researcher in a multicultural environment, in C. A. Grant (ed.) *Research and Multicultural Education*. Lewes: Falmer Press.

Wellman, D. T. (1977) *Portraits of White Racism*. Cambridge: Cambridge University Press.

Wheatley, E. (1994a) How can we engender ethnography with a feminist imagination? A rejoinder to Judith Stacey. *Women's Studies International Forum*, 17: 403–16.

Wheatley, E. (1994b) Dances with feminist: truths, dares and ethnographic stares. *Women's Studies International Forum*, 17: 421–3.

Wilkins, R. (1993) Taking it personally: a note on emotion and autobiography. *Sociology*, 27 (1): 93–100.

Williams, J., Cocking, J. and Davies, L. (1989) *Words or Deeds: a Review of Equal Opportunity Policies in Higher Education*. London: CRE.

Williams, P. (1991) *The Alchemy of Race and Rights*. Harvard, MA: Harvard University Press.

Willis, P. (1977) *Learning to Labour*. Farnborough: Saxon House.

Wilson, E. (1985) *Adorned in Dreams*. London: Virago Press.

Woods, P. (1986) *Inside Schools: Ethnography in Educational Research*. London: Routledge & Kegan Paul.

Woods, P. (1990a) *The Happiest Days? How Pupils Cope with School*. Lewes: Falmer Press.

Woods, P. (1990b) *Teacher Skills and Strategies*. Lewes: Falmer Press.

Wright, C. (1986) School processes: an ethnographic study, in J. Eggleston, D. Dunn and M. Anjali (eds) *Education for Some: The Educational and Vocational Experiences of 15–18 Year-Old Members of Minority Ethnic Groups*. Stoke-on-Trent: Trentham Books.

Wright, C. (1988) 'The school experience of pupils of West Indian background', unpublished PhD thesis, University of Keele.

Wright, C. (1990) Comments in reply to the article by P. Foster. *British Educational Research Journal*, 16 (4): 351–5.

Wright, C. (1992a) Early education: multiracial primary school classrooms, in D. Gill, B. Mayor and M. Blair (eds) *Racism and Education: Structures and Strategies*. London: Sage.

Wright, C. (1992b) *Race Relations in the Primary School*. London: David Fulton Publishers.

Zack-Williams, A. (1995) Development and diaspora: Separate concerns? *Review of African Political Economy*, 65: 349–58.

Index

THE MAKING OF MEN
MASCULINITIES, SEXUALITIES AND SCHOOLING
Máirtín Mac an Ghaill

Wayne: 'You can't trust girls because of what they expect from you . . . And you can't be honest with your mates because they'll probably tell other people.'

Rajinder: 'There's a lot of sexuality . . . African Caribbeans are seen as better at football . . . and dancing . . . the white kids and Asians are jealous because they think the girls will really prefer the black kids.'

Richard: 'Okay sharing the housework and things like that are fair. But it's all the stuff not making girls sex objects. It's ridiculous. What are you supposed to do. Become gay?'

William: 'We wanked each other one night when we were really drunk. Then later on when I saw him, he said he had a girlfriend. I knew he hadn't. We just had to move apart because we got too close.'

Gilroy: 'It's the girls who have all the power. Like they have the choice and can make you look a prat in front of your mates.'

Joanne: 'You lot are obsessed with your knobs . . . all your talk is crap. It's just to prove you're better than your mates. Why don't you all get together and measure your little plonkers?'

Frank: 'My dad spends all his time in the pub with his mates. Why doesn't he want to be with me? Why doesn't he say he loves me? . . . It does my head in.'

Máirtín Mac an Ghaill explores how boys learn to be men in schools whilst policing their own and others' sexualities. He focuses upon the students' confusions and contradictions in their gendered experiences; and upon how schools actively produce, through the official and hidden curriculum, a range of masculinities which young men come to inhabit. He does full justice to the complex phenomenon of male heterosexual subjectivities and to the role of schooling in forming sexual identities.

Contents
Introduction: schooling as a masculinizing agency – Teacher ideologies, representations and practices – Local student cultures of masculinity and sexuality – Sexuality: learning to become a heterosexual man at school – Young women's experiences of teacher and student masculinities – Conclusion: sociology of schooling, equal opportunities and anti-oppression education – Notes – References – Index.

224pp   0 335 15781 5 (Paperback)

RACISM AND ANTIRACISM IN REAL SCHOOLS

David Gillborn

- How are 'race' and racism implicated in education policy and practice?
- What does effective antiracism look like in practice?
- How can teachers and school students be encouraged to think critically about their racialized assumptions and actions?

In exploring these questions David Gillborn makes a vital contribution to the debate on 'race' and racism in education. He focuses on racism in the policy, research, theory and practice of education, and includes the first major study of antiracism at the level of whole-school management and classroom practice. The voices of teachers and school students bring the issues to life, and illustrate the daily problems of life in urban schools. This is a fascinating picture of the key matters facing managers, classroom teachers and their students as schools struggle to develop strong and workable approaches to anti-racist education. It is accompanied by a critical review of current debates and controversies concerning 'race', ethnicity and identity.

Arguing for a critical return to the concept of 'race', *Racism and Antiracism in Real Schools* represents an important addition to the literature on the theory and practice of education in a racist society.

Contents

Racism and schooling – Part I: 'Race', research and policy – Discourse and policy – Racism and research – Theorizing identity and antiracism – Part II: 'Race' and educational practice – The politics of school change – Antiracism and the whole school – Antiracism in the classroom – Student perspectives – Rethinking racism and antiracism – Notes – References – Name index – Subject index.

240pp   0 335 19092 8 (Paperback)